"Stretching" Exercises for Qualitative Researchers

Fourth Edition

SAGE was founded in 1965 by Sara Miller McCune to support the dissemination of usable knowledge by publishing innovative and high-quality research and teaching content. Today, we publish more than 850 journals, including those of more than 300 learned societies, more than 800 new books per year, and a growing range of library products including archives, data, case studies, reports, and video. SAGE remains majority-owned by our founder, and after Sara's lifetime will become owned by a charitable trust that secures our continued independence.

Los Angeles | London | New Delhi | Singapore | Washington DC

"Stretching" Exercises for Qualitative Researchers

Fourth Edition

Valerie J. Janesick
University of South Florida

Los Angeles | London | New Delhi
Singapore | Washington DC

Los Angeles | London | New Delhi
Singapore | Washington DC

FOR INFORMATION:

SAGE Publications, Inc.
2455 Teller Road
Thousand Oaks, California 91320
E-mail: order@sagepub.com

SAGE Publications Ltd.
1 Oliver's Yard
55 City Road
London EC1Y 1SP
United Kingdom

SAGE Publications India Pvt. Ltd.
B 1/I 1 Mohan Cooperative Industrial Area
Mathura Road, New Delhi 110 044
India

SAGE Publications Asia-Pacific Pte. Ltd.
3 Church Street
#10-04 Samsung Hub
Singapore 049483

Chapter-opening icons from www.clipart.com.

Printed in the United States of America

Library of Congress Cataloging-in-Publication Data

Janesick, Valerie J.

"Stretching" exercises for qualitative researchers / Valerie J. Janesick, University of South Florida. — Fourth Edition.

pages cm
Revised edition of the author's "Stretching" exercises for qualitative researchers, 2011.

Includes bibliographical references and index.

ISBN 978-1-4833-5827-7 (pbk. : alk. paper)

1. Social sciences—Research—Methodology. 2. Observation (Scientific method) 3. Qualitative reasoning. I. Title.

H62.J346 2016
300.72'1—dc23   2015015154

This book is printed on acid-free paper.

Acquisitions Editor: Helen Salmon
Editorial Assistant: Anna Villarruel
Production Editor: Melanie Birdsall
Copy Editor: Diane DiMura
Typesetter: C&M Digitals (P) Ltd.
Proofreader: Sue Irwin
Indexer: Joan Shapiro
Cover Designer: Karine Hovsepian
Marketing Manager: Nicole Elliott

15 16 17 18 19 10 9 8 7 6 5 4 3 2 1

Brief Contents

Detailed Contents

Preface

I did not want to write this book. Yet here I am beginning a fourth edition. Many changes have occurred in the field of qualitative research since the third edition of this book in 2011, let alone since its inception in 1998. To use just one example, it is a part of everyday job listing now to actually announce faculty position in Qualitative Research Methods. In addition, numerous journals, books, handbooks, encyclopedias, websites, electronic mailing lists, blogs, discussion boards, and conferences are now part of our everyday existence. This was not the case when I began my journey in qualitative methods teaching and research. I see this fourth edition as something of an extension of the previous editions with additional new exercises. As I reflect on my own career in teaching qualitative research methods to doctoral students in the arts, sciences, and humanities, this edition is rewritten to walk through each additional moment in constructing our field of study as it continues to evolve.

Those of you who used the third edition know that I like to reimagine and create spaces for integrating the arts into the research process. In fact, I see the work of the qualitative researcher most like that of the artist. I use the metaphor of dance and stretching once again with incorporation of yoga as a metaphor cast in the light of contemplative activity. While the stretching metaphor is obvious in both, each relies on a strong history and at the same time a strong commitment to change, adaptation, and metamorphosis. Also, since my study of yoga and meditation has intensified, I am writing here about contemplative qualitative inquiry throughout this book. I am using Zen as a metaphor for understanding how important reflection and a quiet mind can be in terms of advancing our understanding of qualitative inquiry (see Janesick, 2015).

This edition will have many new components. The new components here include an entire new chapter on Technology as a Habit of Mind, a major section on Zen as a metaphor for understanding qualitative inquiry, and ten new exercises that cover reflection, writing, creativity development, technology, and writing poetry. In addition, new examples of interview analysis, new ways to represent data, and ethics are revisited in light of new material which has been generated in our field.

POETIC AND CONTEMPLATIVE RECONSTRUCTIONS

In addition, I will concentrate more fully on *narrative and poetic writing, analysis,* and *presentation of data to tell a story and the integration of technology into our work.* I am keeping the theoretical frame of John Dewey's habits of mind. I cannot think of or find a better way to look at our work. If we look at our work as observers, interviewers, reflective journal writers, photographers, and web-based connoisseurs as habits of mind, the dancer's and philosopher's idea of "practice makes perfect" prevails. Likewise, I am integrating in this edition an overall exercise of writing a research reflective journal upon doing all the exercises and to develop each particular habit. After reading this text, my goal is for you to practice narrative writing in the researcher reflective journal. Having recently completed a book on *Contemplative Qualitative Inquiry: Practicing the Zen of Research* (2015), I will include some exercises that foster Zen approaches to our work. Put another way, this book is about *critical literacy* and *critical writing.* Observations must be understood through a critical lens while documenting and writing. Interview transcripts eventually are reinvented in new forms, such as poetry, as a critical edge in representation of data and pushing writing into a poetic mode. The researcher reflective journal is all about critical writing, thinking, synthesizing, and communicating. The use of photography and video as research tools enriches our stories as well. Thus, the text is recast with an eye to history, to the digital era, to art and poetry, and to writing skills and development, with one foot still in the trenches of day-to-day negotiations with the Institutional Review Boards (IRBs) and various public stakeholders who are our partners.

I have been teaching qualitative research methods since my doctoral studies at Michigan State University. There, I became obsessed with Dewey's work on art as experience, experience as education, and habits, and this struck a chord with me that resonated with my work as a qualitative researcher and choreographer. His elegant thoughts on habits of mind have always inspired me. I hope to continue to add to our field by using habits of mind as the organizer for this book. While you will find many new exercises in the book, I have not abandoned the existing exercises, for they naturally set the stage for developing good habits of mind and researcher muscles as the researcher is the research instrument in true qualitative work. By using the arts, specifically poetry and photography, as components of qualitative research projects, I hope this fourth edition extends and strengthens our understanding of content knowledge, theory, and practice.

A HISTORICAL GLANCE AT QUALITATIVE METHODS

We are fortunate to live in this era of qualitative inquiry and its development as a serious locus of study. Having lived through the 1980s and 1990s with numerous discussions about the qualitative and quantitative differences, similarities, issues, problems and possibilities, I think we can now move forward. Historically, we still focus on the fact that the types of questions we ask are suited to our methods; our theoretical frames are suited to our inquiry and the way we tell stories of lived experience in the best way possible. The exciting changes in our field continue and are unstoppable. For example, now we see job announcements specifically for professors who teach qualitative methods of research. We have a wide range of journals on qualitative methods, content-specific major journals devoting sections specifically to qualitative work, and a growing number of qualitative methods texts, conferences, colloquia, and webinars.

Our persistence has paid off. We are still here and excited to move forward. I have found that readers of the previous edition have written or stated to me that they want to be better at interviewing, observing, and writing. I am motivated to move forward with this fourth edition to do just that. I am hopeful that through this book, you will develop curiosity, creativity, consciousness, and care about qualitative inquiry in a mindful way.

GOING FORWARD

Since the previous edition of this text, the context of our field has been illuminated by more than a dozen handbooks related to qualitative research methods and by new online and hard copy journals numbering well over five dozen. These journals include and name many of the approaches of qualitative researchers: narrative research, arts-based research, a/r/tography, action research, ethnographic research, oral history, life history, autoethnography, biography, autobiography, case study research in all its forms, phenomenological studies, grounded theory studies, feminist research approaches, netnography, and Internet inquiry to name the most prominent. In addition, websites, electronic mailing lists, blogs, social network sites, and Internet dissertation coaches, for example, have widened the repertoire of making overt all the resources that assist qualitative researchers. Furthermore, the number of conferences devoted to qualitative research projects is only growing. Many key professional organizations have divisions and special interest groups devoted to qualitative research methodology. In fact, their major journals welcome qualitative work specifically. Not only that, we see today on a regular basis, job opportunities advertising specifically for qualitative researchers. When many of us started out in this field, this was unheard of! All in all, it is a good time to test the boundaries of and to develop new and better ways to do qualitative research. I hope this edition contributes to emphasizing stretching and development.

In this fourth edition, I have reconstructed some of the exercises from the third edition and added new exercises. New examples are used from current works throughout the text and in the appendixes. New in this edition, you will find the following:

1. A focus on developing good habits of mind, including the observation habit, the interview habit, the writing habit, keeping a researcher reflective journal habit, the creative habit, the analysis and interpretation of data habit, contemplative habits, and the technology habit.

2. A focus on keeping a researcher reflective journal, and in fact, by the end of the book, the reader should have a substantial researcher in training portfolio and researcher reflective journal: its possibilities, its problems, the ethical implications of using digital settings in research, the use of the Web, social networking sites, interviews online, software products, and exercises for practicing digital techniques.

3. Expanded information on the habit of doing interviews in general, especially the need to pilot the interviews and to use new forms of representation such as interview data in the form of poetry.

4. An integration of the habit of writing in multiple forms, such as narrative writing, poetry, and practice, with the researcher reflective journal as a data set.

5. A section on contemplative approaches to qualitative inquiry especially using concepts from Zen.

6. Developing analytical habits that include creating categories, themes and models, and a discussion of analysis of qualitative research data.

7. New samples and examples of student work, including the use of found data poems, that is, poetry created with words from transcripts and documents, identity poetry, and other poetic forms.

9. New exercises, including the oral history/life history interview.

10. Completion of your own researcher reflective journal following from the exercises here.

In this version of the book, as in the previous editions, the arts function as the core metaphor. My life has evolved this way. From dance, which really has never left me, I have become a serious practitioner of yoga and meditation. In fact, I apply some of the concepts from Zen thinking such as non-self, impermanence, and nirvana to qualitative inquiry. You will see many references to the arts and to yoga here. There is integrity to movement in dance and in yoga that resonates with the entire shape of qualitative research techniques and processes. As one of my teachers told me, "The body is a clear place. It never lies. Once you understand your body you understand your mind." Similarly, the word *practice* is used to describe yoga and meditation as a practice. This resonates with qualitative research as a practice in itself. Qualitative research skills and techniques need development on a daily basis. This is like practicing yoga postures called *asanas*. Meditation is a reflective practice akin to the thinking time qualitative researchers need to make sense of the data collected. Thus, the Zen metaphor fits nicely with our work.

Like the arts, in qualitative research we never know who might attach themselves to our work. Nevertheless, this book has been written for any person interested in learning how to observe and see what is in front of them. It is for any person who wants to know how to interview, listen, and communicate with another human being. It is also the case that, because the qualitative researcher is the research instrument, one has to sharpen that instrument by training the eyes to see, the ears to hear, and the mouth and body to communicate. You must train your hands to write. Like a dancer or a yoga and meditation practitioner would do, one can achieve this only by practice, discipline, diligence, focus, and perseverance. Reimagining this text took on a life of its own, and the result is before you. I hope you will find these exercises useful and inspiring as you move on your journey toward becoming a better qualitative researcher, a better educator, a better writer, and a better person. Like the yoga and Zen meditation teacher who strives for mindfulness and the dancer and choreographer who strive for unity in movement, this book offers another way to view our work.

Acknowledgments

F irst and foremost, to my current and former students, I must say thanks for taking part in this adventure and always raising the bar by using imagination. To colleagues, friends, reviewers, and critics, I am most grateful. Those who contributed to the text with samples of their works in progress are generous, and I thank them for their graciousness. They are Beatrice Smith, Carolyn Stevenson, David Thornton, Angel Hernandez, Lisa Piazza, Gary Padgett, Dustin De Felice, Elizabeth Visedo, Daryl Ward, Maggie Saturley, Jose Sanchez, Oksana Vrobel, Patricia Williams Boyd, Jill Flansburg, and Ruth Slotnick. A special nod of gratitude to my yoga and meditation teachers at the Deepak Chopra Center, Chicago Yoga Center, and my teachers in Tampa for always inspiring me to stretch further. Finally, thanks to Helen Salmon, my editor, and all at SAGE who made this process creative, challenging, and caring. I am grateful.

PUBLISHER'S ACKNOWLEDGMENTS ●

SAGE gratefully acknowledges the contributions of the following reviewers:

Ruth Ban, Barry University

Vicki Chartrand, Bishop's University

Joy C. Phillips, East Carolina University

Dave Shen-Miller, Bastyr University

Wenfan Yan, University of Massachusetts Boston

About the Author

Valerie J. Janesick (PhD, Michigan State University) is Professor of Educational Leadership and Policy Studies, in the department of Leadership, Counseling, Adult, Career and Higher Education, LCACHE, University of South Florida, Tampa. She teaches classes in qualitative research methods, curriculum theory and inquiry, and ethics in leadership. Her latest book, *Contemplative Qualitative Inquiry: Practicing the Zen of Research* (2015, Left Coast Press), argues for the use of Zen approaches to qualitative inquiry cast as Contemplative Qualitative Inquiry. Her chapters in the *Handbook of Qualitative Research* (first and second editions) use dance and the arts as metaphors for understanding research. Her book, *Oral History for the Qualitative Researcher: Choreographing the Story* (2010, Guilford Press) incorporates poetry, photography, and the arts to capture lived experience. She serves on the editorial board of *The Qualitative Report* and the *International Journal of Qualitative Methods*. She continues to take classes in yoga and meditation. Correspondence to vjanesic@usf.ed.

I dedicate this text to all of my students, teachers, colleagues, friends, and mentors who continue to inspire me. Likewise, this is dedicated to the memory of Elliot W. Eisner who changed the way we think about qualitative inquiry.

1

Qualitative Research and Habits of Mind

Storytelling reveals meaning without committing the error of defining it.

—Hannah Arendt

B eginning and framing this book relies on the fact that you are the research instrument in qualitative research projects. Thus, it is important for you the researcher to practice and refine techniques and *habits of mind* for qualitative research. Habits of mind in this text will include observation habits, interview habits, writing the researcher reflective journal habit, the narrative writing habit, the habits of analysis and interpretation, the technology habit, contemplative habits, and the habit of writing poetry found in the interview transcripts. In addition, the creative habit and the collaborative habit will also be discussed. Combining and working on all these habits will also prepare you to be a reflective researcher in terms of Internet inquiry along with the issues surrounding the use of blogs as data and representing data in visual format and visual text, all with an eye toward the ethical questions embedded in our research approaches. You need to fine-tune your observation skills, your interviewing skills, and your narrative and poetic writing skills, and this edition of the book will provide exercises to assist you in this journey on the path to being a better qualitative researcher. In addition, in this technology-centered world, you need to know how to use and critique the latest technological artifacts that may or may not make your work easier. In fact, you need to practice like a dancer warming up, or the yoga student stretching and striking the perfect *asana*, or pose. You need to reflect on what works for you, like a yogi who meditates and stretches before yoga class begins. All these bodily activities help to jump-start your brain, the primary center for you, the research instrument. Thus, you need to practice seeing what is in front of you. You need to practice hearing the data, that is, listening skills to hear what your participants are telling you. You need to flex your arm muscles and write in both narrative and poetic forms. In other words, you have to be present in the study. Like the dancer or practitioner of yoga, you need the body to reflect what the mind can produce. In this fourth edition, I rely on continuing work in the classroom and in the field along with my ongoing dialogue and debate with my students, peers, and critics. As a teacher of qualitative research methods, I have been fortunate to have been both inspired and tested by my doctoral students. No matter what the geographical setting, the questions they have raised remain nearly the same:

1. How can I become a better qualitative researcher?

2. How can I improve observation skills?

3. How can I improve interview skills?

4. How can I become a better writer?

5. What can I do with these skills?

6. How can I become more creative?

7. How can I become a qualitative researcher?

8. How can I become more contemplative and reflective?

Most recently, another question has been forthcoming:

9. Can I get a job as a qualitative researcher? (A resounding yes!)

Realizing that the first seven questions have no simple answers and realizing that there is no one way to respond to these questions, I am using the concept of *stretching exercises* once again to frame this fourth edition coupled with the notion of habits of mind as a response to these questions. I have written elsewhere (Janesick, 1994, 2000, 2001, 2007) using dance as a metaphor for qualitative research design and I am extending that metaphor by using the concept of stretching through yoga, meditation, and the metaphor of Zen. Zen allows for creativity, consciousness and compassion all helpful as part of qualitative research in general and in particular. Stretching implies that you are moving from a static point to an active one. It means that you are going beyond the point at which you now stand. Just as the dancer must stretch to begin what eventually becomes the dance, the qualitative researcher may stretch by using these exercises to become better at observation and interview skills, which eventually solidify as the research project. These are meant as a starting point, not a slavish set of prescriptions. Also, in yoga, stretching is critical because you stretch not just the body but the mind as well. In fact, in yoga, every cell is activated by a series of asanas, or postures. The idea is that by activating your cells through stretching, breathing, and successive postures, you not only stretch the body, but you also stretch emotionally, mentally, and spiritually. Furthermore, meditation is a way to stretch the mind by clearing the mind of clutter (see Janesick, 2015). The notion of contemplative qualitative inquiry will also permeate this book. As a qualitative researcher in training, so to speak, you will grow in many ways as well. In fact, no matter how many tweets, Twitter accounts, Facebook postings, blogs, or Web-based activities you the researcher in training participate in, in the end, you still need to rely on yourself as the research instrument and rely on the two basic techniques of all qualitative work, observation and interviewing. Then you must write about what you observed, what you heard in the data, and what all that means. You become a master storyteller. In this book, you will find exercises to assist you in your development and hopefully assist in your definition of your role as the researcher you strive to become.

IDENTIFYING, PRACTICING, AND DEVELOPING HABITS ●

As a starting point, I see these exercises as part of shaping the prospective researcher as a disciplined and reflective, contemplative inquirer. *Disciplined inquiry*, a term borrowed from the renowned educator and philosopher John Dewey (1859–1952), assumes that we begin where we are now and, in a systematic way, proceed together to experience what it might mean to inquire. Furthermore, his notion of "habits of mind" resonates here. In this case, practice exercises are used to help in identifying a disciplined inquiry approach and to develop habits of mind. To use ballet as an example, the ballet dancer in training takes a series of beginning classes, intermediate classes, and various levels of advanced classes before going to performance *en pointe*. There is no way an individual can skip from beginning to advanced stages in ballet, or in modern dance for that matter. In fact, the modern dance student is often required to study ballet at advanced levels in order to have a stronger ability to do modern dance. So it is with yoga. You can imagine that in a discipline where your goal is to integrate breath, body, mind, and spirit, you must proceed through levels of beginning, intermediate, and advanced study. It is the same for you, the qualitative researcher in training. You work toward developing as a qualitative researcher by developing habits of mind to enable you to move toward your goal.

One has to develop habits and skills and train the body and mind incrementally. Likewise, the qualitative researcher has to train the mind, the eye, and the soul together as a habit. By doing these exercises, we allow for an interchange of ideas and practice, self-reflections, and overall evaluation of one's own progress through each of the chapters described in this text: (a) the observation and writing habit; (b) the interview and writing habit; (c) the creative habit; and (d) the analysis and writing habit, which include making sense of the data, ethics, intuition, interpretation of data, Internet inquiry, and interaction with the Institutional Review Board (IRB); (e) the contemplative habit; and (f) the technology habit. By assuming a posture of disciplined inquiry and assuming development of sturdy habits of mind, the prospective qualitative researcher is an active agent. This is not about memorizing a formula. Nor is it about dropping into a research project and finishing up quickly. This is about constructing a critical space for serious observation and interview skills habits and development of those habits. By actually constructing this space, the prospective qualitative researcher automatically begins a labor-intensive and challenging journey. This is like the journey of a dancer from first dance class to performance, or a student of yoga from beginning stretches to amazing handstands, backbends, headstands, and other postures that truly test the body and mind at every known level. This requires time, patience, diligence, ingenuity, and creativity, all of which are required for the qualitative researcher. Just as a dancer keeps track of movement phrases and critiques on performance, in the exercises described here, you will also keep track in a researcher reflective journal throughout the use of this book to reflect upon your own habits of mind as they develop. What better way to get to know yourself as a researcher and writer?

GETTING FEEDBACK AND WRITING ABOUT IT ●

Consequently, some exercises here may also provide a way to work on the role of the researcher by helping researchers to know themselves better. This can be helpful only when researchers are engaged full-time with participants in the field. Participants will trust the researcher if the researcher trusts himself or herself. It goes without saying that the researcher must have a solid knowledge of the self. One of the great things about graduate study is that if done correctly the student should grow and change remarkably. I have often remarked that graduate school is for stretching the mind and using parts of the brain that have not been used so actively previous to graduate study. One of the great things about teaching is watching that process unfold. Also, I like to think of the classroom as something of a studio space, a laboratory if you prefer, to see the various levels of habits of mind displayed in behavior. Graduate school or any learning space allows for the practice of the exercises and allows for space to fail, to receive feedback, and to redirect. Just as in a dance studio or yoga studio, constant feedback is given to allow for progression toward performance, so too in the studio of the qualitative research classroom, is there a space for critique, feedback, and redirection and not just from the instructor but from fellow researchers in training. The feedback loop is essential in this process. The dancer as artist is accustomed to the constant feedback loop of performance, critique and feedback, redirection, and then a new performance. After that performance, we do it all again with feedback and redirection to the next level. Another good example to illustrate this point can be seen in the performances at the Olympics. Judges assess the athletes through a rating system. They give feedback with that score, and then the coaches of the athletes go in depth into the redirection for the next time around. The athlete has to take part in the redirection or suffer in the ratings. All of this conveys a sense of action, dynamism, and movement forward. Now we can begin on the habits we need to develop to become a qualitative researcher and refine existing habits.

FINDING YOUR THEORETICAL HABIT ●

Research is an active verb. It is a way of seeing the world that goes beyond the ordinary. Thus, this series of practice exercises is designed to help learners along the way. In any class, there are beginners, mid-level learners, and advanced learners. The exercises written here help individuals find themselves in terms of their levels of expertise in observation, interviewing, writing, and analysis. This also requires self-knowledge.

These exercises are not a formula. I created them, and I have tested them for years. They resonate with students, and they work for me, provided students make the effort to really go the distance. In that sense, the qualitative researcher starts with two basic questions:

- What do I want to know?

- What set of techniques do I need to find out what I want to know?

This is the starting point for any research project. In qualitative work, the fact that the researcher is the research instrument requires that the senses be fine-tuned. Hence, the idea of practice on a daily basis sharpens the instrument. Many individuals can look at something and not see what is there. It is my goal to have readers of this text try to sharpen the following skills:

- Seeing through the habit of observation

- Hearing through the habit of interviewing

- Writing as a habit (researcher reflective journal, narrative writing, and poetry)

- Conceptualizing and synthesizing as a habit of mind (developing models of what occurred in the study)

- Being contemplative with a Zen-like approach and thereby reducing anti-oppressive practices

- Communicating through ordinary language

- Reflecting on and using Internet resources and tools that may help in refining yourself as the research instrument and become adept at the use of technology

One of my dance teachers once said that dancers are, in the end, architects of movement. So, before an architect builds a building, he or she must understand, for example, the use of structure and the grammar of architecture, steel, plastic, and stone. Likewise, the qualitative researcher must understand the functions and feel of observations, interviews, writing, and so on, before the final written report of the study is created. Prior to that, the researcher also needs to know the theoretical foundations that guide his or her research. In this book, exercises are designed to allow for finding your theoretical framework. What is the *ology or ism* that guides you? Is it phenomenology? Is it social reconstructionism? Is it feminism? Is it critical theory in any of its forms? Your job by the end of this book and at the end of your researcher reflective journal artifact is to identify and describe the theory that guides your work and why and how you might use that to inform your observations, interviews, and writing.

I have found that learners respond to being actively involved in these practice exercises for a number of reasons. They have told me that these exercises strengthen their confidence, imagination, and ability to cope with field emergencies. (See Appendix F for reflective journal samples.) In addition, students appreciate the fact that all of these exercises are understandable, because the language used to describe them is ordinary language. I have always found students more responsive and enthusiastic when ordinary language is used to include them in the active engagement of qualitative research. They are more excited about theory, practice, and praxis when they are not excluded from the conversation. The reader of this text will see that the exercises are described in ordinary language, following in the tradition of bell hooks (1994), who pointed out that any theory that cannot be used in everyday conversation cannot be used to educate. In addition, the actual experience and practice of these exercises in observation and interview activities often help to allay fears and misconceptions about conducting qualitative research projects. Four of the most common misconceptions stated in classes or workshops are the following:

- Doing qualitative research is easy, and anyone can do it. Many students actually tell me that they are sent into my class because they were told it is easier than doing statistics. They then discover how qualitative research projects are time intensive and labor intensive. They discover they must be an above average writer.

- You should only learn qualitative research methods to augment quantitative work. In fact, this is a most woodenheaded notion. I find myself constantly working upstream to counter this default notion of research, that research must first be quantitative.

- Most people can do interviews and observations with little or no practice. Because in the workplace an individual may interview someone at the Auto Vehicles Bureau, there is an assumption that all interviewing is the same. By contrast, in the dance world, one would never attempt a performance without years of training, practice, and movement through beginning, intermediate, and advanced-level class work.

- Anyone can write a journal with no practice, preparation, or quiet time. Writing takes time and practice and should be a daily ritual if you are to effectively communicate your findings from a given study. Writing every day is a must.

In a sense, this text is a response to these four misconceptions. I see these exercises as an opportunity to continue the conversation with individuals who want to take the plunge and develop strong habits of mind that allow for developing observation and interview skills. This of course means developing habits of mind for vigorous descriptive writing and powerful poetic writing if need be. This is one approach to learn qualitative research methods. Although I have used these exercises with doctoral students in education and human services, there is the continuing hope and possibility that beginning researchers at the master's degree level may also find these exercises useful, not only in education and human services but in other disciplines as well.

● DEVELOPING HABITS OF MIND

I engage learners in these exercises over a period of 15 weeks, the artificial constraint of the given semester time line. In the best of all possible worlds, I would prefer a year or more, perhaps three semesters or even three courses over three semesters. Habits practiced include

1. **The Observation and Writing Habit.** Here, observation and narrative writing are connected, demanding time in terms of preparation and implementation and space for feedback and rewriting.

2. **The Interview and Writing Habit.** This includes both narrative and poetic writing. Interviews may be rendered in poetry constructed from the data, found data poems, or evocative poems, sometimes called evocative texts, prompted by all the data sets. In addition, technology has enabled us to make short videos and integrate those into the narrative.

3. **The Reflective Journal Writing Habit.** This allows for specifying all that encompasses your role as the research instrument.

A clear and descriptive statement of the role of the researcher in any project can only help to strengthen the final product. This includes looking at qualitative research as a contemplative activity, and I will include some concepts from Zen philosophy to describe contemplative qualitative research.

4. **The Analysis and Interpretation Habit.** Here, time is needed for thinking, rewriting, and eventually constructing a model of what occurred in your study. This may also involve critical use of software or Internet data resources.

5. **The Creative Habit.** This is where intuition and creativity come into play and should be documented in addition to detailed documentation of any ethical issues that arise in a given study.

6. **The Contemplative Habit.** This is about framing your research by knowing yourself, living in the present moment and taking a Zen view of your research. This implies reducing anti-oppressive practices in research and pedagogy.

7. **The Technology Habit.** Qualitative researchers use technology throughout the research project in various ways and at many points in the study. Using free software for assistance in transcriptions, voice-to-text software or applications, stunning graphics and models for capturing findings, or the use of photography and video clips—we must be tuned into technology.

   Increasingly, Internet interviews, social network research, and complete integration of technology is becoming more commonplace and useful to the researcher.

Learners simultaneously design, conceptualize, and conduct a mini-study. Within the study, each learner must conduct interviews and observations and keep a researcher reflective journal. During the first third of the class, learners practice exercises in and out of class that focus on observation, writing, getting feedback, rewriting, and the role of the researcher. The next third of the class is spent on interviewing exercises and practice in ongoing analysis. The learners also share their journals-in-progress with one another in small groups. Here, students may wish to create poetry from the interview data from documents received from participants in the study and from their own researcher reflective journals. The final third of the class is devoted to the final analysis of data, issues regarding intuition in research, and ethical issues. Ideally, the observation exercises and role of the researcher exercises are practiced for about five or six weeks, at which point the learners are asked to develop a plan in writing for their mini-studies. Then, as they go into the field, they work simultaneously on interview exercises and role of the researcher exercises for the remainder of the semester, all the while reading selected books and articles in the area. They immediately begin to keep a written record in the form of a researcher reflective journal in order to keep track of their thoughts about the readings and engagement with the written text. This also prepares them for entry into the field. Although this series of exercises grew out of my work with students and workshop members, surely others may be interested in this book. Likewise, the reader of this text can be immersed in these exercises at any pace he or she may choose. However, as my meditation teacher once told me, "It takes thirty days to develop a habit." Similar to John Dewey's concept, the learner has to develop the habits of mind that allow for being better at writing, interviewing, and observing. Also, in the social world, because of the vast number of hours spent at the computer, online, video gaming, Facebooking, tweeting, and all the investment in Internet time frames, prospective researchers are using parts of the brain that do not typically engage what is needed to observe and *see* or to interview and *hear*. I am almost convinced that even creativity may be at risk if Web-based activities distract from development of the research instrument, you, the researcher. Basically, this book is an attempt to begin a conversation with individuals who may not have had the time, energy, or interest in practicing qualitative techniques but are now ready to jump into the studio of the social world and stretch. Of course, there are always complications. For example, just the number of terms used to refer to qualitative research alone could confound anyone. Take a look at the list in the following section.

● TERMS USED TO DESCRIBE QUALITATIVE RESEARCH

The terms on the next page are just those I find myself using when working with students on their research projects. It is not exhaustive. The point of listing them is to alert the reader to the numerous terms. Just as there is no one way to learn ballet or no one way to learn yoga, there is no one way to learn how to be a qualitative researcher. Find your personal velocity. Which approach resonates with the person you are? When you know that, learn all you can about that approach. By now, there are many examples in textbooks, articles, the World Wide Web, and dissertation abstracts to name a few resources. Then, like the dancer and the yogi, practice, practice, practice. Practice also includes feedback, critique, redirection, and rewriting. For example, I took my first yoga class in the 1970s, a hatha yoga class. Since then, I have taken classes in Bikram yoga, Ashtanga yoga, Iyengar yoga, and Kundalini yoga. Yet after all this, I have returned to totally immerse myself in hatha yoga. I returned to my starting point. So, from my experience, I suggest you find your niche from the approaches listed above. It is surely not meant to be all inclusive, but rather, a starting point for understanding the complexity of qualitative research approaches. I refer you to *Qualitative Inquiry: A Dictionary of Terms* by Thomas A. Schwandt (2001) for more definitive information. In addition, qualitative work has certain characteristics, such as the following:

Some Terms Used to Identify Qualitative Work

A/r/tography	Field research	Narrative study
Action research	Historiography	Netnography
Arts-based inquiry	Interpretive interactionist study	Oral history
Autoethnography		Performance inquiry
Case study	Interpretive policy analysis	Philosophical analysis study
Descriptive study		
Ecological study	Life history	Portraiture
Ethnoarcheology	Microethnography	Teacher research
Ethnography	Narrative research	Webography

Furthermore, in qualitative work, certain questions resonate with the techniques and approaches we use. By the questions we ask, we are suited to qualitative work. In the following list of characteristics of qualitative work, you may see a reflection of the kind of questions suited to you, the qualitative researcher.

CHARACTERISTICS OF QUALITATIVE WORK   ●

1. It is holistic: It attempts to understand the whole picture of the social context under study; in education at least, we have trampled on this unmercifully. Often, individuals call their work qualitative when in fact it is not. This is due to the fact that they ask questions ill-suited to any of the main qualitative

approaches. They do not use the foundational frameworks for qualitative work either.

2. It looks at relationships within a system or subculture: Again, this relates to the holistic nature of qualitative work. There is nothing qualitative about doing a survey on Survey Monkey and adding one question that requires a sentence or two. You will simply get a sentence or two of narrative, verbal, self-report data. Yet time and again, individuals will call their studies qualitative without meeting the rigorous standards of qualitative work. Context is everything in qualitative work.

3. It refers to the personal, face-to-face, immediate interactions in a given setting.

4. It is attentive to detail and focused on understanding the social setting rather than predicting and controlling.

5. It demands equal time in the field and in analysis; often individuals rush to meet a deadline and in their haste forget to analyze what is in front of them.

6. It incorporates a complete description of the role of the researcher; too often this is forgotten or recklessly done. The description of the role of the researcher must incorporate the biases, beliefs, and values of the researcher up front in the study. In addition, the actual specifics should be described as to the number and types of observations and interviews, length of interviews, how transcripts were completed, how documents were collected and used, and so on.

7. It relies on the researcher as the research instrument.

8. It incorporates informed consent documentation and is responsive to ethical concerns in the study.

9. It acknowledges ethical issues in fieldwork with a complete discussion of these issues.

10. It considers, in many cases, participants as coresearchers in the project.

11. It tells a story in narrative or poetic forms. A good story based on your data can take you far.

12. It is useful for the reader of the research in terms of the coherence, cohesion, insight, and actual words of the participants.

13. It often incorporates the arts, especially poetry, video, performance, photography and painting.

14. It values the life of the mind, contemplation, compassion, and creativity.

I must return here to the metaphors of yoga and dance. Dance as an art form is one of the most rigorous and demanding of the arts. For one thing, physical tone and health are critical to the survival of the dancer. The hours of working out are not just physical, because the physical and mental connections engage the dance artist totally. The dancer's life is short in terms of performance due to dependence on a superbly functioning instrument—the body. The only practice that is more demanding is the serious study of yoga. I mention all of this to punctuate the fact that the discipline and desire of the dancer and the yoga student are persistent and indomitable, much like the qualitative researcher. As a professor of qualitative research methods, as a former choreographer and dancer, and now as a student of yoga, I see the role of the researcher as one characterized by discipline, persistence, diligence, creativity, and desire to communicate the findings so as to reflect the social setting and its members. This is like the dancer who reflects the dance and the *yogini*, or female yoga practitioner, who reflects inner growth and outer physical strength and endurance. Likewise, qualitative research methods are related to dance in another way, in that the body is the instrument of dance and the researcher is the research instrument in qualitative work. Furthermore, in yoga, the body and mind are integrated in all movement, work, and meditation in order to walk in balance of all phases of living.

QUESTIONS SUITED TO QUALITATIVE RESEARCH METHODS ●

1. Questions of the quality of a given innovation, program, or curriculum

2. Questions regarding meaning or interpretation

3. Questions related to sociolinguistic aspects of a setting

4. Questions related to the whole system, as in a classroom, school, school district, and so on

5. Questions regarding the political, economic, and social aspects of schooling or society

6. Questions regarding the hidden curriculum

7. Questions pertaining to the social context of schooling, such as race, class, and gender issues

8. Questions pertaining to implicit theories about how the social world works

9. Questions about a person's views on his or her life and work

10. Questions that are viewed as controversial

11. Questions related to public policy

12. Questions no one else is willing to ask

13. Questions that point out oppressive practices

● USING THEORY IN QUALITATIVE RESEARCH

As the reader is most likely aware, in qualitative work, theory is used at every step of the research process. Theoretical frames influence the questions we ask, the design of the study, the implementation of the study, and the way we interpret data. In addition, qualitative researchers develop theoretical models of what occurred in a study in order to explain their findings, warts and all. Qualitative researchers have an obligation to fully describe their theoretical postures at all stages of the research process, just as the choreographer fully describes and explains each component of a dance plan. As a choreographer, I was always looking for the asymmetrical movement in order to tell the story in some kind of symmetry. This is what I hope these experiences will help the reader to accomplish. Like the student of yoga, who works for unity in mind, breath, and body, the qualitative researcher ultimately is looking for this unity in the end in the final written report.

Speaking for myself, I have had many influences throughout my career, but the most notable influences from my own experience as a teacher include the work of John Dewey on education and art as experience, aesthetics, and habits of mind. In addition, I've looked to the work of Elliot Eisner on arts-based approaches to educational research and connoisseurship; critical pedagogy, cultural studies, and the work of Henry A. Giroux, Joe Kincheloe, and Shirley Steinberg; feminist theory and the work of Jane Flax and bell hooks; and postmodern sociology and the work of Norman Denzin. My former dance instructors and the texts written by my past teachers—Erick Hawkins and Merce Cunningham, Martha

Graham and various teachers from her school, Margit Heskett and teachers from the Twyla Tharp school—have made a deep impression on my work. I call myself a critical, postmodern, interpretive interactionist with a feminist artistry. In addition, the works of Paolo Freire and Myles Horton have influenced my thinking. Horton's idea that we have our own solutions within us fits perfectly with interpretive work. Likewise, Freire's education for freedom is identical to Merce Cunningham's philosophy of dance. My own qualitative research projects have been guided by the theoretical frames of interpretive interactionism and critical pedagogy. This does not mean that other frameworks are incompatible or not useful. I have great affinity for phenomenology as described by Max Van Manen, the work of Valerie Yow on oral history, and the work being done in medicine by Atul Gawande in terms of narrative case studies. In qualitative research methods, of course Harry Wolcott, Norman Denzin, Yvonna Lincoln, Egon Guba, Judith Pressle, Irene and Herbert Rubin, and Valerie Polakow have influenced me in many ways.

A great deal of the debate over qualitative methods has to do with the issue of theory and its place in the research project. I would characterize this as a struggle of values. Many feel there is definitive knowledge about how to proceed in research substantively, theoretically, and procedurally. Others see research as a way to pursue moral, ethical, and political questions. I ask learners to think about and read many texts to get a feel for what resonates with them, what makes sense given their points of situation in doctoral studies. I often say that, in order to do qualitative research, you must accept that there is no universal truth, that all findings are tentative and context based, and that we live in an irrational and chaotic world. For those who want a neat and tidy social world, this is definitely not for you. We begin with a serious and prevailing curiosity about the social world. The focus is on formulating good questions. Many scientists, artists, and writers agree that formulating a question and problem is the essence of creative work. As Einstein and Infeld (1938) said

> The formulation of a problem is often more essential than its solution, which may be merely a matter of . . . skill. To raise new questions, new possibilities, to regard old questions from a new angle, requires creative imagination and marks real advances in science. (p. 35)

What this means for the purposes of this book and the study of qualitative research methods is that we transform ourselves by looking and seeing what is before us in our observations. In addition, we hear the data as it is spoken to us in interviews. We refine our narrative writing skills to be able to put forth a trustworthy, credible, and authentic story. We incorporate technology and we are sensitive to ethical issues and informed consent. We inform our participants about the study throughout the study. (See Appendix A.)

The world for the qualitative researcher is tentative, problematic, ever changing, irrational, and yes, even chaotic. Many qualitative researchers see research as participatory, dialogic, transformative, and educative. It may be a constructivist, critical, and transformative approach to research. In this text, I am using the metaphor of stretching in dance and yoga as an art form to illuminate some of the many components of qualitative work—observation skills, interview skills, and the role of the researcher skills—in order to arrive at that level of participation, transformation, and education. One way to think about all is in a nutshell is

Decide (what you want to know and how you will find out about it)

Initiate (by finding participants)

Practice (observing, interviewing, writing, reflecting)

Write (constantly and faithfully)

Rewrite (constantly and faithfully)

Connect and share your writing (to get feedback and rewrite once again)

Compose (the final narrative)

● **ARTISTIC APPROACHES TO QUALITATIVE RESEARCH**

There is a long and embedded theoretical history for me starting with John Dewey's (1958) *Art as Experience* (*AAE*). In fact, for Dewey, art was not about daydreaming but about providing a sense of the whole of something, much the same way qualitative researchers see the whole picture in their slice of the case under study. In *The Early Works* (*TEW*), Dewey (1967) states

The poet not only detects subtler analogies than other (men), and provides the subtler link of identity where others see confusion and difference, but the form of his expression, his language;

images, etc. are controlled by deeper unities . . . of feeling. The objects, ideas, connected are perhaps remote from each other to the intellect, but feeling fuses them. Unity of feeling gives artistic unity, wholeness of effect, to the composition. (p. 96)

So for Dewey, especially in *TEW*, imagination was highly valued and was explained in terms of feeling. In 1931, when Dewey delivered the first of the William James lectures at Harvard, the subject was that which became *AAE*. He was roundly criticized at the time. Most problematic was Dewey's suggestion that art is about communication and experience. How history changes us! It would be very difficult today to find someone to disagree with the wisdom of Dewey on this point. Dewey refused to separate art from ordinary experience. He said that the artist should "restore continuity between the refined and intensified forms of experience that are works of art and the everyday events, doings, and sufferings that are universally recognized to constitute experience" (1958, p. 97). The qualitative researcher is involved in this artistic activity because he or she must describe and explain the lived experience of participants in his or her study. I have written (2008) on the clarity of art as experience and that we are always looking for that which is beyond the obvious. That is the artist's way, the dancer and choreographer's way, and the way of the qualitative researcher. Furthermore, the notion of developing habits of mind that Dewey spoke of and wrote of in 1938 still resonates for me today. Although he was writing about logic, the main idea of making your mind work is important. It pertains to the dancer and the yogi for mind and body union. In fact, that word *yoga*, means "union" and is interpreted as union of mind and body.

I ask the reader's indulgence here as I try to make the ordinary activities described in this text evocative of Dewey's notions in order for the prospective qualitative researcher to eventually become aware of a critical approach to art and research as experience. This is the only way that makes sense for me. But even those who may not wish to revisit Dewey's ideas on art as experience or on habits of mind can certainly find points of integration and connection in whatever other theoretical framework is used to guide their research.

For the purposes of this text, the description and observation exercises relate to the field-focused nature of the work and to developing the habit of observing, seeing, and writing about that experience. The role of the researcher exercises relates to the self as research instrument and to developing the creative habit. The interview exercises relate to the interpretive, expressive nature of this work, the presence of voice in the text, and developing this habit and writing about it. The analysis of data exercises and Internet inquiry exercises relate to the points of coherence, insight, and utility. As an umbrella for all this, narrative writing is the key to communicating purposes, methods, findings, and interpretation of the study and developing the habit of using the brain for analysis and interpretation. In addition, any use of poetry found in the interview transcripts or documents also fall in this frame. In fact, photography, video, or any Web-based inquiry can also fall into the creative habit and analytical habit of mind. I ask all my students to be above average in writing ability, among other things, in order to complete a qualitative dissertation and subsequent qualitative work. The arduous habit of writing of course demands critical thinking. Here again, the researcher as research instrument must be actively involved in developing insight, creativity, acute observation, sensitive interviewing, and all digital techniques to tell the story of what was found in the research project. This can most often be achieved through diligent practice.

CONTEMPLATIVE QUALITATIVE INQUIRY AND THE ZEN OF RESEARCH

Some may wonder what contemplation, meditation, and Zen have to do with qualitative research. I use the term *contemplative qualitative inquiry* to be an advance organizer or a heuristic tool for understanding the role of the qualitative researcher, ways to represent data and ways to disseminate findings in our research. Zen also emphasizes *mindfulness, consciousness, and compassion*; all of these allow for enlightenment and insight into living. Mindfulness carries with it as well the notion of unlearning oppressive and harmful practices. Recently the term *anti-oppressive pedagogy* has been coined and is exactly what resonates with Zen mindfulness. Thus, the idea of Zen is a powerful stimulus to thinking in a new more expansive way. It has potential for influencing many fields of study. Certainly this has implications for research. It is for this reason that I want to emphasize Zen as a way to understand and advance qualitative research projects given questions that are appropriate for qualitative methods. Three cornerstones of Zen philosophy are **impermanence, nonself**, and **nirvana**. Zen brings us immediately to the awareness that impermanence is a fact of life. Everything changes. This is resonant with qualitative research since we capture our participants lived experience at some moment in time. This capacity to even accept and realize what impermanence means is in itself a big step forward in coming to understanding Zen and understanding qualitative research methods. Put simply, *all findings are tentative*. This is true of all research approaches, but we in the qualitative arena acknowledge this openly and happily. Similarly qualitative work allows for the impermanence in the social world. At any given moment, things can and do change. We embrace that as a fact of life. Furthermore, Zen teachers advise that we think like a beginner. The beginner's mind is open to all possibilities.

In studying Zen meditation, that is what is meant by a beginner's mind. It is wiped clean of the self in Zen. In qualitative research methodology, it is wiped clean of proving something, generalizing and fitting into a formula. It means *giving up permanence*. This is the first step to mindfulness and includes at least an awareness to live so as to avoid oppressive behavior.

In addition, non-self, that is the realization that we are connected to people and the entire universe, is a powerful frame for understanding qualitative research and its theory and practice. So rather than think of the self which is a delusion in Zen thinking, think of being connected to the entire world through the participants in your study. This is like the notion of reflexivity and the ability to take on perspectives of our participants. In other words, we are all in this together struggling to make sense of our respective worlds.

Finally, nirvana, which is the knowledge that we are one with and in the universe can be useful here. The concept of nirvana is that the self is basically a delusion. How can there be a self if we are connected to each other and the universe? Again, this is powerful way of looking at the world that we can learn from Eastern thinkers and writers. If we are aware of our connections we come to a state of bliss, free of suffering which characterizes nirvana. How practical this is for those of us using qualitative methods to make sense of a person's life. We are connected to our participant(s) whether we wish to be or not. All in all, I call this contemplative qualitative research. The contemplative component has to do with the stillness and silence of thinking with a meditative orientation.

WHY TRY THESE EXERCISES? ●

Although these exercises are for those who are interested, they are not for everyone. Not everyone has tapped into his or her artistic intelligence. I am in agreement with those writers who have found that we all have an artistic side as well as multiple intelligences (see the work of Howard Gardner), but I have also found that the learner must take an *active* role in discovering his or her artistic intelligence. I am constantly amazed at learners who tell me that they cannot draw. When we do the drawing exercise in class, they are doubly amazed that, to some extent, they can draw, and when they revisit that exercise later, they have to admit that they can indeed draw. More on that topic will follow when we arrive at that exercise. In addition to this active stance, the artistic theoretical frame that drives these exercises is critical, transformative, educative, and ethical. These exercises were created from a lifetime and career of reading and action. More or less, these writers were part of my dialogue with myself: John Dewey, Elliot Eisner, Myles Horton, Henry Giroux, Maxine Greene, Joe Kincheloe, and Paolo Freire in education. Twyla Tharp, Erick Hawkins, Merce Cunningham, and Martha Graham have influenced my thinking about dance and choreography. Yoga writers who influenced me are both contemporary like Rodney Yee and historical like Yogi Sachitananda. Just as the dancer might look before leaping, so the reader of this text might look with a critical and enlightened eye. I must ask the reader to do something that is very difficult: Give up one view of the world and imagine another.

In other words, just because there are exercises for all levels, this does not mean that in the final product, that is, the creation of a work of art and science, it will be easy. It takes persistence, determination, preparation, passion, diligence, and above-average writing skills to do all this. Nevertheless, I purposely chose to write in a clear, descriptive, narrative style. I write in ordinary language and in my voice for the following reasons:

1. **To *disrupt* what some have called academic writing, which distances the reader from what is written and denigrates the reader's experience.** Academic writing often excludes many people who want to be part of the conversation. By eliminating thick jargon and tired phrases, we open the space for a creative use of ordinary language. Thus, more people may read our stories.

2. **To *educate and engage* the reader, who may not, up to now, have had an interest in qualitative research.** I am writing both for people who love qualitative research and those who think they hate qualitative research. In addition to this, I like to educate my coworkers. I often tell my students that they must show all the texts they have read to the professors who sit on their committees, if for no other reason than to let those members know of the vast array of written texts about qualitative research. Another point of educating is to make the learner aware of the amount of time, money, and energy involved in

the undertaking of a qualitative study. (See Appendix J for the recent documentation of the cost of a recently completed qualitative dissertation, for example.)

3. To *inspire* **the reader to go further and read the writings on theory and practice in qualitative research.** Students who are turned on to qualitative research purchase all the texts referred to in whatever they are reading on the topic at the moment. They also join discussion groups and electronic mailing lists, and they scan dissertation abstracts regularly for the latest qualitative dissertations. Later in this text, you will find numerous examples of Web-based resources to inspire further study. In fact, since the second edition of this book, Internet inquiry has evolved into a mainstream research genre in many fields, and that will be discussed later in this fourth edition.

4. To *demystify* **the research process by the use of ordinary language, thereby opening up the pool of researchers in our field.** *In a very real sense, qualitative research is contributing to a more democratic space for doing research.* As in the past, currently, the language of quantitative research is off-putting to many students, and as a result, educational research at least has been disavowed or overlooked. For too long, research has been cloaked in secrecy and jargon, and behavior to keep things hidden has been the rule. We call it the curse of the ivory tower. In addition, when research reports are published with all the jargon and formulas, there is a distancing of the reader from the report. Here, in this paradigm, the reader is part of the report because it is made understandable. With the questions of the postmodern era forever before us, we have no choice but to deconstruct and demystify the research process. One way that qualitative researchers are ahead here is that we already value and use ordinary language. We already value ordinary people in ordinary life. We want to describe and explain the social world. Some researchers even go so far as to hope for a better world through application of research findings. We are researchers of subjectivity and proud of it.

5. To *democratize* **the research process.** Qualitative research techniques open up the process of research to many more researchers who take responsibility for the rigor and high standards of this work. Consequently, there is less emphasis on only a few elite individuals taking ownership of these approaches. In this postmodern era of social constructivist models of learning and teaching, which open up knowledge acquisition, qualitative research is a part of opening up all research processes to those previously excluded from the conversation.

The Internet and all its strengths and weaknesses have given us a new and bold democratic path. The wiki world, for example, invites the viewer to add content with verification to a knowledge base, such as Wikipedia. Our job is to be critical agents who tune our bodies and minds to adhere to the rigor of qualitative research methods and to disseminate the research findings with care, with precision, with ethical awareness, and with authenticity. This is in short taking part in the democracy of the research process. We also commit to anti-oppressive practices—also a cornerstone of democratic process.

6. **To *revive an awareness of the importance of the arts* specifically through poetry, visual arts, performance arts and music.** Qualitative researchers tell a story of what occurred in a social setting. More and more researchers are using journals with drawings to represent data, poetry for the literature review and data presentation, and video and audio digital components in the project to describe and explain various stages in the research process. The arts are helpful to the qualitative researcher.

● HOW TO USE THIS BOOK

The whole idea of this text is to get the reader to stretch and open new possibilities of doing research in a given social context. These exercises should get you started in the actual experience of doing observations and conducting interviews. After all, fieldwork is mostly work, so you must strengthen your body and spirit to do it well. You may wish to scan the book before beginning the exercises. I begin with observation exercises in order to force you into another way of thinking about and seeing the world. Think of these exercises as making you a stronger, more flexible, and more fluid researcher, just as the dancer becomes stronger, more flexible, and more fluid after stretching. Likewise, the practice of yoga, if done correctly, can strengthen body, mind, and spirit. There is a regularity and discipline to fieldwork, much like that of dance and yoga, and these exercises are progressive in difficulty in each of the major sections. The next set of exercises is about interviewing, writing, creativity, and contemplation.

The exercises provide a process for developing skills in the main techniques of qualitative research methods, that is, observation and interview. The shape of these exercises developed over time and will continue to develop. In dance, there are no static points. Likewise, in qualitative research, there are no static points, only reshaping the approach and continually questioning and analyzing. The reader may also notice that many of these exercises refer to the arts in order to broaden the conversation and thinking about the research process. I have always found that my own background in drawing, photography, drama, and dance has provided the foundation for activities that eventually provide access for many students to improve as interviewers and observers of the world. For me, research is alive and active. It is the most exciting use of many ways of looking at and interpreting the world. I hope these exercises will convey a portion of that enthusiasm for knowing. By the way, enthusiasm and passion for your research project is essential to sustain you in the many hours of labor in the field. Fieldwork is indeed hard and demanding work after all is said and done. This work needs to be documented, and a favorite and emancipating way to do this is through writing a reflective journal while reading this book and doing the exercises. Starting in the next chapter, and at the end of every chapter, you will be asked to compile entries through various exercises in journal writing. Thus, after reading and working through the exercises you select, you will have your research reflective journal started as a test drive, so to speak, for your actual dissertation or other research project.

THE AUDIENCE FOR THIS BOOK   ●

This text is for anyone who wants to practice the two most prominent techniques used in qualitative research projects: interviewing and observation. At the same time, writing skills and digital inquiry skills go hand in hand with these two cornerstones of our work. In addition, some exercises included in the text are for the purpose of developing a stronger awareness of the role of the researcher through writing, reflecting upon ethical issues in qualitative work, and developing the creative habit. Furthermore, using Zen concepts such as compassion, consciousness, mindfulness, and contemplation can only increase awareness. I have become aware, since previous editions of this text, that it is also for teacher-educators, nurse educators, and teachers in training. Because the fields of teacher education and nursing often rely on action research, critical case studies, and teacher research, this book may assist those members of the educational community. As an educator, I would include the group of students of research as a major portion of the audience. Colleagues who wish to practice qualitative research methods are certainly included as well. Finally all those who think they hate qualitative research may adjust their view by taking a look at this book. May the reader of this text have a passion for disciplined contemplative inquiry, a high tolerance for ambiguity, a rich imagination, an open mind toward ordinary language usage, and a very good sense of humor.

SUGGESTED RESOURCES

The following references are resources to help you navigate this text and learn more about qualitative research. They have been remarkably helpful to students.

Berg, B. (2007). *Qualitative research for the social sciences* (6th ed.). Boston, MA: Allyn & Bacon.

Best, J. (2004). *More damned lies and statistics: How numbers confuse public issues.* Berkeley: University of California Press.

Cole, A., & Knowles, G. (2001). *Lives in context: The art of life history research.* Sherman Oaks, CA: AltaMira.

Charmaz, K. (2000). Grounded theory: Objectivist and constructivist methods. In N. K. Denzin & Y. S. Lincoln (Eds.), *Handbook of qualitative research* (pp. 509–535). Thousand Oaks, CA: Sage.

Creswell, J. W. (2013). *Qualitative inquiry and research design: Choosing among five approaches* (3rd ed.). Thousand Oaks, CA: Sage.

Denzin, N. K., & Lincoln, Y. S. (2002). *Handbook of qualitative research* (2nd ed.). Thousand Oaks, CA: Sage.

Denzin, N. K., & Lincoln, Y. S. (2003). *The landscape of qualitative research: Theories and issues.* Thousand Oaks, CA: Sage.

Denzin, N. K., & Lincoln, Y. S. (2003). *The strategies of qualitative inquiry* (2nd ed.). Thousand Oaks, CA: Sage.

Denzin N. K., & Lincoln, Y. S. (2006). *Handbook of qualitative research* (3rd ed.). Thousand Oaks, CA: Sage.

Dewey, J. (1938). *Experience and education.* New York, NY: Collier.

Dewey, J. (1958). *Art as experience.* New York, NY: Capricorn.

Dewey, J. (1967). *The early works.* Carbondale: Southern Illinois University Press.

Eisner, E. W. (1991). *The enlightened eye.* New York, NY: Macmillan.

Janesick, V. J. (1994). The dance of qualitative research design: Metaphor, methodolatry, and meaning. In N. K. Denzin & Y. S. Lincoln (Eds.), *Handbook of qualitative research* (pp. 209–219). Thousand Oaks, CA: Sage.

Janesick, V. J. (1999). A journal about journal writing as a qualitative research technique: History, issues, and reflections. *Qualitative Inquiry, 5*(4), 505–523.

Janesick, V. J. (2000). The choreography of qualitative research design: Minuets, improvisations, and crystallization. In N. K. Denzin & Y. S. Lincoln (Eds.), *Handbook of qualitative research* (2nd ed., pp. 370–399). Thousand Oaks, CA: Sage.

Janesick, V. J. (2001). Intuition and creativity: A pas de deux for the qualitative researcher. *Qualitative Inquiry, 7*(5), 531–540.

Janesick, V. J. (2007). Oral history as a social justice project: Issues for the qualitative researcher. *The Qualitative Report, 12*(1), 111–121. Retrieved from http://www.nova.edu/ssss/QR/QR12-1/janesick.pdf

Janesick, V. J. (2008). Art and experience: Lessons learned from Dewey and Hawkins. In J. G. Knowles & A. L. Cole (Eds.). *Handbook of arts in qualitative inquiry: Perspectives, methodologies, examples and issues* (pp. 477–483). Thousand Oaks, CA: Sage.

Janesick, V. J. (2015). *Contemplative qualitative inquiry: Practicing the Zen of research.* Walnut Creek, CA: Left Coast Press.

Leavy, P. (2015) *Method meets art: Arts-based research practice* (2nd ed.). New York, NY: Guilford Press.

Knowles, J. G., & Cole, A. L. (Eds.). (2008). *Handbook of the arts in qualitative research.* Thousand Oaks, CA: Sage.

Pascale, C. M. (2011). *Cartographies of knowledge: Exploring qualitative epistemologies.* Thousand Oaks, CA: Sage.

Paulus, T. M., Lester, J. L., & Dempster, P. G. (2014). *Digital tools for qualitative research.* Thousand Oaks, CA: Sage.

Piantanida, M., & Garman, N. B. (2009). *The qualitative dissertation: A guide for students and faculty* (2nd ed.). Thousand Oaks, CA: Corwin.

Rossman, G. B., & Rallis, S. F. (2003). *Learning in the field: An introduction to qualitative research* (2nd ed.). Thousand Oaks, CA: Sage.

Rubin, H. J., & Rubin, I. S. (2012). *Qualitative interviewing: The art of hearing data* (3rd ed.). Thousand Oaks, CA: Sage.

Schwandt, T. A. (2007). *The SAGE dictionary of qualitative inquiry.* Thousand Oaks, CA: Sage.

Wolcott, H. F. (2002). *Writing up qualitative research* (2nd ed.). Thousand Oaks, CA: Sage.

2

The Observation, Reflection, and Writing Habit

Research is formalized curiosity. It is poking and prying.

—Zora Neale Hurston

When Zora Neale Hurston wrote these words, they caused many in her field to appreciate research. It reminds me of one of my favorite dance teachers in New York City, from the Merce Cunningham School at Westbeth, who once asked all of us in class to observe her movement closely. The reason to observe so carefully, she said, "was to become more aware of your own body and mind" and to "internalize" the movement. She emphasized that until we could observe ourselves and each other, we would not be able to dance with freedom. Another of my teachers said, "The body is a clear place." It always tells the truth. From this, I began to learn that observing carefully was so focused an activity that, in order to teach others to observe, I needed a way to introduce observation practices that allow the learner to develop this habit of mind and develop narrative writing skills. Similarly, Alfred Nobel emphasized that observing the world in its similarities and differences is the basis of all human knowledge.

Likewise, in a recent yoga class, my teacher demonstrated a variation on a headstand that prepares one for a headstand. First, the teacher demonstrated it to give an idea of what it should look like. Then, he asked us to write down in our yoga practice journals all that we had observed. Next, we read them to each other and the class before we started practicing the pose. We started out with one step, and moved to the next, and moved to the next. Many of us thought there would be no way we could ever do a headstand! By breaking down the movements of the headstand step by step, the teacher proved he was correct. We all did headstands of all types, partial headstands, full headstands, for example, to punctuate the importance of oxygen flowing to the brain. Then we wrote about it in our journals. The exercises described in this section start out simply and grow in complexity as the learner becomes more practiced in each activity. Think of this being similar to oxygen flowing to the brain. Again, this is not meant to be a slavish following of a recipe. Each person may improvise at any given point so that he or she continues to claim an active part in the activity. One size does not fit all. In fact, one size fits few.

I begin with an exercise taught to me by my favorite high school art teacher, which is simply to observe a group of objects. Although this exercise was meant originally for drawing, I find it helpful when introducing prospective researchers to the activity of description. Also, this exercise may help to place observation in a historical context as a step in an ancient and continuing journey. One aim I have for all of my work is to understand qualitative inquiry in a historical context that goes back ages in order to recognize a common history. I like to frame the history of observation of one's environment from an art history perspective that begins in 3000 BCE, when the Chinese master painters began recording their observations of everyday moments in their environment with descriptions of trees, orchids, rocks, plants, water, and so on. I start arbitrarily with the Chinese artists because of their long history of appreciation for nature, observation, and aesthetics and because of their systematic and methodical approach to documentation. Likewise, I stress the meaning of the term *empirical* at this point to reflect its meaning, "relying on direct experience and observation," as the cornerstone of qualitative work. It is confounding to me that many students think the word empirical is a synonym for statistics or numbers. It takes a while for them to realize that numbers are one, two, or three times removed from the actual experience being described! In addition, I ask students to find the definition for the word *empirical* in three different dictionaries. This gets them thinking in a new way. In this first exercise, we start with a still life scene because it grounds learners in observation, and it is less demanding than observing and describing people. While every single detail seems impossible to document, learners are advised to get as many details into their descriptions as possible.

EXERCISE 2.1   Observing a Still Life Scene

Purpose:

To observe and describe an assortment of objects on a table in 5-minute increments twice.

Problem:

To see these objects from your position in the room.

Time:

Take 10 to 20 minutes of observation time and another 10 to 20 minutes of reading to the group or to someone what you wrote to get feedback and try again.

Activity:

Set up a table in the center of the room so that viewers will have multiple positions and vantage points as they observe at least five objects, each of a different shape, texture, size, and color. Select any objects you wish. For example, I recently arranged the following:

1. A coffee mug with various photos on it encased in a plastic outer shell with a circular, fingernail-size Starbucks logo

2. A 5-inch by 7-inch, framed, empty, stand-up photo holder

3. A deep purple steel water bottle

4. A pile of newspapers approximately 4 inches high

5. A *Webster's Dictionary* in a red, textured cover

I placed the items listed above on a portable table for all to view from their seats. I envision a room of worktables arranged in a rectangle so that each person has a direct view of some portion of the scene. If the reader is working on these exercises alone, the reader selects a space for this activity. Space and how it is used are as critical for the qualitative researcher as they are for the dancer. The second time around with the description, try moving yourself to another vantage point to get a sense of the importance of the placement of the observer.

Aim:

In the time allotted, describe what you see on the table. Use descriptive terms and field note format. Although there are countless ways to take field notes, for the purposes of the group, we all agree to use one format that includes space for the researchers to write notes to themselves on the left third of the page and to write the actual descriptive field notes on the right two thirds of the page. In the upper right-hand corner, there is space for the following information: date, time, place, and participants. Learners are urged to develop a system of pagination and classification of notes. For example, for descriptions of settings, one may use a color code at the top of the page or select a different color of paper. For descriptions of interactions in a social setting, another color code at the top of the paper may be used and so on. In any event, the object is to encourage learners to create their own systems of coding that work for them. Figure 2.1 shows a sample of a field note page in the format and style we have adopted because it is effective for our purposes. My students and I find that this format is helpful because part of it is for the field notes and part of it is for notes to ourselves.

In this exercise to observe objects, the learners take notes as the observation takes place. After 10 minutes, they change seats and observe and describe the objects for another period of 10 minutes. The purpose for doing this is to experience the change of seating and viewpoint for description. Later, we discuss the reactions of the students. An interesting result of this, for example, is that one person may simply write something like, "there is a vase of flowers on the table," whereas another may describe that same vase of flowers with the precise Latin names for each flower; the type, shape, and size of the glass; and the tints and hues seen in the vase. Learners share their field notes with class members and get feedback from the group members as well as myself. We then repeat the entire process. When taking field notes for description, be sure to write notes to yourself as reminders and memos. See the fine example of field notes by Ruth Slotnick (2010).

Figure 2.1 A Sample Field Note Format

FIELD NOTES

By Ruth Slotnick (2010)

University of South Florida (USF)

Date: January 27, 2010

Time: 10:17–11:17 a.m.

Location: University Medical Clinic

Type: Nonparticipant observation

USF Health Dermatology and Cutaneous Surgery	
Notes	*Observations*
I pretend to look at my watch because I feel an older man observing me. To help blend in, I glance at the time to appear to be less of a stranger. Need to look up glass barriers on the Web.	10:17 a.m. **Getting to** I am sitting in cubical-like fishbowl located between sections A and C of the university medical health clinic. From the main entrance of the clinic, one can get to this space by walking straight ahead through the automatic double-glass doors and proceeding along the industrial-carpeted, fluorescent-lit corridor passing the Quest Diagnostics waiting room on the right. Also on right and left sides of the wallpapered hallway, there are a series of 45-inch by 39-inch reproduced watercolor paintings depicting Florida sea and landscapes. When the hallway comes to a dead end, make a left and continue down corridor until intersecting an adjoining hallway. Make a hard right and walk past patient check-in desks A and B on the right and left, respectively.
How many patients frequent the medical clinic each year?	**Just Outside the Clinic** To get to the clinic, immediately upon passing patient check-in station A, make a hard left into the waiting room outlined by two 15-foot by 20-foot, separately placed and freely standing, floor-to-ceiling, C-shaped transparent glass walls with frosted, horizontal bands ranging from 2 to 3 inches running through the middle. The glass structure is framed by a dark brown plastic molding that outlines the tops and bottoms. The vertical edges are lined with a 1-inch stainless steel, silver-matte border.

USF Health Dermatology and Cutaneous Surgery	
Notes	*Observations*
Need to look up the type of footer for ceramic form.	**Entering** 10:33 a.m. Advancing through the opening of the two C-shaped glass dividers, one passes a large 16-inch diameter, oxblood-red, fishbowl-shaped, mass-manufactured, low-fired planter with a wide-mouth flange. The ceramic pot sits on top of a plastic, faux-Japanese, footed plant stand.
Note to self: Older patient signals to me that he cannot hear the nurse when she calls out his name.	The plant is not real. It is an artificial, leafy palm tree plant with three perfectly placed stalks, one high and to the right, one low to the left, and one in the middle. To the right and to the left of each glass wall are two sets of high-density, foam-filled, heavy-duty triplet plastic seats (each with a separate cushion and backrest) mounted on top of a tubular steel frame that is a matte blush color. The metal framing is a glossy rose. The sets of metal chairs are joined together by a half-moon-shaped table that stands about two feet from the floor. This surface is made of a wood composite laminate, which is also the color of dusty rose. A clear plastic pamphlet holder is stacked four deep with trifold pamphlets. One pamphlet advertises the "Cosmetic and Laser Center" on 60-lb., glossy white paper. A second pamphlet is labeled "Your Dermatologist." The color for this brochure is benthic blue with white Times font lettering. In the center of the half-moon-shaped coffee table is another 8.5-inch by 11-inch, tri-stacked, clear plastic brochure holder. The bottommost row holds a multicolor, oversized bookmark with a five-step guide on how to examine your body for melanomas. Each step is allotted its own space with a gesture drawing of how to examine your body. Two other pamphlets remain in the stack: a placemat-like, double-sided sheet describing how to examine your skin and also how to improve tone and treat sun-damaged skin. Another one-page, high-gloss, professionally printed, full-size brochure shows how skin cancer is "treatable and beatable with early detection." There are eight steps given on how to protect and prevent skin cancer.

(Continued)

Figure 2.1 (Continued)

USF Health Dermatology and Cutaneous Surgery	
Notes	*Observations*
	Two spiral-bound half notebooks adorn the middle of the table. A laser copy color print is placed inside the front sleeve and displays a photo of a male doctor.
	He appears to be in his mid-50s. Gray hair and mustache. Friendly smile. He is wearing his doctor's overcoat with a sky-blue, button-down shirt and colorful, silk tie. A pair of reading glasses hangs around his neck. His name is Dr. Sam Fiske, and he is both the professor and chairman of the Dermatology and Cutaneous Surgery unit as well as the local newspaper correspondent. The caption written over Dr. Fiske's image reads "Ask the Expert." The university logo is prominently visible inside each notebook as are various newspaper and magazine articles on skin cancer, acne, how to remove moles, rejuvenate skin, remedy facial veins, smooth flaky feet, and combat fungal infections. Other articles include such topics as Vitamin D, eczema, and premature skin aging, useful information on how too much sunscreen can be harmful. All these articles have been written by Dr. Fiske. A final brochure, also a trifold, is advertising Humira, which is used to treat psoriasis. This brochure includes a hologram that shows a before and after effect of using the drug.
	Left Side of Glass Cubicle
	11:05 a.m.
	Two sets of seats are in the middle, placed back to back in a set of three and a set of two. Inside this cluster of seats is a white cubicle containing a yellow-pages phone book and a black, touchtone office phone. A placard above reads "Please Limit Telephone Calls to 5 Minutes."
I wonder if elementary school children are covering the topic of the sun in their science classes.	A gray-colored fabric cubicle about eight feet high, spanning three panels long for a grand total of 14 feet, has a 10-foot by 4-foot white poster created by a local elementary school. The word *shade* is spelled out in big, black, block lowercase letters. About 500 names surround the word.

Date: January 28, 2010

Time: 8:47–9:47 a.m.

Location: USF Medical Clinic

Type: Nonparticipant observation

USF Health Dermatology and Cutaneous Surgery	
Notes	Observations
How do people know what clinic they are supposed to go to or sit in? The clinic waiting rooms are not clearly labeled beyond a letter A, B, or C, etc.	8:47 a.m. I am sitting in the waiting room of clinic A. Not a single patient is waiting. Clinic D check-in desk is busier. At D, there appear to be a few individuals in line. A heavyset Black female in her 40s, wearing jet-black sweatpants, a charcoal-gray T-shirt, a hooded, zip-up, black jersey sweatshirt, and a cobalt-blue, loosely woven knit cap, converses about a missed appointment with the receptionist.
Appears to be quite a few Black women working in the receptionist area. I notice people wearing denim jeans and sweatshirts. Does this mean that people are either too sick or not interested in getting dressed up for the doctor?	A White man in his 30s, wearing a pair of faded denim jeans, Puma sneakers, and a chocolate brown-colored, hooded sweatshirt, drinks a can of ginger ale or Sprite, sniffling and sneezing while waiting his turn in line. He rocks from side to side. A receptionist from section C (across from D) escorts "Ms. Miller," a Black woman in her 40s, into the neighboring clinic waiting room. Still, no patients are sitting in the Derm Clinic area of A.
Who is the patient?	9:00 a.m. First couple enters the waiting room. After checking in, they place a medical file in P. Weinberg's mail slot, which is affixed to the brick wall next to the clinic door. A nurse quickly opens the door and retrieves the file. The couple is in their late 70s. He is dressed in a pair of dark blue chinos, is 5 feet 9 inches, and is wearing brown Dexter shoes, white nylon socks, and a blue denim, button-down shirt. He has a heavy gold watch on his left wrist. He is holding his head in his left

(Continued)

Figure 2.1 (Continued)

USF Health Dermatology and Cutaneous Surgery	
Notes	*Observations*
	hand, which is slightly cocked to the left side, with his elbow resting on the armrest. He wears a pair of wire-rimmed prescription glasses. His hair is salt and pepper. The woman sitting to his right is wearing a winter, reversible, black and red down coat. The nurse pops her head out of the clinic door and calls, "James." The couple stands up and goes into the clinic with James leading.
This couple seems to be low income. Something smells? These people perhaps? Not bathed? Clothes unwashed?	Moments later, the next couple sits down exactly where the last couple was seated. The woman speaks to the man, "You got all my papers?" They place their paperwork in Dr. Weinberg's mail slot. The woman is rotund. She is wearing a stonewashed denim jacket with a small pocket over the elbow. The woman appears to be in her mid-50s. She also leans, but to the right. She appears to be resting or catching her breath. Maybe she is listening to a message on her cell phone? Her back is to me. Can't tell. Suddenly, she turns her head left toward the clinic door. She is not using her cell phone! Her partner, who has gone to the men's rest room, returns, scuffing his black leather sneakers against the carpet as he walks. He is wearing a red and black-checked flannel shirt. His dirty blond, unwashed hair, which is shoulder length, is tucked under a gray-blue baseball cap. He is also wearing prescription glasses and a very worn pair of denim jeans. He has a mustache. I cannot tell if he is shaven. She is mumbling something like, "We can't go downtown . . ." when her name "Leslie" is called. She continues this thought in breathy tones, "Try to take that lady those papers?" She is extremely bottom heavy and is wearing a pair of dark brown sweatpants with two lime green vertical stripes running down the sides. As she enters the clinic, she slowly shuffles and waddles painfully, teeter-tottering down the clinic hallway behind her nurse and her partner.

USF Health Dermatology and Cutaneous Surgery	
Notes	Observations
	Another man arrives; he is in his late 40s. Dark skinned. Maybe Hispanic? Wearing a pair of dungarees and a light gray-colored sweatshirt with an untucked T-shirt hanging out the back of his pants.
At first I thought this was a lesbian couple. The son was so obese that he had breasts. His hair was cropped very short. I only realized that he was male when he disappeared to the men's room after his visit. Earlier, a man had been directed to the men's room so I knew where it was. The man seems to be high-functioning autistic. He is clean but overweight. Slurred speech. Some kind of speech impediment. Has a library book tucked under his arm so is therefore literate. Mother also comes with a novel.	A female arrives. Also for Dr. Weinberg. She smells like a cigarette smoker. This woman is in her 70s. Directly behind her, another female in her 40s—very large and out of breath with short, buzzed-cropped brown hair—sits down next to her. She is having trouble sitting down due to her large body size. Loudly, she whispers in slurred speech to the older woman, "No wonder why! Pants are twisted." She has on a pair of slip-on, black leather shoes with Velcro straps, and cotton, white socks are on her feet. Her pelvis area is very full and extended. Suddenly, the clinic door opens, and her name is called. In her surprise of being called so soon, she bolts toward the clinic nurse, running—all 200 pounds of her. The older woman (maybe her mother?) is following quickly behind. They exit at 9:45 a.m. The older woman, wearing a pair of dungarees and a light blue cotton sweater, goes to check out. The larger woman goes to bathroom around the corner. Wait, that's the men's rest room. Maybe she is not a she? Maybe he? Yes, male!
So far all the patients are coming for Dr. Weinberg. The mother and daughter couple is clearly dressed up for the doctor. The mother has an Eastern European accent.	Next patient: A well-dressed older woman in her 80s enters the clinic with a woman in her 50s or 60s escorting her. The impeccably dressed elderly woman is about 5 feet with cropped-short silver hair, wearing a matching pants and top outfit. Her osteoporosis makes her stoop, causing her pants to rise slightly above her ankles when she walks.
Based on the headscarf and seeing no hair, I wonder if this woman is undergoing chemo.	The blond woman escorting her is also well dressed. She holds onto the older woman's arm as they exit the clinic. They had come in earlier in the same fashion but did not appear to wait. The nurse opened the door to

Figure 2.1 (Continued)

USF Health Dermatology and Cutaneous Surgery	
Notes	*Observations*
	the clinic, and they were simply ushered in with the nurse commenting, "We were just looking for you." In response, the older woman stated, "It's like you were waiting for us! Such service."
	An older female in her 70s enters the waiting room, wearing a sandy-colored headscarf and a suede jacket of the same color and black slacks with a row of buttons tapering down to her ankle. She has on a pair of slip-on black flats. Just when she sits down to fill out paperwork on a clipboard, she is called in. Her glasses are black, square-framed bifocals. "Petal," the nurse beckons.
For some reason, I found myself bored by this description.	An army vet in his 70s arrives in the space. He is wearing faded fatigues, an ochre-colored rain jacket, and a sandy-colored, button-down shirt with his glasses case (brown) placed in a pocket over his heart. He is wearing a pair of slip-on leather Bass shoes. The tops appear worn, but the soles are in good shape. He is clean shaven. Tufts of white hair spill out from under his marine army cap with a Marine seal embroidered on the brim. The word *Marine* is sewn on with golden thread. His socks are cottony white. He steps up to leave and greets the Hispanic man who entered earlier in a businesslike manner. The very first couple, 9:37 a.m., exits too.
Lots of women using the women's bathroom. No public-use bathrooms in the clinics?	The woman with the headscarf exits the clinic to use the women's bathroom, walking briskly for her slight frame. Her large, pouch-like, soft, matte-black leather bag is slung over her left shoulder.
	It has golden buckles at the corners. Her bag is now slung over the right shoulder on her way back.
Exit space, 9:47 a.m.	9:43 a.m.
	The waiting room is empty. Only one older White female with black hair signing in at station A.

DESCRIPTION OF A STILL LIFE SCENE ●

I begin with the coffee mug. The mug appears to be approximately 8 inches tall, made of plastic that covers various travel photos. It is shades of beige, brown, blue, and red. It stands with a black plastic lid with a flip-up flap that allows for drinking or stays closed, most likely to keep the coffee hot. The photos, which I call travel photos, are scenes about the size of a postage stamp. One scene is at the beach, another is a sailboat alone in a cove near a rock formation. Next are three photos of children. One is a giggling child approximately three years of age, wearing wide-brimmed white sunglasses, near a sandy shore. The photo is too small to identify the lake or body of water. The next photo has four children, toddlers, and one adult sitting on what appears to be a picnic blanket. The next photo is a young boy and girl, heads together, smiling, approximately seven or eight years of age. About a half inch below the screw-top lid is a rectangular box with the words in script saying, "Create your own tumbler." I can only see from where I am sitting, just to the right of the mug approximately 12 inches away, the words, "Twist off the base and remove this template." I will return and review this later as my time is up.

Beginning the research reflective journal and discussion: How did you approach this exercise in the first 5 minutes? The second 5 minutes? Did you do anything differently in the second observation after you changed seating? What did you learn from the feedback from the class? Following this discussion, write about this in your newly created researcher reflective journal.

What was most difficult for you in this exercise? Find a good notebook or set of notebooks to accomplish this performance task. You may wish to have a separate notebook on observations, one on interviews, one for poetry, and one for photography and other categories. Or you may wish to keep your journal continuously, integrating all of the above in various eventual volumes. By the end of any set of these exercises, you will have a written product that traces your thoughts and feelings, memories and dreams, stories and partial stories. Continuing on, write at least 10 minutes on each of these questions. Each day, you will see yourself wanting to write more. Feel free to backtrack and edit, add to, or delete from your researcher reflective journal.

Rationale: The questions are designed to discover how learners approach the task and how others approach the same task. Some begin by describing one object at a time from left to right, forgetting to situate themselves in the room. Others begin by describing the room and working their way to the table and then to the objects. By sharing their personal experiences, class members begin to see the wide variety of approaches to the task. They also see which members are skilled at description and which need to practice more of the art of description. There is no better teacher than example, so in class, when a skilled observer and describer reads a powerful description to the class, the lesson sinks in. After all, the researcher is the research instrument, and these practice exercises in observation and description are designed to bring home this very point.

Evaluation: In addition to my evaluation of individual work, I ask the students to evaluate themselves. They are asked to fill out the following form, shown in Figure 2.2, or to write me a letter and return to discuss it at the beginning of the next class before starting the next exercise, the observation of the classroom setting. For those working alone, write a letter to someone you trust evaluating this process. I use this form to facilitate an active agency as evaluators of one's work. The questions are meant to be a heuristic tool and a starting point for the evaluative process. Most often, I ask learners to keep a journal of all their thoughts related to the class and these activities. Although many are intimidated by writing a journal, this

Figure 2.2   A Sample Formative Evaluation

Evaluation of: (Name the exercise)

Date:

a. Things I learned about myself as I described the objects under observation:

b. Things I need to continue to work on for the next observation:

c. How I describe my progress:

can be a good evaluation tool and a valuable historical document for charting the role of the researcher in a given project. Journal writing is my first choice and suggestion for self-reflection and evaluation. Of course, the point is to allow the individual to become a stakeholder in self-evaluation.

This baptism into self-evaluation continues with each practice exercise and is part of another overall system of self-evaluation, which looks like Figure 2.3. In addition, students begin to build their own portfolios and integrate these evaluations into researcher reflective journals as researchers in training and add components as we go through the exercises.

CONSTRUCTING A RESEARCHER REFLECTIVE PORTFOLIO ●

Individuals build portfolios throughout the semester of their work and self-evaluation of their work. This allows for the opportunity to evaluate externally and internally, a requirement for the qualitative researcher. They may add and or remove items as they see fit, and if they need to do more than one observation of a still life or a person, they are free

Figure 2.3 A Summative Evaluation for This Cycle

Progress Chart:

Name:

Date:

You may rate yourself on the system you devise. Explain it here and continue the rating process for each exercise.

Here is my assessment of my own work to date:

Exercise: (Name the activity)

Observation of a still life scene:

to do so. The contents of the qualitative research portfolio look something like this:

1. Samples of narrative descriptive observations

2. A log of interview activities

3. Samples of transcripts

4. Video and photographic samples

5. Models developed from data

6. Found data poems from transcripts and documents

7. Researcher reflective journal entries

8. Any sample letters to recruit or sustain participants (see Appendix A)

9. Ethical issues in field work as encountered or wondered about and proof of informed consent (see Appendix B)

10. (Optional) A website designed to situate all these components and tell your story

11. Reflections on your role as a researcher

12. Description of your theoretical framework

13. A reading list of your favorite books and articles that helped you in becoming a qualitative researcher, including books in various fields as they influenced you, sometimes called a working bibliography

● **TYPES OF PORTFOLIOS AND ASSESSMENT**

Portfolios have long been a key method for presenting what a student has learned. It is a multifaceted and complex product. It may have a theme and surely will be judged against a set of criteria usually evidenced in a given rubric. It is similar to the artist's portfolio. It makes sense then to compose a research portfolio.

A rubric shows the viewer of the portfolio levels of performance. Constructing portfolios and assessing them takes time, effort, and dedication to the task. Many practitioners define a portfolio as a historical record of student work. It is more than a collection of papers in a folder. It is evidence of a student's work over time and may include accomplishments, capability records, a history of a person's development, and critiques of one's work by both student and teacher. Of course, the items included can be many, but whatever is included should be an authentic measure of what the student has learned. Usually, the tasks that the student performs show evidence of learning and may fall into the following major areas:

1. The tasks performed were done in multiple ways and for a variety of purposes over time.

2. The tasks provide evidence of learning and growth and sample a wide spectrum of cognitive tasks.

3. The tasks show evidence of work at many levels of understanding.

4. The tasks are tailored to the individual learner and offer opportunities for the learner to show what is known.

There is no one sacred model or type of portfolio. Depending on the discipline of study (e.g., reading, math, physical education, art, music), the portfolio construction varies. However, in looking over the body of literature on portfolios, there seem to be at least three categories of type of portfolios: the working portfolio, the record-keeping portfolio, and the showcase portfolio. Students invariably construct a combination of all three of these categories for their personal portfolio. See the following:

The Working Portfolio

This type of portfolio is mostly the work of the student, on a daily basis, that gives evidence of ongoing learning in one or more areas of study. Teachers and students freely comment on all aspects of the work. The samples for the portfolio are most often selected by the student, described fully, and critiqued by the student. This type of portfolio offers the learner the opportunity to be self-aware and more articulate about learning and his or her own growth process. Many schools begin portfolios at the elementary level and carry through to high school. By the time students come to the qualitative research course, they already have had one or more experiences with the working portfolio.

The Record-Keeping Portfolio

This type of portfolio may be used along with or even integrated into the working portfolio or the showcase portfolio. As the name implies, it is a history of records. It may contain samples of evaluative remarks, assessments, and so on. It is also devised and monitored by the learner with input from the class members and from me. Keeping a diary or journal may assist in the record keeping portfolio.

The Showcase Portfolio

This is the most known and used type of portfolio assessment. Here, the learner constructs a showcase of samples that best describes the learner's progress to date in a given area or multiple areas. It is something like the portfolio a photographer or artist might put together. Usually, this includes completed works that are excellent or outstanding. It is meant to be the record of the student's best work. Thus, we see at least three types of portfolios that provide a record of authentic tasks and learning. Many states have encouraged the use of the showcase portfolio, and in fact, some use the portfolio in electronic format. I offer students the option of doing the portfolio electronically or in hard copy. Most select the electronic portfolio. Now, students may even have their own webpages to upload all their work for restricted viewing within the class and for me. They are actively selecting what to put in the portfolio and webpage and what to leave out or change periodically. It is a dynamic and immediate activity.

● HOW THE ELECTRONIC PORTFOLIO WORKS

In past few decades, with the growth of technology and computers in the classroom, electronic portfolios are a valuable method of assessment. Electronic portfolios allow for easier storage and retrieval of information and also allow for easier inclusion of parental input and feedback. Portfolios are kept in digital files, on websites, or on a thumb drive. A big bonus with the use of the electronic portfolio is the ability to store material that a traditional notebook portfolio cannot. For example, songs, poetry, performances, music, and dramatic readings are more easily stored in digital form, and they capture the activity visually and more accurately. Furthermore, with an electronic portfolio, a new dimension may be introduced: interactivity. Students also may create podcasts or short videos for their websites or for featuring in class. With the wonderful software available for electronic portfolios, students can be more creative and use digital means to verify and adjust their portfolio contents. Most students use a Mac or a PC and update their software regularly. It is always a good idea to invest in good equipment for your work as a researcher. Be aware that technology is advancing so quickly that from the time you enter your doctoral program to the time you finish, your digital voice recorder, iPod, and computer may be outdated. Be sure to get the upgrades you need to be the best researcher you can be. Many ask, why use an electronic portfolio? The benefits are obvious.

1. Work can be stored digitally more efficiently, allowing for more student options.

2. The display of best examples may be represented more elegantly and more often with the flexibility of the digital format.

3. We now have access to the cloud for storage or Dropbox.

Students love it because it allows them to edit, cut, paste, and play back what they have entered. Just as in any research process, all work is at the same time a work in progress. It may be altered throughout the duration of the study and even afterwards. Thus, the prognosis is very good for portfolio assessment. Because most students do their own dissertations on a portable notebook computer anyway, it is no trouble to continually work on their portfolio to showcase their progress in the qualitative research course. Students also remarked that they can do more with field notes on the computer, take notes during interviews, and send reminders to themselves, as well as track other points of data entry, such as references and interview transcripts. Furthermore, individual researchers in training may use social media sites as a research lab. In later parts of this text, software for analyzing interview and observational data will be discussed.

Although teachers and students get into the computer age and all that it requires, one can imagine that the transition to electronic portfolios is gradual and not necessarily easy. Yet, the benefits of the electronic portfolio can surely be persuasive as we move to the electronic record. If we ask why we should use an electronic format, many benefits may be listed. For example, consider the following:

- Electronic portfolios foster engaged learning, active learning, and student ownership of ideas.

- Electronic portfolios are repositories of feedback in a medium familiar to many of today's students. This is similar to artistic work as artists have always received feedback on their work and immediately redirect. In dance, for example, notes are given to the performers after each rehearsal and performance by the choreographer.

- Electronic portfolios are the basis for students' discussion of their own progress and a record of their reflections on what they have learned.

- Electronic portfolios are easily accessible, portable, and able to store vast amounts of data and information and remain effective and efficient.

● PORTFOLIO CONTENTS

The creative activity of constructing a portfolio rests on the learner. Any system may be used. For example, some portfolios are displayed in binders, boxes, display cases, or any combination of the above. Currently, electronic portfolios are in digital formats, thumb drives, podcasts, websites, and can be uploaded at the discretion of the researcher on various websites such as YouTube. Whatever method of display is used, reason dictates that it should be manageable, accessible, and portable. Samples are created, selected, and evaluated by the learner. The contents of the portfolio may include the following:

1. Works in progress, such as writing samples in various drafts and revisions that show evidence of learning. Feedback from the class or the instructor can be included here, as well as the learner's responses to the feedback on the record. Thus, the idea that research is a work in progress is punctuated once again.

2. Outstanding products such as poetry, photographs, artwork, cartoons, descriptions of activities, audio recordings, video recordings, interview transcripts, and field notes. Most important, it should include the researcher reflective journal.

3. Evaluative comments by the student, teacher, and class members. Feedback is critical to the researcher in training. While learning to be a researcher, ethical standards to protect participants and the researcher are in place. Informed consent is standard procedure. (See Appendixes A and B.)

Remember that the portfolio is at the end of the process chain. Prior to the portfolio development, all of these exercises and opportunities in the field were planned and executed. The researcher reflective journal is alive and changing throughout and is a key component of the portfolio. The portfolio is a perfect spot for the written record of events and what they mean. Portfolios widen the repertoire of reflective and contemplative assessment strategies and provide solid evidence that students can do this work. It is testament to what the learner has accomplished and learned. Thus, portfolios are a critical element in the qualitative research process. It is extremely valuable throughout the entire dissertation or other research project. To create and shape an individual portfolio is, in itself, a work of art for many. This also affords the opportunity to review and monitor the examples of any work on a regular and sustained basis.

Using what we learned from the still life description, we move on to the next level of complexity: description of a setting.

EXERCISE 2.2   Physical Description of This Setting

Purpose:

To observe one section of the room in which we are seated.

Problem:

To see this section of the room.

Time:

20 minutes.

Activity:

Select a section of this room that is immediately across from where you are seated. Describe this section of the room in detail. Then, add your reflections on this in your researcher reflective journal.

Evaluation:

Continue with self-evaluation and overall evaluation for your journal and portfolio.

Discussion:

1. How did you approach this exercise?
2. How is this exercise like the previous exercise? Unlike?
3. What was the most difficult part of this activity?

Rationale:

The movement from a still life description to the setting is a step in complexity. Now, the learner is faced with a number of additional possibilities in how to approach this assignment and how to execute it. Beginning the journey to become a better observer includes this challenge, which is to describe a large physical area. Some individuals add a floor plan and rough sketch of the setting only to return later and measure the floor, the room, the furniture, and so on. Others may take a photo of the setting. Later, the learner tries to capture in narrative form what was captured in the drawing or the photograph.

EXERCISE 2.3   Observation in the Home or Workplace

Purpose:

To continue developing observation skill with a setting. Observe an area in your home or workplace.

Problem:

To see your own space as you never have before.

Time:

30 minutes.

Activity:

Select an area to observe and describe part of your living or working space. Set aside 30 minutes of quiet time to describe a portion of your room or office. Set reasonable goals of description. For example, select one half of the room to describe or one section of the office. Again, after taking notes, type them in field note format and return to class with these data. After discussing these in class, be sure to write in your journal.

Discussion:

In class, we will share our descriptions and frame our discussion around the following questions:

1. How did you approach this description of a setting?
2. How did this differ from the previous exercise in class?
3. What was the most difficult part of this exercise for you?

Evaluation:

Continue with self-evaluation and overall evaluation for your journal and your research portfolio.

Rationale:

By this time, individuals have completed two observation exercises and now move to another level. The learner has a wider band of options to reflect and act upon. Will I select home or workplace to describe? Once selected, on which area of the site will I focus? With the luxury of 30 minutes of observation time, how do I use this time to my best advantage? All are encouraged to think about how this exercise goes beyond both the description of a still life arrangement and a description of the classroom for writing about in the journal.

EXERCISE 2.4   Description of a Familiar Person or a Stranger

Purpose:

To describe a person sitting across from you, either one whom you know or a stranger.

Problem:

To see someone as never before.

Time:

15 minutes. Stop, read to a partner or to the group, get feedback, and repeat again. See if your description changes after the feedback given.

Activity:

Select a person to describe physically. Arrange your 15 minutes to your best advantage. Remember to use descriptive behavioral terms and work for accuracy.

Discussion:

1. What can you identify as major differences in observation of a still life, a setting, and a person?
2. How did you approach this exercise?
3. What was difficult for you in this exercise, and what do you want to do about it?
4. Is there anything about describing a person that relates to your role as the researcher?

Evaluation:

Continue with self-evaluation and overall evaluation for your journal and portfolio.

Rationale:

The shift from describing objects and settings to describing people is major. For one thing, people are animated. Previous to this, learners had an inanimate, static environment to describe. Now, learners must move to other complicating factors in their observation practice, factors of activity, movement, and life. This exercise is designed to prepare them for observations of people in their future research projects or in the classroom if they do case studies as teacher education projects. I am including an example (p. 54) for your careful study. I mentioned earlier that teacher-educators and preservice teachers often take to these exercises. Here is an example where a middle school teacher went further with the observation of a person in his own classroom. He used this technique to develop his own critical case study. Inevitably, students tell me that this is the most difficult observation exercise because people are always moving, changing, and expressing themselves. Take a look at the critical case of a middle school teacher observing a student and how powerful observation becomes in this case.

The Critical Case Use of Observation of a Student (Edited)

By Patricia Williams-Boyd (2005)

Professor, Eastern Michigan University

One of the most critical characteristics of effective teaching, particularly in the middle grades, is a deep, abiding, and constantly challenged understanding of young adolescents as complex, unique, and ever changing human beings. Upon the robust knowledge of who students are, how they think, and why they act as they do is built a developmentally and culturally relevant pedagogy. This paves the way for teachers to meet the needs of and to set high expectations for all students. Case study research can be a form of action and revelatory research in which the educator-researcher contextually studies a student in greater depth and breadth. The teacher-researcher examines the student both within the community of the classroom as well as within the larger culture of the family. The single case study design and, in particular, the critical case format contribute not only to knowledge and theory building but also uncover areas of weakness, assumption, and limited understanding in the engaged, often hectic, and active environment of the classroom. The case study is a legitimate form of social inquiry because the study is instrumental in furthering the teacher-researcher's understanding of a given problem, concept, issue, or behavior in students. It also represents a contemporary phenomenon—namely, students—in a real-world context—the classroom—where the boundaries between the home, the community, and the school are blurred, given the effects they have on students. Often, however, because of the number of students, the demands of a standards-driven system, and a lack of formal training, teachers see the classroom sphere as existing alone rather than as multiple, overlapping spheres.

When given the charge of conducting a critical case study, my graduate students make some very studied decisions: whom to study, for how long, when during the day, how to ask questions that elicit the kind and depth of information they need but which leave their student in a zone of comfort, how trust can be established so disclosure is not as painful as it could be, how the case study can be written to ethically and powerfully capture the angst and sometimes trauma of the young adolescent world. The master's degree program in middle-level education at Eastern Michigan University includes a course in the theory and practice of middle grades policy, philosophy, program, and practice. Because that course is the first of the cohort classes for middle grades majors, it relies heavily on developing the student's deliberateness both in technique and in perspective. In other words, it asks them to think meta-cognitively by examining themselves and their students. It

(Continued)

(Continued)

asks, Why do you do what you do? Who are the students with whom you work? What kind of environment do you construct for their learning? What variety of instructional techniques is effective for all your students? Why do you make the assumptions about your students that you do? And most important, are there students with whom you feel you have been unsuccessful, students whom you felt you did not reach, much less teach? And did these students, across time, share any common characteristics?

Initially, the most difficult decision the teacher-researcher must make is the selection of one student to study. Separating a piece (a student) from the greater whole (the classroom) is usually based on the teacher-researcher's notion that the selected student is unique or that the student has a distinct identity within the classroom. When the critical case is chosen from the group, we frame the understanding of *group* in sociological terms: a collection of people who interact, who identify with each other, and who share expectations about each other's behavior . . . even if they may not share group membership, in this case, referring to kids who may be left out of peer groups for various reasons. Since the critical case uses the individual student as the focus of the study, it is often called *microethnography*.

Critical Case Study

Purpose:

To conduct a critical case study. This will lead learners to the point at which they can construct their own meaning and answers to these questions. The study tends to be illustrative and is conducted inductively. Induction helps with understanding the qualitative research process.

Problem:

To examine the classroom as a constellation of individuals rather than as a group of young adolescents, to confront myself and challenge assumptions, and to develop a sense of self as a teacher-researcher and as an action researcher who can identify and solve problems.

Time:

Gather data in the field for 6 to 7 weeks. Leave the field, and begin the analysis and interpretation of data.

Activity:

Select a student who causes you to ask some critical questions. Gather data through personal interviews, and triangulate both the source and interpretation of data. Present your study in five to seven pages with a minimum of seven bibliographic sources. Use respected journals in the field. Use APA style. Your paper must have a title page and must have a creative title. The body of the paper should follow the research design: study question, propositions, the student (with care and protection of the student's identity and with written permission from the student, the family, and the building principal), research interpretation, theory, and conclusions. Address key issues or general concepts. Organize your paper in the following fashion:

- Start with the presentation of the case. Describe the boundaries of that case.
- Next, present the research interpretation of the case.
- Then, discuss the extension of the study or the ways in which the study has influenced you as a professional.
- After the paper's conclusion, offer several discussion questions that will help the reader focus his or her own perceptions of the study's key issues.
- Finally, present your bibliography and suggested readings if they are significantly different from the works cited.

Discussion:

1. How did you select the student you studied? What criteria did you use?

2. What kinds of questions did you ask that offered you the depth of information you sought?

(Continued)

(Continued)

3. How did you establish trust? How did your relationship with the student change across time?

4. What did you notice about yourself, both personally and professionally, as you moved through the process?

5. What challenges did you encounter?

6. How did this study affect your professional development and relationships with students?

Rationale:

This tends to be a pivotal experience for master's students. It provides the opportunity for them to experience the power of their own research and analysis to more fundamentally understand who their students are. Consequently, the learning activities that they construct will look different. They see themselves as advocates for their students, for they challenge themselves to develop a more responsive classroom. And, they talk about themselves as teacher-researchers, as action researchers who are agents for change.

In the analysis of what is required in both the final presentation as well as in the conduct of the study, my students and I engage in a collaborative discussion of the skills requisite to an effective case study. Together, we decide on the following:

- The researcher should be able to ask good questions—questions that are open-ended—encourage the student to disclose an often sealed-off area of his or her experience and move the student incrementally from his or her zone of comfort. The researcher should then be able to interpret those answers.

- The researcher should be a good listener and should not be trapped by preconceptions. The thoughtful researcher listens for how things are said, watches for body language cues, and often listens for what is not said as well as what is said.

- The researcher should be adaptive and flexible to the extent that newly encountered situations can be seen as opportunities rather than threats or deficits.

- The researcher must have a firm grasp of the issues being studied.

- Perhaps even more important, the researcher must be willing to deal simultaneously with multiple ideas and possibilities and must be comfortable with ambiguity. The researcher's willingness to research the literature in an ongoing fashion helps him or her to better understand the unexpected twists and turns of interview data and better positions the researcher for the next interview session.

- The researcher should be aware of preconceived notions, including those derived from theory. Therefore, the researcher should be sensitive and responsive to contradictory evidence. Look for what does not make sense.

- The researcher must be respectful of and sensitive to the total person being studied.

THE QUALITIES OF EXEMPLARY CASE STUDIES ●

The Case Study Must Be of Interest to the Researcher

- Underlying issues you suspect may be present are globally important to your field in either theoretical or practical terms. The individual case must be unusual, not typical of the average young adolescent, and it must be of general public interest.

- The case may be revelatory in that it reflects a real-life situation that other social scientists may not have been able to study in the past. It will be revelatory for you as the researcher in training.

The Case Study Must Be Complete and the Boundaries Defined

- Give explicit attention to the boundaries of the case or the distinction between the phenomenon being studied and its multiple contexts. Describe what the boundaries of the case include.

- The collection of evidence must be thorough, relevant, and sufficient, and it must be triangulated.

The Case Study Must Be Composed in an Engaging Manner

- The reader must be able to see the person and the environment as described through the use of rich and descriptive language.

- Although many design models are effective, the following is a friendly way to introduce practitioners to the dynamic world of qualitative analysis.

The Research Design

The Case Study Should Answer the Following Questions:

- **Who:** Explain who the individual is and what the immediate setting looks like.
- **Why:** Describe why you chose that particular student, why you are doing the study, and what if any changes you propose making at the conclusion of the study.
- **How:** Discuss how and where you are going to conduct the study, what questions you will use, and how you are going to develop some assumptions that you will interpret.
- **Where:** Describe the sociocultural context of the classroom, the school, the family, and the immediate community.

Making Sense of Data

- Engage in research.
- Interpret the field research through literature.
- Develop your own theories and test them against the literature.
- In explanatory cases, examine the facets of your argument.
- In exploratory cases, debate the value of the work.

Criteria for Interpreting Findings

- Match patterns; look for points of tension in the data rather than for a single, consistently explanatory conclusion; look for emerging patterns or themes; triangulate data sources; and find multiple analysts such as peers, other teachers, and parents.
- Develop analytic statements based on physical and cultural artifacts as well as on fieldwork.
- Draw conclusions.
- Ask what implications this new knowledge has on your own practice; what professional as well as personal changes did you experience?

These guidelines may easily apply to researchers in training. See this example of a case of reflecting on one's own writing by David Thornton (2014).

The Case of an Antique Worth Restoring in Letter Format (Edited)

By David Thornton

David composes this case in the form of a letter to his professor after reading materials required for the Qualitative Research Methods beginner class.

Dear Professor,

I hope you are seated in a comfortable and relaxing place. This should be a place with good light, a place of your own, as you review my letter reflecting on some of the readings and my development as a researcher. You know in fact, Stephen King (2000) recommended this for writers and readers so they might conduct a sort of telepathic time travel. I hope we are carrying on a similar experiment at this very moment. I have positioned myself to allow for mental work with only minimal worldly distractions. Please realize if I were to be unabridged with you in this letter, reading it might take a much longer time than either of us have. As it is, I will aim to be as brief as possible touching on areas which pop most frequently into my mind as I write and move toward increasing skills of observing, interviewing, and reflective journal and narrative writing. These skills are all vital for qualitative researchers (Janesick, 2011).

Upon starting Qualitative I class my expectations were neutral. Experience typically yells not to expect too much, particularly on anything showing potential to excite the spirit. Well, this is not to be a typical class. If the material in the books was a meal, I inhaled my food. The books I completed were *Stretching Exercises for Qualitative Researchers* (Janesick, 2011), *On Writing: A Memoir of the Craft* (King, 2000), *Cartographies of Knowledge: Exploring Qualitative Epistemologies* (Pascale, 2011), and *Understanding and Evaluating Qualitative Educational Research* (Lichtman, 2011). With two of these I used a Kindle reader. I may tell you about this later

(Continued)

(Continued)

as this is an unfolding story in itself (see reflective journal). As for the optional reading selection, as soon as possible, likely within a week or less, I hope to read the two additional books listed.

I must tell you, during class discussions and while submerged deep in a text or writing, I find my mind running wild all over the landscape of qualitative analysis. My researcher reflective journal records some of this. Incomplete as they are, my skills as a qualitative researcher are taking root in a nurturing soil. Hope within me is building. I might find self-awareness or at least heightened understanding of just who I am. I believe you might be interested in how this is going for me, so I will share some of this with you now.

Finding reading material of interest upon which to reflect is not difficult. Moments without reflection on the reading are in fact quite rare. Waking with visions related to qualitative study seems to begin many of my mornings. This is not what I expected. I actually enjoy writing thoughts down or even just writing. Although I was not quite sure at the beginning, I found some exercises that made sense to me. Some of these exercises I have entered into my journal. I see value in this for me as a researcher, and it is fun.

Along with developing writing skills, the purpose of the reflective journal is to assist in the development of a reflective nature or specific "habits of mind." I find recording into the journal helps me focus my thinking. This focus hones one's reflections, writing, thinking, and ability to communicate. I believe you feel this as well. Strengthening my reflective nature and writing is, undoubtedly, important for me as a qualitative researcher.

As a researcher involved in qualitative studies, I must consider unexplored areas of my mind. The meditative focus on which reflective writing is dependent aides in piecing together the story from the jumbled mess (Janesick, 2011). I enjoy taking time out of each day to write and reflect. Often my thoughts may not seem to focus on any particular aspect of qualitative study; then I find words falling on the document. Then, thoughts grow appendages and wander down roads not previously taken or roads overgrown with brushes and brambles from years of neglect. When this happens, I look at surroundings differently, see areas previously unnoticed, and learn of other worlds. This component of qualitative research is a joy for me and needs little encouragement.

Although all various skills necessary for a qualitative researcher support each other in many ways, the skill of narrative writing shares a direct physical link with reflective journal writing. I use my reflective journal to practice narrative writing as well. For me, this is a must; I already notice differences in my personal writing. Narrative writing is, after all, the "key to communicating purposes, methods, findings, and interpretation of the study and developing the habit of using the brain for analysis and interpretation." Including narrative portions in my reflective journal, I see as challenging myself to grow in this area. I found King's (2000) thoughts here quite constructive.

Possessing what I feel is a sound ability to communicate in writing, I was not sure the "Horror King" would serve anything useful for my writing. I was wrong. Like a lunatic jumping out from one of his novels, King got my attention quickly. He led me on a story regarding his development as a writer. Then turning the corner, he again provided assistance by offering me a toolbox. As I listened, he described the tools and the appropriate use of each. I learned.

I learned some of what I have is good; other tools are either missing or in need of a good cleaning, years of rust and all. One tool called the "bread of writing" and referred to as "the commonest of all" tools is the writer's vocabulary. Vocabulary is different for each individual. When a writer uses the vocabulary correctly, in a manner where the words used get the greatest degree of torque possible, the key to successfully communicating is held.

I work to grow my vocabulary. I have a habit of writing down new or unfamiliar words whenever they are encountered. I find myself looking up the meanings and trying to build these words into the existing framework occupying my mind. Some of these words eventually get covered by other words and may never again surface. Others, words identified as more interesting or having a more practical nature, I find myself using now and then until I feel comfortable implementing them into my everyday

(Continued)

(Continued)

use. I know as a researcher this will assist me in efforts to clearly communicate. The tool of vocabulary is used in conjunction with other tools. Grammar and elements of style are two fine tools surely helpful in all qualitative writings.

Grammar gets better with frequent use; otherwise it becomes rusty as King pointed out. Different writing types used in qualitative writing, such as narrative and descriptive, all benefit from fluent grammar use. As for my skills with grammar, in some ways they are better than average, while in others maybe more rust has accumulated on stored grammar tools. Getting writing correct is a commitment I make every time I create with words. Monitoring grammar requires constant vigilance on my part as a researcher. Repeat after me. Proofread. Proofread. Proofread.

The style of writing, as elaborated on by King (2000), differs among writers and various tones used to express thoughts. There are many unique styles and any one might work. Wow, what a tool for studying human beings! A tool allowing for multiple settings and adjustments is of great value for communicating various story interpretations. Frequency of adverb use is a direct component of style, and on this issue of style King is passionate. He frowns upon the use of adverbs. I found his arguments ~~quite~~ compelling and have been ~~judicially~~ implementing efforts to adjust adverb use. The idea of cutting unnecessary adverbs works ~~masterfully~~. Repeat after me. Practice. Practice. Practice.

One additional area I enjoy but have been reluctant to practice is the inclusion of metaphor and simile in my writing. Until now, I typically only think of the metaphor; I keep it inside. After reading the books for this class, however, I started riding this magical creature. I am enjoying the ride on its comfortable yet strange saddle. As it flies in and out of a story, I get glances of meanings hidden without such a positioned view. And, let me tell you, when it breathes its fire onto an object, that object is sure to shine or burn to ash.

Remember, I included observation and interviewing as additional skills in need of advanced training for qualitative researchers. It is possible to see this illustrated in ethnography, where common to ethnographic studies is the idea of "thick description." The setting and person(s) of study are described in a manner expressing great detail and producing clear mental images. Detail of this type might even pull at strong emotions from within the reader as well as the writer (Lichtman, 2011). Writing about a simple experience, such as traveling to the store for groceries, provides practice for upcoming qualitative researchers. Heck, this might even be fun! How did you travel to the store? What are you looking for there? Is it all you buy? Why did you select this store? Was there any difficulty on your journey? Did you walk near a bakery? Did you want to? How much detail can you place into this description? Activities designed to sharpen skills of narrative writing are linked with increased observation skills (Janesick, 2011).

Reflecting on this more brings to mind thoughts from Eliot Eisner (1991). When making observations of "teachers and classroom life" (p. 81), there is an abundance of detail seen best through an experienced and enlightened eye. I know I am fortunate. I have had experience observing teachers and uncertified staff as well as buildings and school programs during 11 years of administrative work. My evaluations were filled with narratives on my observations. Some were shorter while others ended up recording substantial data. Although I realize I have a great deal to learn, this experience benefits me as a developing qualitative researcher.

Interviewing skills are interwoven with those of observation quite closely. For what other purpose might an interview be given than to observe the comments, both verbalized and the nonverbalized? These observations are "the act of taking notice of" (Janesick, 2011, p. 99)—in this case, what is being communicated, how it is said, and what is the intended meaning. Interviews allow focus from the researcher, focus on the message or voice of the interviewee. This is important as different voices carry different messages even when they appear to be saying the same thing. In my mind, the variety of voices is quite endless and includes those mentioned by Thomas Green (1999). Green identified several voices of conscience (craft, membership, sacrifice, memory, etc.). Pascale (2011) indicated when social communication occurs, the interpretation of what is being said is more likely to get a response than is what is actually said. (I recognize this in interactions with others.)

In education, I recognize how many voices are vying for attention. Another key for interviewers is listening to and hearing the particular voice and then recognizing from where it originates.

(Continued)

(Continued)

Voices differ according to relationships between people involved in the communicative effort. Historical and cultural climates produce impacts on language and, therefore, meanings (Pascale, 2011). Norms operating under *Gemeinschaft,* familial/friend relationship, or *Gesellschaft,* contractual/professional relationship change in formality of communication and this influences messages (Greene, 1999).

With all the different voices and interpretations, qualitative researchers also get to handle situations which mold themselves right in front of the researcher's eyes. This is exciting. It is not the "average" or "standard deviation," but what is living and what is happening now to people and to individuals. The practice interview currently undergoing my transcription skill, or lack thereof, is a valuable exercise. I am stretching here to build my reach there. I feel transcribing the interview on my own is proving a valuable experience. Not only am I learning about the time commitment, I am also building insight for aspects of the interview that without the rehearing and recording were unnoticed by my hearing eye.

Considering all I wrote to you, the development of an Enlightened Eye is assisted by regular writing in my research reflective journal as it grows in importance to my development as a researcher. As descriptions and interpretive thoughts are recorded and considered, I see where connoisseurship develops and sharpens my focus as an educational researcher. This is where a critical eye develops, not solely the judgmental eye, but an eye connected to a stilled heart and a helping hand, a hand able to provide constructive thought.

Oh, look at me. I have only touched briefly upon the issues above in my letter, and I have already taken so much of your time. I would like to say goodbye with a final thought. I feel there is a bit of irony found while conducting qualitative research. No matter how experienced I may become, there is always much more to learn, but you already know this.

See you in class,

David, the Antique, Thornton

Thus, from working out cases in any format as part of a reflective portfolio, we see some fine examples of thoughtful writing about that which is involved in the research act. Next, we go on to description in a public place, the art museum.

EXERCISE 2.5 Observing at an Art Museum or at a Movie

Purpose:

To observe and describe two areas of an art museum, such as the lobby or gift shop, or an area of the museum where you find two paintings, sculptures, or any works of art of interest to you. Alternately, if you have no access to an art museum, then a movie will be a good substitute. Currently, I am fortunate to be able to have a field trip with my students to the Salvador Dali Museum nearby.

Problem:

To see the art museum as a place of movement, activity, silence, and so on. Watch for interactions of people with artworks. See this place as you never have before. If you go to the movie house, apportion your time to describe the movie house, the movement of the patrons, and the movie itself. Recently, for example, students observed the movie *The Blind Side*, observed and described the patrons in class and the movie house along with the setting of the movie, and selected one character from the movie to describe. If selecting the movie, obviously stay for the entire film.

Time:

15 minutes for each of the three areas, 45 minutes total. For the movie, stay for the entire film and do the best you can once you select the one character to describe.

Activity:

Take time to select and focus on these public spaces. If you need to do so, that is, if someone asks you what you are doing, introduce yourself and explain that you are doing this to become a better observer. Assure them of confidentiality, that no harm will come to them, and that you are doing this for a class. Most people will be delighted that you are there. In fact, you may have to stop them from speaking to you so that you may go on with your observation. After 45 minutes of observation and field note taking, return to the group—if you have the benefit of a class, for example—to discuss this experience. If on your own, take a few minutes to write down your thoughts about this exercise. Of the two exercises, students love the movie exercise better, and if they select the art museum, they always say they wish to return and redo the entire exercise. They also remark that they are forever changed, and at every subsequent visit to the museum, this exercise has changed how they view art and how they view the context in a public space.

Discussion:

1. Identify what you were thinking as you selected your areas.

2. How did this differ from previous observations?

3. What was most difficult for you in this activity?

Evaluation:

Continue with self-evaluation and overall evaluation and write in your researcher reflective journal about this exercise.

Rationale:

Learners move to yet another level when they begin to realize what it is like to observe and describe in a public space. They begin to realize what gaining access and entry to a social setting feels like, although admittedly, they are in a safe environment at this point, and one that is somewhat familiar to them. In addition, learners have firsthand experience in articulating their goals of observation. They are working on multiple levels of observation and description. I like to suggest finding a quiet place to work afterward to reshape the field notes, review notes to the self, and render the description in standard sentences and grammar. This will help later in studies when an individual is trying to make sense of mounds of data.

EXERCISE 2.6   Observing an Animal at Home, the Zoo, or a Pet Shop

Purpose:

To describe an animal at home or at the zoo.

Problem:

To see and recognize the complexity of the animal's movement.

Activity:

Go to the zoo or a pet shop or observe an animal in your household. Physically describe the animal—how the animal eats, moves, and shifts position and attention. Can you make a list of five adjectives that describe this animal? Do you see inner qualities as well as outer qualities? Isolate your description to include limbs, eyes, head, and mannerisms. Find two traits of the animal that you also find in human beings. Construct a metaphor for this animal. Use the following as examples:

> *This cat is a princess.* (Then, the writer describes physical and behavioral characteristics to convince us that this cat is a princess.)

> *This gorilla is a prizefighter.* (Again, the description of physical and behavioral qualities should convince.)

> *This dog has become the caretaker of the family.* (Continue with physical descriptions and describe interactions with family members.)

Time:

Take as much time as you like with the observation.

Discussion:

1. What did you notice about yourself as an observer as you began this exercise?
2. What was difficult about describing an animal?

Evaluation:

Continue with self-evaluation and overall evaluation for your journal and portfolio.

Rationale:

Individuals may learn something about the difficulty in observing people by beginning with observing animals. Like human beings, animals are animated, unpredictable, and active. This is a good beginning step in complex description in a complex setting. Learners often remark that, although difficult, this exercise was challenging and enjoyable at the same time.

EXERCISE 2.7   Drawing to Become a Better Observer: Drawing Upside Down

Purpose:

To try some drawing exercises, which are the heart and soul of observation, in this case, an upside-down drawing of a famous painting.

Problem:

To see this painting and view it in a new light—upside down.

Time:

45 minutes.

Activity:

I use a drawing by Picasso (1881–1973) suggested by Betty Edwards (1999) in her text *The New Drawing on the Right Side of the Brain*. The drawing is a pencil drawing called *Portrait of Igor Stravinsky* done by Picasso in 1922. There are variations of this exercise in virtually every art book on drawing. I amend it here to serve as a strategy for developing the role of the researcher, to awaken one's artistic intelligence, and to serve as a catalyst for good narrative writing. Learners are given a copy of the drawing and asked to turn it upside down. They often mention they simply cannot draw, and some teacher in their educational history made note of that fact.

Instructions:

- Copy the image as you see it upside down. Use your pencil and your eyes to follow the lines, starting anywhere you wish. Find your personal velocity, and start where you decide is best for your concentration level.

- Use a pencil and plain white paper.

- Copy it any size you wish.

- Start drawing at any point you wish; there are no sequences. Some start at the top and work left to right, others start right to left, some start in the middle and carefully add lines on one half of the page, and so on. Some start with an article of clothing, say the jacket sleeve. All the while, attention is focused on the upside-down drawing. Do not turn it right side up until you are finished.

- When complete, turn your drawing right side up.

- Begin discussing the exercise. Students are amazed when they realize that indeed they can draw if they are careful with observation, they have the time, and they concentrate.

Many students are so inspired by this exercise that they actually devise some additional work of this nature and share it with the class at future meetings. The point most often made in the discussion that follows is that there is a strong tendency for some to want to turn the drawing right side up. I might point out here that the silence in class is complete and utterly poignant, so intense is the concentration in this exercise. For qualitative researchers, it is a valuable exercise because it shows clearly how we can switch modes in our thinking. In the field, one is often required to do this at various points in the research process. Just as you are forced to think differently when viewing something upside down, you see things differently. For the qualitative researcher, this awareness is helpful later in the research process, because we are called upon at the oddest moments to see things differently. After doing this, learners realize that in fact they can draw, that they need to practice in order to draw, and that they need to see what is in front of them in order to draw it! Now, you have progressed through seven exercises that will sharpen you as a research instrument. You are developing the habits of observation and reflective journal writing, which will prepare you for the exercises in the next chapter to advance these techniques.

3

Advancing the Observation, Reflection, and Writing Habit

If you do not breathe through writing, if you do not cry out in writing, or sing in writing, then don't write, because our culture has no use for it.

—Anaïs Nin

Having completed the exercises in Chapter 2, you are ready to go into the field in a public space. One of the wonderful things about doing qualitative research is that you know you are capturing individual lived experience in the social setting. You are also capturing collective experience of given context. *Research* after all is an active verb. It is vibrant and alive. For qualitative researchers the social setting and context is our life force. You have successfully completed a series of observation exercises that took you into various levels of difficulty, starting with the observation of a still life scene. You progressed to describing people and action, then drawing, and now it is time to test your abilities as a research instrument and start a new habit. This first exercise is for developing the habit of nonparticipant observation in a public setting and strengthening your beginning habits of reflection and journal writing. Practice makes perfect as they say.

EXERCISE 3.1 Nonparticipant Observation Assignment

Place:

Restaurant, coffee shop, shopping mall, book store, zoo, place of worship, museum, health club, funeral parlor, dog park, beach, skating rink, park, movie theater, library, technology center, or any public setting.

Purpose:

To observe, describe, and explain a complex public setting. There should be natural public access to the setting and multiple viewing opportunities for you.

Activity:

Nonparticipant observation. Go to this social setting more than once in order to get a sense of the complexity and to maximize what you learn. Go at least three times at different times of the day. If you wish to return at any other time, of course, feel free to do so. Take notes. Make a floor plan. Discover what you are able to hear, see, and learn just by observing. Take photographs if possible, but ask permission first.

What to Look for:

1. The setting: Look around you and describe the entire physical space. Draw a floor plan or take a photo if permitted.

2. The people: Look around you and describe the people in this setting. Focus on one or two of the people. What are they doing in that social space?

3. The action: What are the relationships between people and groups? Try to discover something about the people in the setting.

4. Describe the groups and any common characteristics, such as age, gender, dress codes, speech, activity, and so on.

5. Focus on one person in your viewing area to describe in detail, for example, a waitress, a caretaker, or a salesperson, depending on your setting.

6. If you had all the time in the world to do a study here, what three things would you look for upon returning to the setting?

7. Be sure to give a title to your report that captures your study.

8. Be sure to use references from a minimum of seven texts.

Time:

You have 4 weeks to complete this assignment. Be sure to include a self-evaluation.

Discussion:

1. Of all the exercises so far, how has this one challenged you?

2. How did you approach this assignment, and what difficulties did you encounter in the field setting?

3. What would you do differently if you were to return?

Evaluation:

Continue self-evaluation. And at this point, you need to complete a summative evaluation of this observation cycle for entry in your journal.

Rationale:

At this point, the individual has direct experience in nonparticipant observation, observation of action, and self-evaluation and has been given the opportunity to discuss with peers his or her progress to date. These exercises give the learner a taste of what it will be like in the field in terms of the mini-study for the class and quite possibly in terms of his or her own dissertation or future research activities. Also, there is growth in terms of thinking like a researcher and developing a role for oneself. In the context of a course, the mini-study may be used as a pilot study for a dissertation project if it is reasonable to do so. The learner also begins a research reflective journal and starts, in most cases, an electronic portfolio. No matter what the situation of the individual reader of this text, throughout the practice of these exercises, learners must continue reading from a series of reading lists. Here is an example of a completed project. It is edited in some portions. It was selected because it shows how observation, interviewing, and analysis come together in a practice exercise.

Example: A Square Peg in a Round Hole: A Music Teacher's Perspective on Her Evaluation Process (Edited Class Assignment)

By Daryl Ward

Introduction

All animals are equal, but some animals are more equal than others.

—Orwell, 1996

A hallmark of any qualitative research approach is its ability to give voice to people who have been silenced by a hegemonic system. By detailing the lived experiences of individuals, research can begin to transcend its purely academic formulations and develop narratives that not only reveal inequities, but also serve to supersede them. As I considered the topic for my project, the new teacher evaluation system, I couldn't help but be reminded of these inequities and of Orwell's classic quote referenced above. It would appear that in an attempt to create a one-size-fits-all approach to teacher evaluation, the state of Florida (and its subservient school districts) has instead created an approach that actually fits very few—and some teachers not at all.

At the heart of any of the "value-added models" (VAM) currently popular with policy makers and political pundits is the contention that a consistent causal relationship can be found between teacher behaviors and student achievement. The VAMs attempt to eliminate any variables that may exist from class to class, teacher to teacher, and student to student—and thus equate any learning (or lack of learning) squarely to the effects of the

(Continued)

(Continued)

teacher in question. Despite studies that consistently question whether these models are appropriate for teacher evaluation (Hill, 2009; Hill, Kapitula, & Umland, 2011; Newton, Darling-Hammond, Haertel, & Thomas, 2010), inherent in their use is acquiring accurate student achievement data. An often-over-looked (as far as research goes) concern is the equity of this data across teachers of wildly differing subjects. For example, can the effects of a high school English teacher's instruction as measured on the Florida Comprehensive Assessment Test (FCAT) be fairly compared to a physical education teacher's instructional impact? Here, I studied a music teacher and her perspective on the new, external, prepackaged teacher evaluation system.

Thus was the impetus for my interview choice: a high school chorus teacher who will be evaluated under a new teacher evaluation system that attempts to quantify her instructional techniques using a nonstandardized assessment. My goal was to allow this teacher to have a voice in this process and to be able to articulate her specific concerns of equity as it relates to professional practice. Formulaic, homogenized evaluative processes should not diminish the twin notions of equity and professional practice. These notions are at the heart of what Kenneth A. Strike (2007) means when he says,

> It is not true that to know if we have achieved some end, we must be able to *measure* [emphasis in original] it. What is true is that we need a way to *recognize* [emphasis in original] whether we have achieved our ends. These are not the same thing. (p. 118)

My participant articulates her concerns regarding the "measurement" of her teaching.

The First Interview

I have known Suzi Lambert for seven years. Four of those seven years, her husband worked with me in the Harrison School for the Arts, where I am a principal. She is an educator with seventeen years of teaching experience and is nationally board certified. She has taught elementary, middle, and high school chorus and other ancillary music classes. In addition to voice (chorus) classes, she currently teaches music theory. Suzi is active in her professional organizations and committees. I chose Suzi as a participant for two distinct reasons. First, she is a skilled art teacher. Her choirs have won numerous commendations; her students consistently score well on music performance assessments; her pedagogy is multifaceted—it involves teacher-directed activities as well as student-centered practices. Her goal to have her students "sing to her" has them creating music that is rich in emotion and vast in tonal quality and precision. Simply put, she is a consummate educational professional.

I also wanted to interview her for another reason. I am impressed with her commitment to the craft of teaching. Never the kind of teacher who sits back and lets things be "done unto" her, she actively seeks professional development with the specific purpose of developing her pedagogy. I knew that an interview with her would produce an honest reflection on the current teacher evaluation process. She is not a person who reacts against change, nor is she one to question reform efforts that have the potential to create a richer classroom experience for students. If she has qualms about the teacher evaluation process, I knew these issues were arrived at through thoughtful and reflective means.

For the first interview, I used the following interview protocol questions:

1. Please explain how you came to be a teacher. Tell me the history of your career choice.

2. Describe how you understand (or what you don't understand) about the new teacher evaluation process?

3. How does teaching a performing art differ (in your mind) from teaching a traditional academic subject?

4. What's the most difficult part about being a teacher?

5. What's the most satisfying aspect of being a teacher?

These interrogative conversation starters served as the impetus for me to probe specific aspects of how Suzi felt regarding her

(Continued)

(Continued)

profession and her place along the spectrum of that profession. The interview took place on a Sunday afternoon at a local Panera Bread franchise. Though the interview location presented specific problems (more on that below), the inviting nature of the restaurant—it's difficult to beat the smell of fresh bread and pastries—allowed for open conversation between Suzi and me. After settling on comfort drinks of coffee (for me) and tea (for her), we began our discussion.

The results of this interview (and its subsequent transcription) revealed some areas for further exploration. Specifically, I was intrigued by her response to the questions regarding her perception of the new teacher evaluations system. A major component (50.3%) of the teacher evaluation "score" is student achievement data. A teacher of a core subject (math, science, English, etc.) will have FCAT data to use in determining student learning gains. Teachers of noncore subjects (art, business, physical education, etc.) must rely on some other type of assessment to garner that data. This revealed a concern for Suzi:

> the big one [problem] is that it [the assessment] is not standardized. It is kind of a teacher-created test.... It's very subjective ... if you want to change something, you have that freedom to change your work and make a choice that the kid is actually doing well because it's subjective.

This subjectivity would lead to later discussions and deeper probing regarding equity. In essence, Suzi was frustrated by what she believed is an inequitable application of the metrics used to measure student achievement. For example, some teacher's students will be judged by a standardized assessment such as the FCAT. Other teacher's students, however, will be assessed by a district or teacher-created test. Though this is legal under the state statute, it presents a teacher evaluation system that is rife with potential inequity. Simply put, districts or teachers can create assessments that are less rigorous than the respective standardized assessments. This means some teachers' evaluations will be connected to differing levels of fidelity than other teachers.

Another strain of inquiry was discovered in the first interview related to her views of teaching as an art-craft. She was primarily concerned for the creative spark that certain aspects of teacher accountability measures serve to curtail. Her views echo the sentiments of many in the profession:

> Teaching, to me, is an art-craft. You have to have that freedom to do what is your strength—your certain creative strength to get that student where they need to be, whether it's math, whether it's English, whether it's piano—anything. This model pigeonholes it to where it impacts [the] spontaneous environment [of teaching].

This, too, led to further exploration in the second interview. Specifically, Suzi expressed reservations that the new teacher evaluation system creates an assessment structure that relegates teaching to measurable, easily coded processes that remove the power of spontaneity from the pedagogical act.

This concern is not without merit. In a discussion concerning the focus of education, Strike (2007) notes "what has happened is that instruction has tended to emphasize comprehension and skill acquisition over analysis, discussion, interpretation, and argument" (p. 23). This emphasis on lower order cognitive skills requires pedagogical principles that are more easily assessed and therefore more easily recognized on an assessment rubric.

A final aspect of the preliminary interview that I found to be noteworthy was Suzi's concept of shared accountability for the teaching-learning process. Strike (2007) speaks to this notion of education as a communal effort as well when he notes, "Our society, quite sensibly, views the education of its children as a shared project between parents and the state" (p. 104). He is also cognizant that accountability need not require only quantifiable assessments. "There is a great deal about what constitutes a good education that schools will not be held accountable for if the only form of accountability is the accountability to the legislature for meeting benchmarks defined by test scores" (p. 109).

Suzi echoed Strike's sentiments with her own formulization of her experience. "The biggest [concern] for me is that we don't work on a bell curve," she stated. "When it comes time for a performance, if I'm at 80% mastery, my choir is not very effective." She clearly illustrated the importance of distinguishing between

(Continued)

(Continued)

effective assessments in an arts classroom compared to that of a traditional classroom. She also was quick to point out that performing groups have a different component to consider in regard to pedagogy. "I have to get them to all be able to like each other because that's an issue," she said. She went on to review the importance of teaching diversity in an arts-based classroom.

Suzi Lambert elevates the concept of teaching to include a powerful relationship dynamic. "Teaching is a gift. Effective teachers have a calling and a drive to know more. They want to know their students," she stated. Her passion for making the learning process a communal experience is evident. "I don't know how a classroom exists without looking at the unique qualities of your students and what they bring and what they can bring to others," she said. She later describes this as a "community of learners" and this idea is explored in more depth during the second interview.

After the initial interview and an analysis of the transcript, I began to see potential themes emerging. That allowed me to create a more focused set of questions for the second interview protocol:

1. Part of the concern about the new teacher evaluation system (TES) is about equity. Explain how you think the new TES is not equitable in the ways and methods it uses to evaluate teachers.

2. Describe your reasoning and thoughts on teaching as an art-craft. What components of *art* does it utilize?

3. Describe for me what *spiral learning-teaching* is? How would you differentiate it from another (more traditional?) way of teaching? Give me an example lesson.

4. How does a "team" model of teaching-learning work—one in which everyone, teacher and students, has a stake in being accountable for student achievement?

The second interview took place on Monday, November 14, in her office at Harrison School for the Arts. By allowing Suzi to conduct a member check of the transcript and by providing her with a more refined interview protocol, our second session provided data to inform my analysis of emergent themes.

First Theme: The Equity of the Teacher Evaluation Process

The first theme that emerged was specifically related to the perceived equity of the teacher evaluation process. The concern of equitable evaluations is noteworthy in many regards. Hill (2009) notes that there is an implied assumption that "in a properly specified value-added model, teachers/school scores are accurate enough indicators of the above traits to sustain their use in accountability systems [and that] schools and teachers can be accurately distinguished from one another" (p. 702). In essence, it should be a required component of any evaluation system that all teachers within that system be afforded equitable evaluation opportunities—that is a "highly effective" rating for a math teacher should be commensurate with a "highly effective" rating for a visual arts teacher. Polk County's new teacher evaluation system does not illicit confidence in its approach to consistency. Suzi states,

> That evaluation tool, I know it has to exist, but I don't feel like it's differentiating. I don't feel like it's diverse enough or content-specific enough. It doesn't help the administrator be able to meet the needs of that teacher through an assessment and proper feedback.

Suzi also has concerns that inherent subjectivity in the evaluative process is pervasive enough to bias an administrative evaluation. While she understands that any human endeavor involves an element of bias, her anxiety is heightened by the high-stakes nature of this new evaluation process:

> The [teacher evaluation] rubric is set up to make it more objective, but in the end it is subjective. It's what one person sees in that moment in time. I've come to respect high levels of expectation from my administration, however, another director may be evaluated at another level—ultimately scored at a higher effectiveness.

(Continued)

(Continued)

She is worried that due to the varied administrators' levels of content expertise, it is possible for one choir director to score lower (due to his or her administrator's more sophisticated content knowledge) while a colleague might score higher (due to his or her administrator's lack of content knowledge). This, she feels, creates for an unequal application of the evaluation process.

If I'm being honest with you, I have a principal that knows what's considered effective and not effective in a performance situation [choral music] as opposed to someone else who has a principal who does not [have that knowledge]. So I might be evaluated at a higher rubric [level] in the mindset of my administrator than someone else.

Suzi also addressed a perceived inequity in the teacher evaluation system as it related to teachers of different subjects. She voiced specific concerns that students in performing classes (chorus, band, visual arts, etc.) are taught differently than students in traditional core subjects (math, English, social studies, etc.). These differing pedagogical approaches, she felt, could lead to inaccurate and unfair evaluations. She gave a specific example suggesting that in an English class, the entire class would likely be discussing the same section of *Hamlet*, however in her piano class, the differentiated instruction that is required presents challenges. "What happens if all of my students are working on piano skills at the time [of evaluation]? I'm working with one student. Am I going to be able to address everyone [the other students] on that one concern?" The need to offer specific instructional strategies, she felt, could impact her score on the evaluation instrument. Thus she felt, traditional academic subjects allow the teacher to "implement some summarization tool," that might not be available to a performing arts teacher.

If I tried to improve my choir based on an LFS (learning-focused solutions) model, I'm not going to get anywhere. I have to have the ability to get them to sing in tune and an LFS graphic organizer is not going to do that.

She also noted that different subjects seem to have certain advantages when it comes to the assessment used to evaluate student achievement. These advantages also promote inequity. Her main reference was the FCAT. Teachers who teach in FCAT-tested subjects have "had lots of practice with that model. There are even professionally produced [practice] tests." Whereas with her subject, chorus, her students are going to be assessed on a district-created assessment with performance criteria gleaned from expectations of eleventh-grade students. Therefore even her "ninth graders are going to be assessed at eleventh-grade requirements." This presents a vastly unfair teacher-assessment system when the student performance metrics are allowed to have such significant disparity between teachers. And ironically, Suzi points out that this type of evaluation system would never be allowed if it were being used on students.

> It's just so vague and I don't like when you're holding someone accountable [for such a vague outcome]. If I did that as a teacher in the classroom, and the parent complained, I would have to change. . . . I would have to delete the grade.

Suzi's concluding thoughts on the new teacher evaluation system's inequity are telling in and of themselves: "It's very unprofessional. If I were to evaluate the model, *it* [emphasis in original] would be ineffective. So how can ineffective produce effective?"

Second Theme: Teaching as an Art-Craft

A seminal debate among educators and educational philosophers is the degree to which education is an art-craft or a science. And while practitioners would unequivocally state that education is both art *and* science, there remains a debate as to the attempt at quantifying (and hence assessing) the teaching act. This is the entire premise behind all of the valued-added models of teacher assessment: that observations of teachers and student achievement scores can somehow be quantified into a data set that can then be used to make personnel (and payroll) decisions. Noted educational philosopher John Dewey offers a salient perspective of the dichotomy of teaching as a science and an art. He champions the idea that although pedagogical principles exist and can be taught (and perhaps assessed), there

(Continued)

(Continued)

is a distinct element of teaching-learning that is akin to the creative process of an artist. This is also a notion supported by my interviews with Suzi Lambert.

She related her sentiments that the new evaluation process has the potential to inhibit the spontaneous creative process that is good teaching. "I strongly feel the evaluation assessment tool and implementation plan stifles many of the traits of highly effective teachers," she stated. She was particularly concerned with what she perceived as the constrictive nature of a mechanical approach to teacher assessment. She described a recent incident concerning a teachable moment in one of her classes:

> We were in theory the other day and we were starting four-part. And I had my little check-off system—what I was going to do. We're going to do this, this, this. And all of the sudden, one of my high-thinkers—one of our composers, someone who actually composes in jazz for ensembles— said, "Let's talk about this." [He] wanted to talk about how he thinks as a composer and what the text was bringing to him. [Next we had] three, four, five, guitarists who write for themselves and sing with their guitars and they were all sparking. Well, what do I do? Do I snuff that out? Do I take the opportunity to [let it] go? Do I break that moment, again, put the blanket over it and say, "Okay, I've got to check this off; let's go back to the lesson essential question?"

Suzi expressed frustration that the observation rubric would "penalize" her for not meeting its expectations (the teacher is supposed to refer back to the lesson essential question). She further explores the theme of a loss of artistry due to the new evaluation system by decrying the process's prohibitive structure: "It inhibits me from trusting my instinct, trusting my gifts. Teaching is an art."

Third Theme: Creating a Community of Learners

Suzi described her approach to a communal form of education. "Our group [the choir] depends upon the commitment of all members. I tell my students each one is important." She further explains that it is necessary for "everyone to work together to have everyone achieve their best for the betterment of the group."

Suzi extends this concept, however, into an ethic of care. Nel Noddings (2005) describes this process thusly: "We do not tell our children to care; we show them how to care by creating caring relations with them" (p. 22). Suzi exemplifies this by the example below:

And so the team concept, where I feel I've been most successful, is teaching my students, "I value that you're here." And to yell at them for not being at a rehearsal [they're] just going to say, "Well, she just yelled at me." But if I approach it more like, "I really need you here. You bring this . . .," then they understand where they fit into the puzzle and where we are successful with them. And they feel ownership. And then everybody feels valued and the outcome is stronger.

This approach to teaching as an act of caring has clear implications for student learning. "The thought that comes to mind," said Suzi, "is collaboration or collaborative pairs." She credits this ethic of caring with further engaging students. "We make each other feel better about the overall performance because we're supporting each other. And we're equally honest with each other."

Suzi's desire to share the responsibility of learning with her students is noteworthy. "My goal is to promote a community of learning and to engage students at the highest level of thinking through analyzing, predicting, evaluating, and choosing strategies for improvement." This type of high-order instruction flows nicely with her description of teaching chorus as a "spiral learning" experience. She notes how a musical ensemble may be performing literature from one level early in the year, but later in the year may be able to tackle the challenge of performing more difficult literature. "The literature is very simple—very homophonic—early in the year. . . . If they master that certain skill . . . then we go to where we're developing for our winter concert and the music is very polyphonic." This is what she means by spiral learning—that it starts at one particular level and spirals upwards

(Continued)

(Continued)

toward higher (more challenging) levels. This approach also leads to surprises for the teacher and students.

Suzi notes how in certain classes, an English class for example, the students may read from the beginning of the textbook to the end. In her chorus class however, there is no official conclusion to the learning. "My book is open. I don't know where these kids are going to go and that's what's so amazing about the whole thing. Who knows where they're going to end up?" She continued, my "teaching doesn't stop" as the year winds down. She continues to spiral up with her instruction. "Let's go to the next level," she adds. "Is there more to learn? Yes. And it's usually something totally unexpected that just says, 'Wow. It was worth it from the start'. "

Suzi also notes what she calls a "shift" in education. Her proposition is that students are learning to take responsibility for their own learning and for sharing that learning with others.

> Education is now in a shift. It used to be—and I tell the kids that during warm ups—it used to be you all looked at me and I looked at all of you and I said, "Okay, you don't have your mouth open wide enough," and "You need to close your tongue right behind your teeth when you sing. . . ." Now they turn—we turn every day and we face each other. And so they give feedback to each other because I should be—and I told them this the other day—I said, "I should be the last one to tell you. [If] you can't figure it out, I'm the last resource that you have. Use each other." And that's where I feel education has taken its turn in that it's not teacher-focused; it's more student-focused.

This student-centered to approach to education resonates with Suzi. "I don't take offense to that. I say, 'Let's go,' because it's student-led."

Suzi's belief in a communal participatory educational process is a recurrent theme in her professional beliefs and actions. Strike (2007) again provides support for this philosophy. "If the goal is to advance knowledge through teaching or inquiry, the success of each contributes to the success of all" (p. 17). The notion that everyone benefits from the collective success of individuals is a unique one in education. Inherent in the current educational system is the philosophy of competition and success at the expense of others. This philosophy is one that favors exploitation and not cooperation. Clearly, Suzi Lambert refuses to bite into that ideological poison apple.

Reflection

My impetus for this interview was the perceived inequity of a new teacher evaluation system being enacted in Polk County. As I listened to how this system was being created and implemented, the entire process struck me as one that further deprofessionalizes teachers. I was concerned that teachers would be assessed on student performance—performance that in many instances they had little control over. I was also disturbed by the gross inequity in the types of data used to determine teacher "effectiveness." Who would speak for the marginalized teachers whose subjects do not lend easily to quantifiable, standardizable (dare I say dastardly) measurements? I think that the most important part of this experience was giving voice to a person who felt imprisoned by the silence forced upon her.

Suzi Lambert was a natural choice for my study as she is a teacher at my school and she teaches a performing art (chorus and musical theatre). Her genuinely gregarious personality also contributed to the project in that she felt comfortable sharing with me her personal and professional opinions about her career as an educator and her impressions of the new evaluation system. As a woman of integrity, compassion, and deep enthusiasm for getting students to experience the joy of singing, her thoughts on how a system can stifle and even destroy creativity were poignant.

The actual process of completing the study was also enlightening. Upon reflection, for example, I've learned that choice of interview location is extremely important. In an effort to reduce any work-related perception of power dynamics (as I am Suzi's direct supervisor), I thought it would be best to conduct the interview in a public place that allowed for spontaneity. As such, I chose a Panera Bread location. This turned out to be a mistake. While the digital recorder was able to capture the interview dialogue successfully, the ambient noise was extremely distracting during the transcription process, probably adding more time to the already cumbersome task of transcribing. The second interview, therefore,

(Continued)

(Continued)

took place in a more intimate setting where there were no outside distractions (however, there was no coffee either—an advantage Panera did offer).

The transcribing process was also enlightening. As this was my first experience with converting oral conversation into text, I learned the time-intensive nature of transcription. Steiner Kvale and Svend Brinkmann's (2009) admonition proved insightful: "Rather than being a simple clerical task, transcription is an interpretive process, where the differences between oral speech and written texts give rise to a series of practical and principal issues" (p. 177). I found that I had to decide whether a verbatim transcript was proper for my project with all of the specific speech constructs (*uhmms* and *ahhs*) or whether to use a "written style" as described by Kvale and Brinkmann (p. 180). I chose the verbatim style so as to familiarize myself with attempting to accurately record the interview experience in as much detail as possible. The biggest consequence of this was the actual time it took to transcribe two interviews. Since I was transcribing every *uhmmm, ahhhh,* and *mhhmm,* the process of transcribing took longer than I expected. I would still choose this transcription method, however, as I felt it gave me a clearer picture of the speaker's speech patterns and rhythms.

My final reflective comment is related to the deep passion for students and learning exhibited by Suzi Lambert. In a day when the media and correlated ideological think tanks continue to portray teachers as lazy, underprepared, and concerned only about feeding at the public trough, it is refreshing to converse with a professional who so vividly defies that demonization. I found great comfort (and even inspiration) in her description of what she tries to get her students to achieve:

> That's what I try to teach the kids . . . always think about your resources. Who can you go to? It's better to do it [learning] together than to do it alone. That's just how I've always tried to work, my life is trying the collaboration.

Her desire to teach the power of community and to "not try and do everything on your own" is a testament to what true teaching is all about.

Future as a Qualitative Researcher

As I reflect on this project and my prospective future as a qualitative researcher, I am drawn to the narrative structure of various qualitative approaches. By using the power of story as a research tool, I hope to add to the knowledge of the field. The class visit by Dr. Carolyn Ellis and her sharing of her current work with Holocaust survivors bolstered this desire. I was impressed by her use of interviews and narrative techniques to chronicle the lived experiences of the participants. Especially intriguing to me was her use of various fictive techniques when she shared the story of the man whose mother's instincts for family preservation were contrasted with another mother's apparently selfish actions. The presentation of this research as a short story allowed the reader (in our case, the hearers) of the narrative to engage in the dramatic nature of the tale; it wove a rich dynamic plot with sensual details. This, in turn, produced a powerful communicative experience—one that all research should seek to be worthy of.

I also feel drawn to the phenomenological approach to qualitative research. As John W. Creswell (2007) states, "a phenomenological study describes the meaning for several individuals for their lived experiences of a concept or a phenomenon" (p. 57). Researching phenomena to capture an essence of these shared experiences is appealing to me as I see it as a way to give voice to those who have traditionally not been allowed to tell their stories. As I mentioned previously, this particular interview project was appealing to me because I wanted to allow a chorus teacher to share her feelings of being constrained by a teacher evaluation model that has failed to account for instructional diversity. The idea of exploring similar marginalized groups and people situates itself nicely with my goals of phenomenological research. And while this particular project was not specifically phenomenological in nature, it whetted my appetite for using this approach as a researcher.

I also see my future as a qualitative researcher with an interdisciplinary studies focus. I hope to gain insight and knowledge related to an expansion of my understandings of the field of narrative research. By venturing outside of the traditional Educational Leadership program requirements into such diverse departments

(Continued)

(Continued)

as communication, anthropology, and special education, I hope to continue to broaden my concepts of narrative research. The varied emphases and research directives found within these disparate departments should add to my growing understanding of different methodologies and narrative turns.

I have come to recognize the legitimacy and contributions of qualitative research to the canon of various fields of study. Within education alone, I feel this approach and the numerous methods associated with it offer a more comprehensive way to communicate knowledge than quantitative studies by themselves can do. I hope to someday offer my own contributions to these bodies of knowledge as well.

My Role as a Researcher and a Critique of That Role

As I examine my participation in this interview project, I am struck by the areas I must continue to develop. Most noticeably to me were my experiences in the question-asking department. After listening to the recorded interview, I was able to determine specific times when I reframed or reasked the question without allowing time for the interviewee to process the question and to formulate an answer. It was almost as if I was afraid of silence on the part of the participant and therefore wanted to make sure she understood the question. In retrospect, I don't feel there were times of confusion, but rather some researcher "insecurity" on my part. I feel confident that with continued practice, I will refine my question-asking techniques to allow the voice of the participant to take center stage and to not rely so much on "clarifying" statements that simply mask my discomfort with conversational pauses. I must add, however, that I do enjoy the participatory nature of qualitative research. Instead of trying to maintain an objective distance, I was able to engage equally with the research participant. The fine-tuning of the senses cannot be accomplished without disciplined practice and subsequent feedback. This project revealed to me a need to continue to develop my listening skills. I felt my interview questions were appropriate to my central research objective: to give voice to a noncore teacher about a new teacher evaluation process. However, my listening skills need continued refinement. Instead of thinking about the next question, I need to concentrate more on being "in the moment" with my research participant. Active listening must become a priority for me.

Another aspect of improving my role as a qualitative researcher would be to begin using a researcher reflective journal. Though I have long maintained a journal (mostly concerning books I've read), the concept of journaling on a respective research project is a provocative one for me. Again Valerie Janesick (2011) provides specific insight here when she describes the researcher reflective journal as a device that "allows for all that encompasses your role as the research instrument" (p. 8). Though I did not actually keep a journal for the interview project, this brief exercise revealed to me the benefit of doing so for a more substantial research initiative. I can see how my personal reflections regarding the research process would help refine my skills as a researcher.

Further Research Opportunities With This Topic

If I had further opportunity to expand this interview project, I see numerous avenues for exploration. One area that appealed to me immediately would be to expand the interview pool to include students under the direction of Suzi Lambert. I was intrigued by her participatory teaching style and by her goal to create communities of learning. I would like to see what the students feel about this nontraditional approach to education. Since the students would more than likely have classes that utilize the traditional "drill and kill" or lecture style of instructional delivery as well as Suzi's progressive style of teaching, they would be particularly situated within the phenomena to discuss it. By researching student-specific experiences, a careful dichotomy of instructional approaches could be exposed. This would provide data for a phenomenological study of students' experiences with varied instructional approaches.

I would also like to more broadly explore the concept of equity in teacher evaluation. This would have to include a more detailed review of current literature on the subject and would also involve expansion of the number of participants. For example, as previously noted, Suzi Lambert is a chorus teacher. Would a teacher of

(Continued)

(Continued)

another elective-type class have a similar impression as Suzi does as to the fairness of the evaluation process? Would a business teacher be as critical regarding his or her students' performance assessments not being standardized? Does the nature of teaching a performance-based class (music, art) change the instructor's opinions as to the nature of the evaluative process? A more richly portrayed notion of equity would require these types of questions be asked.

Finally, I would delve further into the concept of teaching as an art. This would necessitate immersion in the literature on the subject and would entail including more participants and recording their impressions. The potential for this to become narrative research is intriguing as I am curious as to the parallels between teachers and artists. I would want to explore the motivations of both groups (teachers and artists) and would seek to chronicle the lived experiences of both as well. Just as in creating art, there is something mystical (magical?) about good teaching. It appears to be a response to a creative spark and must be nurtured. Interviews and observations might garner specific insights into the similarity of both processes: making art and teaching. I also recognize the potential breadth of this topic and that it would perhaps need careful refinement in order to remain manageable as a valid subject of study.

References

Creswell, J. W. (2007). *Qualitative inquiry & research design: Choosing among five approaches.* Thousand Oaks, CA: Sage.

Hill, H. C. (2009). Evaluating value-added models: A validity argument approach. *Journal of Policy Analysis and Management, 28,* 692–712.

Hill, H. C., Kapitula, L., & Umland, K. (2011). A validity argument approach to evaluating teacher value-added scores. *American Educational Research Journal, 48,* 794-831.

Janesick, V. J. (2011). *Stretching exercises for qualitative researchers* (3rd ed.). Thousand Oaks, CA: Sage.

Kvale, S., & Brinkmann, S. (2009). *InterViews: Learning the craft of qualitative research interviewing.* Thousand Oaks, CA: Sage.

Newton, X., Darling-Hammond, L., Haertel, E., & Thomas, E. (2010). Value-added modeling of teacher effectiveness: An exploration of stability across models and contexts. *Educational Policy Analysis Archives, 18*(23), 1–27.

Noddings, N. (2005). *The challenge to care in schools: An alternative approach to education,* (2nd ed.). New York, NY: Teachers College Press.

Orwell, G. (1996). *Animal farm: With connections.* Austin, TX: Holt, Rinehart & Winston.

Simpson, D. J., Jackson, M. J. B., & Aycock, J. C. (2005). *John Dewey and the art of teaching: Toward reflective and imaginative practices.* Thousand Oaks, CA: Sage.

Strike, K. A. (2007). *Ethical leadership in schools: Creating community in an environment of accountability.* Thousand Oaks, CA: Corwin.

Tomlinson, C. A. (2001). Standards and the art of teaching: Crafting high-quality classrooms. *NASSP Bulletin, 85*(622), 38–47.

EXERCISE 3.2   Reflecting to Strengthen the Writing Habit

Important Life Event:

Think of an important event in your life or in a project you are writing. Write the weather for the day it happened. Try to recall what you were wearing. What was happening around you? Write a description of that event and all the subsequent meaning in the event. Aim for five pages to start. Share your writing with another person and get feedback. Rewrite. Add this to your researcher reflective journal as part of understanding your role as a researcher and reflective agent.

EXERCISE 3.3   Writing Your Educational Autobiography

Write seven to ten pages of your educational autobiography with particular attention to your career choice as an educator and how you are progressing on your educational journey. Think of this as your learning autobiography. What inspired you to be a teacher or leader? What influences or setbacks have you experienced? If you could do this all over again, would you still select education as your field? Add this to your researcher reflective journal as part of understanding your role as a researcher. For those who are in other professions, it is always good to reflect back on your educational autobiography. Add a few questions, such as the following: Are you still in the same field in which you were prepared? What outstanding influences did you have during your educational matriculation?

EXERCISE 3.4   Writing a Pedagogical Letter

The Pedagogical Letter: Write a Seven- to Ten-Page Letter to Someone You Know

One of Paulo Freire's (1921–1997) favorite formats of communication was through letters. He described in these letters his political, socio-logical, ideological, philosophical, and contextual beliefs, values, and ideas. Most of his final text, *Pedagogy of Indignation,* evolved and is generated from these pedagogical letters over the course of his lifetime. These letters contained his hopes, his emotions, and his sensibilities. This exercise is for you to do the same.

Write a letter and explain your critical pedagogical beliefs regarding an educational issue you care about and how you apply these beliefs in your everyday world. For example, some students have written to their own children, their grandparent, a spouse, a significant other, another student, or some historical figure, like Mother Jones or Eleanor Roosevelt, or someone who has inspired the writer. Some have written to Paulo Freire himself or one of the authors of a favorite text. Write in a letter format, and include this in your researcher reflective journal.

● NEXT STEPS: SELF-EVALUATION

The next three protocols you will see show some possibilities for becoming an active agent as a researcher. The learner takes responsibility for self-evaluation, as in the sample Figure 3.1, Self-Evaluation for Your Journal. A second option, Figure 3.2, My Story to the Best of My Knowledge, allows for a more introspective turn. Finally, Figure 3.3, Model Format to Explain Your Qualitative Research Study, is to be seen as a working document and a starting point for the learner to begin constructing the mini-study that brings together the practice of and learning from all of these exercises to this point. Now, the learner moves on to the cycle of interviewing. The following self-evaluation is an option for those students who prefer letter writing over the sample forms I have constructed.

PITFALLS IN OBSERVATION   ●

Learners who have the luxury of a class situation or a community of scholars with whom to discuss daily progress have remarked on the following pitfalls to these observation exercises:

1. **Focus and concentration** are the critical elements to doing a decent observation. The first obstacle to overcome is deciding what

Figure 3.1   Self-Evaluation for Your Journal

Self-evaluation of my _____ activity.

List three adjectives that describe what you learned from this activity.

1.

2.

3.

Locate Yourself

Historically, the theories that have most affected me and shaped me are (list at least three authors). EXPLAIN.

1.

2.

3.

The reasons these authors have shaped my thinking are

Figure 3.2   My Story to the Best of My Knowledge

In this exercise, I want you to reflect on your intellectual growth and development. Which ideas have dazzled you? Prompted you to go further in your studies?

Try to remember at least one to three incidents from school, kindergarten to the present, that have profoundly affected your thinking. Describe in detail these incidents—sights, sounds, smells, tastes, the feel of them, key participants, your own memory of how you reacted at the time, and how you view these incidents today.

Add this entry to your portfolio.

Name _____ Date _____

Incident One:

Incident Two:

Incident Three:

You may not see what is in front of you. You may look at something, but you may not look carefully enough to see what is there.

to observe, because you cannot possibly observe everything in a given social setting. The best way to approach this is to settle on a section of a setting, one person, or one set of objects to begin observing and describing. Many describe a feeling of frustration as they have never observed closely before. That dissipates after some practice.

2. **Overdoing it, that is, overdescribing one piece of a setting, for example, may hamper the end result.** Try not to fixate on just one piece of the scene. See if you can gradually add more to your observation as you go along. Once, a student wrote 20 pages while describing a flute. This is an amazing feat and could have even been enriched by placing this flute in a social context with description of the flute player, the actual setting where the flute was being used, and how this observer came there in the first place.

Figure 3.3   Model Format to Explain Your Qualitative Research Study

1. The purpose of this study is to describe and explain: (example: the mentor's view of mentoring)

2. The following theory guides the study: (example: phenomenology)

3. The exploratory questions which guide the study include the following:

   a. What elements or characteristics make up this mentor's beliefs about mentoring?

   b. What variables influence this set of beliefs?

4. The literature related to this study includes the following:

   a. Methodology literature: (name the area)

   b. Topical literature: (name the area)

My rating involves the following:

I still want to work on the following:

Sample Reflection (Edited) for Adding to the Reflective Journal: Self-Evaluation Upon Observing in a Student Laboratory for English Language Learning

By Oksana Vrobel (2009)

Doctoral Student in Second Language Acquisition and Instructional Technology

Challenges on the Way

I am glad that I have done the observation assignment. It was useful and challenging simultaneously. Because I am a beginning qualitative researcher, these are my first steps and attempts to collect data, analyze them, and self-reflect. As many suggest, practice in data collection, analysis, and writing is essential. Therefore, I appreciate that I had this opportunity to practice and receive a valuable feedback on it. Despite the unquestionable benefit of this exercise, it was challenging. This observation work required absolute commitment and concentration. I am a perfectionist by nature and try to do my best. Therefore, it took some time to think over the task itself, to plan how I was going to approach it, to do the observations, and, of course, to write the observation report.

One of the challenges that I had was the time I chose to do observations. During the first time when I came to observe a setting, the place was empty, and I had known that it would be empty because it was just the beginning of the semester in the English Language Institute (ELI). The lab was still closed. I had enough time to look at the details of the setting. However, when I went there for the second and third times, I had to evaluate the situation to determine whether it was the best time for observations. There were only three students there and they were leaving. So, I decided that I should choose a different time to complete the second and third observations. I know that planning observations is also one of the skills I need to practice, but at the same time, there are conditions that I cannot predict. Thus, one of the lessons that I learned was always to leave some time for a back-up plan in case I could not do an observation due to some unexpected obstacle.

In addition, it was rather hard to focus on the details of the setting and people's appearances. I think that it is just one of my traits of character; I am always absorbed in my inner world and not used to focusing on small details that exist around me. Though I realize that small details, such as a hand position while writing, may tell a researcher some essential information about a participant of a study, it was hard to focus and go over the entire setting. While doing it, I just remembered that it is always hard the first time. I also did not know what details I needed to pay attention to most. So, I just followed the rule, "The more I can describe, the better it will be." I think it is possible to think about some details that can be crucial to observe. However, I need to observe and describe many nitty-gritty things that, as a result, can provide important information.

Moreover, I found some internal resistance that made me hesitate, whether it was the best time for observation, for self-reflection, and for writing the report. I think this resistance is the result of my inexperience. I need to overcome the resistance with constant practice. I agree with those who think that it is always possible to find something that seems more important than writing. Even such a humble thing as dishwashing can seem to have importance when we try to block the resistance to write and practice constantly. I found I need to work at writing.

Approach to the Assignment

I think I clearly see this assignment as a means to practice and have a hands-on experience in observation. I have never done an observation before. Therefore, I carefully planned and tried to think over what I needed to do for an observation, for example, times and stages of it. I tried to plan it at home. However, when I came to the ELI, I still had to take a table to jot my observation notes down. I did not use a laptop to put down notes. I thought that, for the first time, it would be more convenient for me to use a pencil than to type and organize the information at home. I think that next time, I will bring my laptop to put down notes. I wonder what could be the most effective way to write down notes and what literature says about it. My guess is that it depends on each researcher's preference. Later, I discovered my own style and preferences.

(Continued)

(Continued)

After each observation, I tried to write and organize my notes to be more prepared for the next observation. I think doing it step by step was a good decision. It makes the process more planned, organized, and meaningful for me. It also gives me more time to focus on each of the stages separately instead of having just a holistic overview of the experience. Fortunately, I had an opportunity to take pictures of both the setting and one of the students I observed. I asked for permission of both the administration and the student, and they allowed me to take pictures without hesitation. I think that I was lucky because the person whom I observed during my second observation was a student of mine two semesters ago. In my opinion, this contributed to her eagerness and quick agreement to be photographed. However, I think it could be challenging if the person were a stranger. Then, it could raise suspicions and unwillingness. I definitely have to keep this in mind if I am going to observe strangers for my future studies. This is also applicable to the setting. I chose the place because I feel that I have some personal connection to it as an international student and an instructor. However, it is also a convenient sample simultaneously. The ELI is my place of work now, and I had no problem getting permission from them to observe it and take pictures of it.

As for the writing, it is my first time, and I am not writing a paper part by part. This time, I tried to focus on my inspiration and internal readiness to write different aspects of this assignment. I think this nonlinear approach to writing is a little bit confusing at first, but I was so inspired by the book *Writing Down the Bones* by Natalie Goldberg (2005) that I decided to follow her advice to start writing about anything that I was up to at the moment. In my opinion, this experiment was a success; I enjoyed it more, though I think the process of editing will be more time consuming this time. While writing, I had to stop to think, then to write, teach, read, and write again. It was not an easy process. Writing always requires a lot of effort. I am exhausted after it, but it is self-rewarding at the same time.

Difficulties in the Field Setting

In addition to the challenges described in the first part of my self-evaluation, I think it was rather difficult to do the third observation. I needed to observe people in action and to take notes about everything around me. However, it was extremely hard because there were several groups of students in the lab, and when I focused on a group, I could not take notes about the others. Moreover, I felt that even when I took notes and got distracted for seconds to write, something important might happen, and I would not see it. I realize that this was just a practice, but I wonder how experienced researchers deal with this question and whether they have this concern at all.

As I have mentioned above, I did not have any difficulties with getting permission to observe a setting and to take photos of it. However, I still felt uncomfortable observing people and their actions. I did not want to make them think I was staring at them. This could have caused misunderstandings and changes in their behavior. In the worst case, they could have left. Therefore, it is important to think about possible difficulties that can occur at the setting ahead of time and eliminate them if it is possible.

Second Chance

If I were to return, I think I would try to use a laptop to take notes and see if it is more effective than to take notes in pencil. I would also try to record my oral description of the setting and people. I think I need to try different approaches to observations to be familiar with the ways to do it. In addition, I will learn what I prefer. I understand that the purpose of this assignment is to practice and take the first steps in qualitative data collection and analysis. Having this experience now, I can try to do observations as a part of my future qualitative studies.

Lessons Learned

I think it was a valuable experience for me. Though I read a lot about data collection for class, there is nothing better than to experience and practice data collection myself. During observation, I learned that I need to focus on the details. It was challenging, but I think it will become easier with practice. In addition, I experimented with different approaches to writing and self-reflection. I tried to write in a nonlinear fashion. That was worth doing.

(Continued)

(Continued)

In addition, I concentrated on my own experience as a researcher. I think this is one of the advantages of qualitative research. A researcher's experience and reflection are essential in qualitative studies. A qualitative researcher is an instrument. A qualitative researcher designs a study, collects data, analyzes them, and provides a rich description through his or her own experience and background. I think it makes a lot of sense, because any study that I design is a part of me. I can do a study and clearly describe connections between this study and me and my role in the study, not only in the rationale but also throughout the paper.

Furthermore, I discovered how much I enjoy the whole process. Sometimes, when I am doing an assignment, I do it for the purpose of simply meeting the requirements of the course. This assignment is not among those. I think I enjoyed every minute of doing it and writing about it. Thus, observation of the ELI computer lab, students, and their actions led to the conclusion that ELI students use the setting to study individually and in groups, socialize with their friends from other countries face to face and online, keep in touch with their families, interact, and use the resources available. Part of their life experiences, emotions, and feelings is invisibly imprinted in that setting.

The observation assignment was beneficial for me as a future researcher because it provided me with a precious experience and practice. I hope that now I can plan to include observations into my data collection for future qualitative studies.

3. **Underdescribing** could harm the overall effect and goal of the exercise if not enough attention is paid to each component. When in doubt, keep writing and refining those observation skills. Take baby steps at first and then move on.

4. **Interacting and communicating with on-site personnel** in the field can be a problem. When entering a public space and in trying to get permission to take photos, realize that some places will allow it and some will not. It is a good idea to explain you are taking a course, and this may help you a great deal. About 90% of people who ask for permission to photograph a setting, for example, get that permission and often a free coffee. As a backup, should you not get that go-ahead

signal, try drawing a floor plan and sketch the scene as best as is possible. Use narrative description as a rule; the better you become as a describer, the less you need to photograph. Also, a note about photographs here is helpful. Photographs should be taken if they add something to the study. They must be purposefully selected for your narrative report. They should add cohesion to the report. It does not make much sense to throw in a dozen photos without a narrative, cohesive reason for doing so.

5. **Use diligence** as you approach these exercises, and take the time to be reflective. As you may already realize, this type of research cannot be rushed. In our overscheduled, overtexted, over–e-mailed existence, we often lose site of the value of silence, reflection, and tapping into our own creativity. The student today spends more time with head bowed over a digital device while walking, crossing the street, dining, in class, and just about everywhere. Part of your job as a researcher is to turn off that noise and focus on the present moment under study.

CHAPTER SUMMARY

In this series of four exercises, the learner has direct experience in advancing further in observational techniques by visiting a public setting three times and describing, explaining, and interpreting that setting for a reader. Next, the habits of reflection and writing are reinforced and advanced through the practice exercises of writing a pedagogical letter, an educational autobiography, and describing and reflecting upon a critical life event. The exercises move forward with increasing complexity in sharpening one's habits of observation, reflection, and journal writing. Each learner is encouraged to evaluate and document in a research reflective journal as he or she moves through the exercises. For each individual activity, the learner then completes a summative evaluation statement on his or her own progress overall as an observer. These exercises are in preparation for progressing to the next series of exercises: interviewing and writing. Furthermore, these exercises have their origin in the arts and humanities. Many are used for the purpose of developing the narrative writing habit.

Because of the hectic pace of many of our lives, being still long enough to observe and describe a setting, an object, or a person requires us to settle down and let ourselves become totally absorbed in the given activity. Most learners seem to get better at this the more they do it. In this case, practice really does allow the individual to improve and proceed in the series. Like the dancer in training, who improves through consistent, relentless, and disciplined exercise, the qualitative researcher in training may improve as an observer of the human condition. Like the student of yoga, the more you concentrate on a given posture and breathe into it, the better you will be able to train your body to hold it. Like the professional writer, the writing habit needs to be developed, and that is best done by writing every day. As we move to the next section on developing the habit of interviewing and writing, digital exercises will also be added to practice and refine skills associated with working on the Web and for the purpose of critical development.

SUGGESTED RESOURCES

Denzin, N. K., & Lincoln, Y. S. (2003). *The strategies of qualitative inquiry* (2nd ed.). Thousand Oaks, CA: Sage.

Edwards, B. (1999). *The new drawing on the right side of the brain.* New York, NY: Putnam.

Eisner, E. W. (1991). *The enlightened eye.* New York, NY: Macmillan.

Freire, P. (2004). *Pedagogy of indignation.* Boulder, CO: Paradigm.

Goldberg, N. (2005). *Writing down the bones.* Boston, MA: Shambala Press.

Leavy, P. (2015). *Method meets art: Arts-based research practice* (2nd. ed.). New York, NY: Guilford Press.

Merriam, S. B. (2009). *Qualitative research: A guide to design and implementation* (Rev. ed.). San Francisco, CA: Jossey-Bass.

Saldaña, J. (2009). *The coding manual for qualitative researchers.* Thousand Oaks, CA: Sage.

Stake, R. E. (2010). *Qualitative research: Studying how things work.* New York, NY: Guilford Press.

Strauss, A., & Corbin, J. M. (1990). *Basics of qualitative research: Grounded theory procedures and techniques.* Newberry Park, CA: Sage.

Sze, M. M. (Ed.). (1978). *The mustard seed garden manual of painting.* Princeton, NJ: Princeton University Press.

Van Manen, M. (1990). *Researching lived experience: Human science for an action sensitive pedagogy.* New York: SUNY Press.

Wolcott, H. F. (2001). *Writing up qualitative research* (2nd ed.). Thousand Oaks, CA: Sage.

4

The Interview and Writing Habit

I asked the zebra, Are you black with white stripes? Or white with black stripes?

And the zebra asked me, Are you good with bad habits?

Or are you bad with good habits? Are you noisy with quiet times?

Or are you quiet with noisy times? Are you happy with some sad days?

Or are you sad with some happy days? . . . And on and on and on and on he went.

I'll never ask a zebra about stripes . . . again.

—Shel Silverstein

nterviewing is the heart and soul of qualitative work in most cases. Not only that, interviewing has taken on a new tone recently with Internet inquiry and interviewing individuals virtually, that is, on the Internet. As a result, many are wondering what will happen to the tried-and-true, face-to-face interview. Usually, the most rewarding component of any qualitative research project is interviewing, and it will never be replaced or never fade away. The same requirements apply to Internet interviews as to face-to-face interviews. Yet, the question of whether we still get good data virtually remains. What are the differences in face-to-face interviews and interviews on the World Wide Web? In some ways, a good interviewer may certainly achieve the connection and trust on the Web as with a face to face interview. In this chapter, I will discuss these points, but I begin with learning about traditional, face-to-face interviews. In addition, I will discuss the issue of how to present interview data, and you will find narrative and poetic examples in the form of found data poems, that is, poetry found in the transcripts of the interviews and identity poems. Interviewing increases your skill set and mind-set as a qualitative researcher, building on your observation skills. Whereas observation is the act of taking notice of something, interviewing is an act of communication. In fact, a major contribution to our history as qualitative researchers is the growing literature on solid interviewing techniques. Since the 1970s, more articles and books have become available (see Janesick, 1998; Kvale, 1996; Kvale & Brinkmann, 2009; Rubin & Rubin, 2005; Spradley, 1980). I consider this a tremendous leap forward because interviews provide such rich and substantive data for the researcher and are also a major part of qualitative research work. Although I have written earlier about the importance and ways of approaching interviews, I would like to frame this chapter in terms of some of those earlier key points, which I will summarize here. A good deal of what I have learned about interviewing ultimately has come from trial and error within long-term interview studies. This chapter is meant to be a nonthreatening and systematic way to approach the complex and challenging act of interviewing another person in person face to face. In addition, we will examine the virtual interview in its complexity.

● TWO PEOPLE TALKING, COMMUNICATING, AND CONSTRUCTING MEANING

Interviewing is an ancient technique, and for the purposes of this text, I define it in this way:

> *Interviewing is a meeting of two persons to exchange information and ideas through questions and responses, resulting in communication and joint construction of meaning about a particular topic.*

As we are always researchers in the process of conducting a study, we rely on different kinds of questions for eliciting various responses. In fact, one of the solid reasons for doing a pilot test of your interviews through a pilot study is so that you, the interviewer, learn which questions are best suited to your study, under what conditions, and when to use particular types of questions. In addition, you may learn how to probe further in a semi-structured interview situation as participants tell you their stories. Writers like Bruce L. Berg (2007), Valerie J. Janesick (2011), Steiner Kvale and Svend Brinkman (2009), Sharan B. Merriam (2009), Elliot G. Mishler (1986), Herbert J. and Irene S. Rubin (2005), James P. Spradley (1980), and Robert E. Stake (1995), and others suggested types of questions for interviewing that have always worked for me and my students. I categorize these as basic, descriptive, big-picture questions; follow-up questions; comparison or contract questions; specific example questions; and structural questions; and overriding all questions is the clarification question. I expand these notions and offer the following as examples of types of interview questions.

TYPES OF INTERVIEW QUESTIONS   ●

Basic, Descriptive, Big-Picture Questions

- Can you talk to me about your life after Hurricane Katrina? Tell me what happened on that evening.

- Describe how you felt that evening.

- Of all the things you have told me about being a critical care nurse, what is the underlying premise of your workday? In other words, what keeps you going every day?

Follow-Up Questions and Clarification Questions Including Example and Experience

- You mentioned that you have no one to talk to about your reactions to the hurricane. Can you tell me some of those reactions?

- You mentioned that you loved going to New York. Can you give me an example or two of what made you love your trips to New York?

- Talk about your impressions of the city.

- You have used the term *socioscientific issues* today. Can you clarify that for me? What exactly can you talk about regarding your teaching of science through socioscientific issues?

- Say something more about what it means to be a prize-winning art teacher.

Comparison, Contrast, or Structural Questions

- You said there was a big difference between a great professor and an ordinary professor. What are some of these differences? Can you describe a few for me?

● PREPARING QUESTIONS

A good rule of thumb for interviewing is to be prepared (see Appendix C). Compose as many thoughtful questions as possible. It is far better to be over prepared than to get caught in an interview without questions. Usually five or six questions of the types just described are reasonable and may yield well over an hour of interview data recorded. A simple question like, "Tell me about your day as a cocktail waitress," once yielded nearly two hours of interview data, leaving all the other questions for another interview time. You will learn to develop a sense of awareness about your participant(s) in the study and rearrange accordingly. Also, always get permission for your interviews in writing. Increasingly, Institutional Review Boards (IRBs) are demanding more of qualitative researchers in their consent forms. See Appendix B for a sample form that has been accepted lately at my university. In order to prepare for testing out some of the questions you create, let us proceed to some exercises that will give you some experience with interviewing. In this section of the text, all of the interview exercises will use the following format:

1. First, be prepared with a digital voice recorder, back-up recorder, and a notebook to take field notes while interviewing. Some interviewers prefer a digital video recorder to upload the interview to their TV sets, computers, YouTube, or their own websites. Currently, most students are using iPhones and iPads for interviewing as they offer applications for voice to text renderings which allow for easier transcription. Note that if you send your interview to be professionally transcribed, most companies prefer digital voice and video recorders rather than the previous generation of tape recorders. One hour of recorded interview yields about 20 pages of interview transcript. On

the open market, the approximate cost for a transcriptionist is about $100 to $120 per hour of recorded interview, so budget accordingly for your dissertations or other research projects.

2.   Before the interview, check your digital voice recorder or video recorder, to see that it is functional. Test your voice on the recorder by noting the *date, time, place,* and *the name of the participant* on the recording. This is helpful later, not only when you do the transcriptions of the recording but also when you need to jog your memory at a subsequent date. You may also find this will serve you later as a coding mechanism for your hours of transcripts.

3.   Whenever possible, carry a back-up recorder and batteries. Many cases have been described where the recorder was malfunctioning, the recorder died, or the batteries wore out! Many newer models can be recharged and have a thumb drive attached to insert into your computer and upload for transcriptions.

4.   Give a copy of the interview questions to your participants ahead of time. Call ahead to remind and verify the exact date, time, and place of the interview, and arrive early. Remember, in the social world, anything can happen, and be prepared to reschedule an interview if requested.

5.   Always have a back-up plan. If someone decides to leave the study, be prepared to replace that person.

6.   Field-test your interview questions with another member in class or someone who will give feedback to prepare you for the first days in the field. Always do a pilot test of your interview questions for your dissertation study. See this example of interview questions from a recent study.

EXAMPLES OF INTERVIEW ●
QUESTIONS FROM A RECENT STUDY

Interview Protocols From Diamonds in the Rough: A Study of a Latino Educational Leader

By Angel Hernandez (2014)

In this study, one Latino assistant principal in Hillsborough County, Florida, was interviewed. The researcher conducted interviews, reviewed digital correspondence and transcripts, field notes, and reflective notes.

(Continued)

(Continued)

Interview Protocol A: The Preplanned Questions

- How do you define *leadership*?
- How about educational leadership?
- Do you consider yourself an educational or instructional leader?
- In your early childhood what influenced you as an individual?
- What influenced your own education (schooling)?
- What path led you to become a teacher?
- What influenced you to enter school administration?
- How do you believe you are perceived as a Latino male assistant principal?
- How has your race or ethnic background influenced your profession?
- If you could change any aspect of your professional career, what would it be?

The study took place over the course of a semester. The researcher introduced the rationale for the study and situated himself in the study.

Values, Beliefs, and Role as Researcher

This work is very personal to me. To portray it in any other way would be false and a disservice to anybody involved, or otherwise interested, in this research. This interview analysis revolves around issues of race, ethnicity, and public schooling in the Tampa Bay area, Hillsborough County to be exact. I am a practitioner in the field of public school administration (middle school assistant principal) and present my ethnic background as Latino (born and raised on the island of Puerto Rico). My parents are both Puerto Rican, my father by birth, born and raised in the mountains of a small, cavernous, rural town called Camuy, and my mother was born in New York City. She moved to the island as a small girl only to find her way back to the United States, this time with her husband and two boys, to follow a childhood dream realized in her second career—becoming a teacher. And so I followed in her footsteps after graduating from Florida State

University and became a teacher in Tampa. After seven years teaching, I am now an assistant principal at the same school that welcomed me with open arms as a new student recently arrived from Puerto Rico in 1994, Quality Middle School.

Middle school education has been my passion and sole professional interest since becoming a middle school teacher in 2004. I value public education and believe that all children should have access to a quality education delivered by teachers and administrators that will not only tailor instructional delivery to their specific needs as individuals but will also have care and concern to make personal connections. It is important that children have access to role models who look like them, talk like them, inspire them, and are taken seriously by students when they say "You and I are not that different. I made it and so can you."

As a researcher, interviewer, analyst, and practitioner in this field of study my roles become intertwined and continuously inform each other. I take notice and opportunity to make known this situational condition in preparing the interview analysis. My role as a practitioner provides passion and intimacy with the topic of Latino school administration based on personal and professional shared experiences with the participants. Simultaneously, my dedication and awareness of my role as researcher and my duty to analyze the data resulting from the interview analysis provide a balance. My goal is to remain cognizant of the different roles and co-construct a shared version of the social reality of Latino middle school administrators in the Hillsborough County School District.

Latinos have been traditionally underrepresented in leadership positions in Hillsborough County schools. In a 2014 brochure titled "FACTS 2014," the School district of Hillsborough County released student and employee demographic numbers. In it, student enrollment for K–12 is listed at 203,506 students. It lists 26,454 employees, 439 of which are assistant principals. Of the 439 in the assistant principal bracket, 15 are assigned to primary schools and 21 are assigned to secondary. For a district with a Hispanic student enrollment of over 65,000 children, this deficiency in properly staffing schools with ethnically balanced administrative teams demands we pay attention to the depressing current state of racial diversity among school leaders in the

(Continued)

(Continued)

Tampa Bay area. To accentuate the problem, it should be noted that this exercise primarily addresses ethnic background, not proficiency of a second language. To include the number of both administrators and teachers employed in relation to the student population that speaks English as a second language or come from homes where English is not the primary language would be sorrowful.

Hernandez then goes on to explain how he conducted his interviews and how he analyzed his data. He used thematic analysis and came up with the following based on the data (see Figure 4.1).

Figure 4.1   Relationship Map of Interview Themes

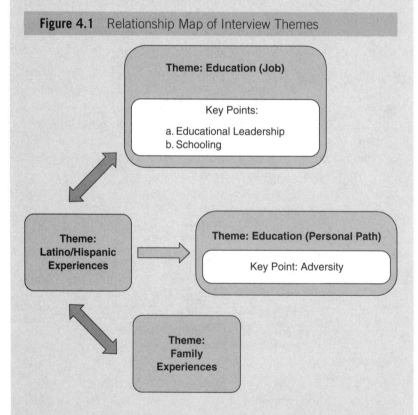

Examples of Initial Categories From the Transcripts

The themes came from a variety of quotations from the transcripts which became categories. For example,

On Leadership

- The important shift in just being an educational leader into an instructional leader is that the kids are here for learning and instruction, so that our solutions need to not take them away from instruction, but rather figure out ways to make the instruction solve the problem.

- I think the big challenge in educational leadership is a lot of people have different perceptions of what education is, and how it needs to be done to be done correctly. When you're using educational leadership specifically, it has to do with addressing the direction. Getting people who have different ideas about a common thing and that they hold dear, because they're all educators, they're teachers, they're people who value education and have this perception of what it looks like.

- What is discipline, what is rigor, what is challenge? How do you motivate students? They have these very different ideas, and you still have to get everybody, sort of, on the same page and working toward a common goal. I see educational leadership as have an extra layer of that perceived . . . a school should look this way, a classroom should be run this way. What one person's class looks like might be completely different and both have excellent results. Sometimes, you have that challenge between a right way and a wrong way, as in different ways, and getting those different ideas together sometimes adds an extra layer.

- A lot of times, I'll talk to teachers or students, and if they're having a lot of passes or whatever, when I talk about what they're doing in class, they seem bored or they're not engaged, they're not working. Part of it is fixing behavioral problems through better instruction. If a class is exciting and the kids are engaged and they're learning, they forget they have to pee. They don't think about talking to their friend because, "I'm so worried about getting done and getting to do the part of the assignment that I'm looking forward to."

On Schooling

- I realized that there were certain aspects of my upbringing, my Spanish-ness, that didn't work with other ethnic groups. For

(Continued)

(Continued)

the most part, I didn't have to be too anything and I realized, I guess maybe part of it is being Spanish, you come at a person a certain way. You come at them sort of expecting respect, and almost demanding it. It didn't work with everybody. My students at Middleton, they needed to feel like it was earned. They had to want to respect you. I will say, here at the middle school, I have learned that being angry, I don't know if it's just my family or not, but the Spanish temper can occasionally get the best of you. You get hotheaded, you just go off. I've found here that if I can control when I have it, it can be very effective occasionally.

- The one thing that was funny, I was thinking when you were on your way here and the one thing I was thinking, it was funny because it actually has to do with your second to last question about the ethnic background. The influence to the profession was, I think as an administrator, you're expected to give up a lot of time. Without question, I'm going to ask you to stay late, I'm going to ask you to spend time away from your family. I was thinking about it, and I was like, "You know, that's one thing that's like completely opposite of at least my upbringing's values." Spending time with your family, having time at home, not bringing stuff home. When you leave work, you come home, you spend time with your family. Whether it's weekends, at a party, going to a relative's house, or cooking food, all the spending time together are things that I think of. My dad . . . I didn't play it, because it was one of his things he didn't think helped him . . . baseball. That spending time playing sports, doing stuff like that together always seems like such a big deal when I'm around my family. When I think about how stuff's set up at school, it was like, "You know, they really don't seem to appreciate it."

Hernandez completes his mini-pilot study with reflections on what he has learned.

What I Learned About Myself as a Qualitative Researcher . . .

I learned to expect the unexpected. In our preparation courses, you hear this time and time again, but you figure it will not apply to you. Equipment can fail, participants can cancel; there are so many things outside of the researcher's control. This is a position that I often face within my professional career as an assistant principal. My days are frequently guided by the unexpected and unscheduled happenings of a school building of 1,100 people, but as a researcher I expect to have the situation under my control. I am supposed to be the in-field expert. I expect for the interview to go exactly as planned and for the setting to be perfect. This was obviously wrong.

When I arrived at Raoul's school and learned he was not there I did not know what to do next. I thought "Well, I don't have his number so I can't reach out to him. Should I leave? I can't believe he forgot about me. Maybe he had some really important meeting to attend and forgot to cancel." Not once did I think I was taking up the time he would normally take to grab his dinner before working an afternoon event at school. Had it not been for the friendly faces that welcomed me, asked me to wait, and reassured me he would be coming I probably would have driven back home only to have to reschedule a conversation that might not have had another chance of happening because of our busy schedules.

I also learned we are incredibly privileged to have the opportunity to look deeply into other people's lives in the name of science or research. I asked Raoul questions I would have wanted to ask him outside of the interview setting but never would have without the formal interview setting. Outside of friendships, people are well within their rights to not have to or want to share personal information with others. The process of interviewing allows us a "fast-forwarding" of sorts into a comfortable zone where sharing of life experiences takes place, and while we do not have carte blanche to ask blindly without regard for the subject, it gives us a credibility that allows the interviewee to "trust" us with their information in the name of research. Qualitative research is very powerful and changes you continuously throughout the process if you allow yourself to be influenced by the work. The result is a co-constructed version of a shared reality.

With unlimited time and money, I would travel the country and expand my number of participants to include Latino assistant principals from other regions of the United States. The experiences are vastly different depending on a variety of factors—age, country of origin, language proficiency, introduction into field of education, structures of the school district for hiring and promotion of

(Continued)

(Continued)

Latinos into leadership, and leadership preparation programs just to name a few.

My strongest desire would be to explore this issue as a phenomenon with a large number of participants. The benefit to large numbers, in this case, is not generalizability. It is the inclusion of different stories and the ability to find ideas that are important to the participants. It would also be interesting to see comparisons of the interview data based on region and being able to match it to practices of school districts to promote or hinder the introduction of more candidates into teaching and school administration.

EXERCISE 4.1 Interviewing Someone You Know

Find someone you know to interview on any one of the following topics for 20 minutes.

1. What are your beliefs about friendship?

OR

2. Describe for me someone you admire, a historical figure or someone alive today. Explain why you selected this person and why you admire this person.

OR

3. Describe your typical workday from the moment you arise in the morning to the end of your day. Remember to end each and every interview with the question: Is there anything else you wish to tell me at this time?

Be sure to record your interview and take field notes to train yourself to observe nonverbal cues and behaviors.

Discussion:

1. How did you approach this exercise?

2. What was most difficult for you?

3. Would you change anything the next time you interview someone?

Learners now get a chance to practice working with recorded interview data by transcribing at least a portion of the interview, if not in its entirety. Later, the group will practice analyzing data from these interviews in groups, with partners, or alone, as they see fit. In the context of the classroom, members pair up, and each member practices as an interviewer and an interviewee to see what it feels like to inhabit each of those roles.

Evaluation:

Learners follow the same evaluation exercises as in the previous chapter, keeping track of their progress, and reflecting on the meaning of the exercise by writing in the researcher reflective journal.

EXERCISE 4.2   Interviewing a Stranger

Learners follow the same directions as above; only now, they must find a stranger to interview. In a class setting, learners go out on campus and find someone. If trying this on your own, use your imagination to find someone in either the workplace or a public place and interview him or her on any of the topics listed above.

Learners are asked to discuss in small groups or in the group at large what was learned from this exercise in comparison to the previous one. Usually, learners find interviewing a stranger easier than interviewing a classmate, neighbor, or colleague. The use of a voice recorder is new to learners at first, but it becomes second nature once they get over the novelty. In the artificial constraint of a class time period, I ask students to find another student on campus at a snack bar, the Starbucks, or anywhere available and interview the student for 15 minutes.

Prompt:

What is your view on the quality of education you are receiving here as you work toward your degree?

Be sure to introduce yourself and ask permission to record the individual. Explain you are taking a class where you need to practice interviewing and how helpful it would be if the person would agree to be interviewed. Get some basic information from the student such as age, how many years at the school, what degree program, why he or she selected this university and this campus, and general descriptive information before beginning the interview. Probe with follow-up questions as needed.

When class members return to discuss this and what they learned from interviewing a stranger, they often remark on how willing people are to talk about themselves. At first, there are awkward feelings talking to a complete stranger, yet in the safety of the university community, people open up. They disclose quite a bit of data and even go into specific classes and experiences that have markedly changed them. Usually, people are ready and willing to be interviewed. That is one thing you can count on in the social word, the fact that people love to talk about their work and their lives. When was the last time you had the opportunity to talk about your work with someone? It doesn't happen very often.

Discussion Points Following This Exercise:

1. How did you select and approach this person, and what did you learn from this?

2. What would you do differently if you repeated this exercise?

3. Rate yourself in terms of the kinds of questions you asked the interviewee.

4. What advice would you give others trying this exercise?

Now, take time to enter into your reflective journal your thoughts on the interview process and how you rate yourself as an interviewer in training.

EXERCISE 4.3   The Oral History Interview

The oral history interview or series of interviews describes the story of one person's life or a collection of individual stories told together. For example, the oral history of one firefighter who was at ground zero on September 11 could stand alone as an individual oral history. A collection of oral histories of multiple firefighters who lived through that experience would be a collective oral history project. The beauty of the oral history interview is that it allows us to capture the memories of people who have had any number of experiences. The meaning made of the storytelling and what we learn from the stories are critical to understanding a given period of time or a specific event or series of events. Oral history is often a vehicle for the outsiders and the forgotten to tell their stories. Currently, as I write this text, many researchers are on the way to Haiti to document the events unfolding there by interviewing survivors of the earthquake. Likewise, we are now seeing many oral histories in print from the various oral histories of Hurricane Katrina. In oral history, we tell the story through spoken text, written text, video text, or all of these media.

Oral history grew out of the oral tradition. Formal written work about oral history has emerged in the last century. Since then, we have experienced many evolutionary stages in the development of the field. Today, we are in the center of a monumental stage, that of the digital movement. This enables us to move forward experimenting with new lenses and technologies.

For this exercise, find two members in your family that represent two generations to interview about their memories of growing up, for example, your mother and grandmother, your father and grandfather, your mother and sister, your mother and brother, and so on. Use a video camera or digital voice recorder.

Goal:

To find out what was experienced as a child growing up including going to school, friends, hobbies, early goals in life, key events, and so on.

Interview Protocol Sample:

1. Can you remember what it was like growing up in (name place)?

2. What memories do you have from that time?

3. What do you recall from your high school days?

4. Do you recall your best friends, and what are they doing today?

5. Can you talk about your hobbies?

6. Can you talk about your dreams or goals that you wished to accomplish?

Ask the same questions of both generational members. Record the interview and take notes if possible. Practice transcribing the interviews. Later, write up your thoughts on what you learned about these two members of your family. Compare and contrast the generational differences and similarities. Are there key themes that emerge from the interviews? What would you like to go back and ask? If needed, do a follow-up interview.

If you do not have family members nearby to interview, try interviewing someone in your neighborhood who is a war veteran or is active in your community or is of general interest in some way. Public servants such as police officers, firefighters, elected officials, teachers, nurses, or physicians may be willing to tell you their life stories and how they came to their chosen paths in life. The point is to document their memories and interpretations of events in their lifetimes. Key oral history resources and texts will be listed at the end of this section. Digital oral histories are prolific on YouTube and on various oral history websites.

EXERCISE 4.4 The Focus Group Interview Demonstration Exercise

Demonstration:

Some learners are anxious to use focus groups as a qualitative research technique, given the nature of their purposes of the study, the time line for the study, and their resources. Focus groups are not a panacea, but they do offer a way for researchers to *focus* on a topic with a given group. I ask learners to immediately read at least one text on focus groups, usually the text *Successful Focus Groups,* edited by David Morgan (1993). I use this exercise when I am fortunate enough to be working on a funded project that allows for learner participation. When on a funded project, I involve all students who volunteer to work at the actual sites. If not working on a funded project, learners may benefit from this demonstration exercise. Remember that focus groups mean just that: *Focus* on one and only one topic. This exercise emerged from an actual case of a study we did of a drug-free school program in northeast Kansas. The topic is one learners and community members can talk about because everyone has something to say about drug usage in a given community. For this demonstration focus group, I ask for volunteers.

Topic:

Drug availability in your school, community, and neighborhood.

Purpose:

To find out how students, teachers, and parents feel about drug usage and drug education in your school.

Sample:

Note that these questions may be modified for each focus group made up of parents, teachers, and students. These were the basic questions used by the trained moderator of the groups, and they were rearranged according to the composition of the group of nine members:

1. Can you talk about whether or not you feel safe in your school or community?

2. Do you have some thoughts on how your school or community is doing regarding alcohol and drug problems with students? Can you describe for me what you know about this?

3. What does your school or community do to educate you about the use of alcohol and drugs?

4. Do you think drugs or alcohol are easily available to students?

5. What kinds of rules do you have about alcohol and drugs?

6. If you ever had a problem with alcohol or drugs, who would you approach to talk about it? Can you explain your thoughts about your choice of this individual?

In this demonstration exercise, I ask for a volunteer for the moderator who must keep the group on task. Also, I give out role-taking cards with a role for each of the seven volunteers for the focus group. Each learner draws a card at random; here are some of the roles taken by participants:

Card 1:   Play yourself.

Card 2:   Play yourself.

Card 3:   Play disagreeable and refuse to answer every other question.

Card 4:   Play overly agreeable and agree with everyone.

Card 5:   Say as little as possible and only speak when asked a direct question by the moderator.

Card 6:   Say nothing regarding drugs and talk about every and any other subject.

Card 7:   Try everything you can to get out of answering any question and keep asking to leave the group.

These seven types can be found from time to time in any given focus group in the real world, which is why I have designed these roles partially to train moderators and partially to allow learners to see that focus groups require a great deal of patience, fortitude, tact, diplomacy, and tenacity. Some warnings about focus groups include being ready to deal with people who cry in the group, people who may lose their temper or composure, people who argue, and so on. If a moderator finds a situation where things get problematic, he or she can stop the group to take a time-out and then make a decision about continuing on or not. Thus, moderators need training in dealing with the public and must have at least the semblance of calm. Also, as the researcher, you should avoid being the moderator, for you cannot be entirely impartial. You need to find a competent moderator and train the moderator in questioning and moving the group along.

Forms, Uses, Strengths, and Weaknesses:

The focus group technique is one of the most common approaches to research in the behavioral and social sciences. A focus group is a group interview with a trained moderator, a specific set of questions, and a disciplined approach to studying ideas in a group context. The data from the focus group consist of the typed transcript of the group interaction.

Uses for and Ways to View Focus Groups:

Self-Contained Research Technique:

Supplemental technique for qualitative and quantitative studies (see Morgan, 1993). While you may get some qualitative narrative data from a focus group, this does not necessarily make your study qualitative. In order to have a qualitative study, you should have a qualitative theoretical frame to guide the study and also good qualitative questions. Most often the focus group is used to augment a survey.

Focus Groups Are Useful for:

1. Orienting oneself to a new field

2. Getting interpretations of results from earlier studies

3. Exposing professionals to the language and culture of a target group (i.e., bridging the gap between the professional and the real-world target group, as with the use of focus groups in medical research)

Strengths:

1. The major strength of focus groups is the use of group interaction to produce data that would not be as easily accessible without

the group interaction on a specific topic. This can also be flipped into a weakness, as it is not contextualized. In other words, the individuals in the group are not interviewed separately to find out their own life stories or the lived experiences that relate to the specified topic of the focus group.

2. Participants' interaction among themselves replaces the interaction with the interviewer, possibly leading to a greater understanding of participants' points of view.

Weaknesses and Disadvantages:

1. Focus groups are fundamentally unnatural social settings when compared to participant observation and interviewing selected participants over time. They are also almost totally decontextualized. In other words, you focus on a given topic without getting all the life stories of the group members and all the related stories to the topic. If, as a qualitative researcher, you are trying to capture contextualized data, you may need to reconsider this choice of technique.

2. Focus groups are often limited to verbal behavior and again only on a specified particular topic. There is no room for additional information to be collected. There is limited opportunity to check back and verify on site if the behavior actually matches what is stated.

3. Focus groups depend on a skilled moderator, who is not always available when needed. The principal investigator of a research project cannot ethically act also as the moderator. The time and money involved in training a skilled moderator is often a major problem when planning a focus group.

4. Focus groups should not be used if the intent is something other than research (e.g., conflict resolution, consensus building, staff retreats, professional development, or attitude changes). Too often, individuals are giddy over the focus group without realizing that, in a qualitative research project, one needs to ask questions of a qualitative nature.

A Sample Approach to Focus Groups:

1. Have a planning phase: Allow for 4 to 6 weeks. *Identify your goals.* State the purpose of the focus group precisely, in one sentence, if possible. Then, identify the ideal membership of the group.

2. Limit the number of groups to perhaps 2 per week over 6 weeks. Members and moderators burn out easily. The logistics of planning the focus group, picking up participants, if need be, and scheduling a site are often overwhelming. Thus, we've found that no more than two groups per week allow us to be true to our study.

3. Transcripts: Plan for 8 weeks or more. Creating transcripts is a difficult and time-consuming task, and we often underestimated the time we needed for completion. Through experience with the drug-free schools case, we learned to allow 3 to 6 months per project, with all conditions being favorable and only a few people backing out of the focus group.

After you identify your goals, I recommend applying these rules of thumb, which were constructed after polling our participants in the project:

Dilemmas:

Again, these dilemmas arose from the actual case:

1. Who brings up controversial issues, the moderator or the group?

2. How far does informed consent go if unusually personal information is revealed?

In working for specificity of, depth in, and understanding of the social context in a given study, the intent of the moderator is always to *get the story.* We found that a skilled moderator is essentially the key to a successful focus group.

Some Myths About Focus Groups:

1. Focus groups are quick and cheap. In fact, they cost money, which varies depending on geographic locations.

2. People will not talk about sensitive issues in groups.

3. Focus groups must be validated by other methods.

The following checklist was developed and modified from experience and suggestions from Morgan's 1993 text for the purpose of assisting learners in this process.

Advance Notice:

☐ 1. Contact participants by phone 1 to 2 weeks before the session.

☐ 2. Send each participant a letter of invitation.

☐ 3. Give a reminder phone call prior to the session.

☐ 4. Slightly overrecruit the number of participants. There are always last-minute dropouts.

Questions:

☐ 1. The introductory question should be answered quickly and should not identify status.

☐ 2. Questions should flow in a logical sequence.

☐ 3. Probing questions should be used as needed.

☐ 4. *Think back* questions (questions that begin with the words, "Think back," for example, "Think back to when you were teaching your first class . . .") should be used as needed.

Logistics:

☐ 1. The room should be comfortable, quiet, and satisfactory in size.

☐ 2. The moderator should arrive early with name tags for everyone.

☐ 3. Have appropriate digital equipment.

☐ 4. Experts and loud participants should be seated near the moderator.

☐ 5. Shy and quiet participants should be seated across from the moderator.

☐ 6. Bring enough copies of handouts, visual aids, storyboards, and so on.

Moderator Skills:

☐ 1. Be well rested, alert, and prepared, and practice your introductory remarks beforehand so as to deliver them smoothly. Remember questions without referring to notes.

☐ 2. Avoid head nodding and comments leading the members to a particular conclusion.

Immediately After the Session:

☐ 1. Prepare a brief summary of key points. Check to see that the recorder captured everything.

☐ 2. Get the recordings to your transcriber or begin transcribing immediately.

☐ 3. Check your field notes as a checks-and-balances tool and keep a list of all participants' names, addresses, and phone numbers.

☐ 4. Prepare your report with excerpts from the transcripts in the body of the report.

EXERCISE 4.5 Presenting Interview Data as a Found Data Poem

Example: Data Poetry Found in an Interview Transcript

Found data poems are essentially *found* in the text of interview transcripts, documents, or even spoken words. For the purposes of this assignment, select a portion of an interview transcript or written text of any kind to practice creating an original poem from the words in front of you. You invent the themes and content based on the words in the transcript or other written text. It is best to keep the words of the interviewee or author as much as possible. Feel free to concentrate on meaning and interpretation.

Create a Found Data Poem of Your Choice:

1. Find at least three lines.

2. Use at least one metaphor or symbol.

3. Develop a clear theme or point of view.

4. Use at least one image that captures the meaning of the text.

Be sure to reference the source of the poem, for example, Transcript A. Include a sample of the text the poem is based upon. You are tapping into the right side of your brain, an often underused portion. We will share this with each other in class in small groups and with the group as a whole.

*Sample Excerpt From an Interview of a
Female Assistant Superintendent in Response
to the Instruction, "Describe a Typical Day"*

This is a part of an hour-long interview where the speaker shared her educational background, her goal of helping kids, and her caring for their well-being while striving for excellence. This was an interview I conducted recently in a project on female leaders.

A: Well, it's been an atypical day so . . . And that's something I've been thinking about. There isn't . . . There are typical days, and they're boring. The typical days are the days when you're sitting and working on paperwork for the state, and working on budgets, and trying to analyze test scores to make them meaningful to the teachers and to the . . . and whatever. So, those are the typical, boring days. This is our second week of school, so there's no typical beginning of the school year. Now, I'm spending more time supporting teachers, right now new staff. Right now, I'm doing . . . pulling on my special ed background. I have a little guy who is in one of our self-contained classrooms, but he's struggling with the transition coming back to school, and mornings aren't good for him, and he's got a new teacher. And the principal in that school is on maternity leave. And the principal who is filling in was a little panicked. And so, we met and talked about strategies for this little guy that, no, you know, in first grade, he's not ready for therapeutic day school. He's not hurt anybody. Everything's fine. It will be okay. We have a controversy going on right now related to curriculum materials that have been selected for students' optional use, optional reading. So, we've been laughing and . . . on one hand . . . and cringing on the other because we're responding to one parent's concern.

Atypically, we have only heard from one parent who has a concern about a book that was on the summer reading list. Kids take home a list of six or seven books that are optional. The kids give a synopsis of the book at school. They talk about 'em. And if you don't like any of those books, you can read any other book in the whole wide world to choose from. And this one is as much young adult literature as it is controversial themes because it gives us the opportunity to support kids as they worry about these things and . . .

Q: Can you tell the name of the book?

A: It's *Fat Kid Rules the World* by Kale Going. And the themes really are friendship, not giving up, perseverance. A student in there contemplates suicide. He's had a very tough time. His mom's died from cancer. His dad's an alcoholic. He's in an abusive home situation. And he is befriended by a homeless teen, who is a gifted guitarist, who asks this kid to join his band and play the drums. And, it basically is about acceptance, and you know it's a great story of redemption. It's a wonderful story. And the parent who objects is objecting based on the proliferation of the F-word. And, it is in there and it . . . kids are in Brooklyn. And, interestingly enough, but it's not really spoken out loud. It's in this kid's thoughts. That she's objecting to the normal, sexual fantasies of teenagers. He's describing a person and saying, "No, not this one, not the one with the large breasts, you know, the other one" . . . physical features. So, you know, things like that. This parent has, you know, not accepted that the fact that her child was not required to read the book and . . . she did not ask for the book to be banned from the library. I think she just asked for it to come off the summer reading list. However, that has snowballed to some right-wing websites . . . Concerned Women for America, the Illinois Family Network. I don't know which all . . . SaveLibraries.org. And, we have been getting interesting e-mails from basically all over the country and Canada.

Q: Like what kind of interesting e-mails?

A: Oh, some that are saying. . . . One was, you know, "If I knew where Osama Bin Laden was, I would turn him in, but first, I would tell him where your school was so that he could bomb it, hopefully, when there were no children . . . on the weekends when no children were present."

You know, "You're responsible for the moral degradation of children and the increase in rapes and murders and school shootings because children have read . . . because we have forced children to read this book." Personally, I, as a woman, I'm not fit to lead, even though Lord knows how that's connected. I'm not sure. We were joking that a bunch of us are Catholic, so we were all damned already anyway, so it didn't matter, so you know. . . . The board's been very supportive. They. . . . You know, they listened to 1 hour and 10 minutes of different people expressing their viewpoints. Some people—I'd heard it on the radio—a board member from a distant suburb came to express her concerns. Somebody from our library board came. The phone call came from one of the mayors in one of the towns that we serve. But, the board was supportive and said that, you know, no, this was not required reading, that the teachers did inform students of that. We did make an error in not informing parents that they might want to be alerted to this fact. And so, we are looking at our selection policy and how we let parents know where to write . . . if they want to follow up. But in all of this time since our last board meeting, and since this started in mid-August, we have only heard from that one parent.

Q: Have you been threatened or has anybody?

A: I have not personally been threatened. The junior high principal has been threatened. You know, "When someone comes and murders your family, it'll be because of how you taught them." Rather interesting. No one from the immediate community . . . No other parents in the community . . . There's an article in today's paper; we had a prepared statement to share with people who called, anticipating . . . And this is the daily paper. This is not like the local Podunk paper. We had one parent phone call with a question or concern. And we did end up sending a note home today, you know, saying that you know we didn't believe that the threat was really credible but that we did have, you know, that there was a police presence.

. . . It (this book) was on the book list for incoming eighth graders, so that would be 13- and 14-year-olds. They talk about these things. And, some statistic that I had recently came across said three to five . . . Three out of five teenagers contemplate suicide at one point. So, um . . . yeah, it's kind of important to maybe say, yeah, there's a place to talk about this. It was . . . It's probably toward the young end of the age spectrum that the book might be appropriate for. And, we did have a parent come and talk in support of the book. Her student had read it during seventh grade. He's a very capable student. And, as a parent, she also read the book and thought it was a perfect avenue to discuss some of these difficult situations, which some of our students live in. You know we don't . . . Not everyone lives in a two-parent home where they go to church every Sunday and their other social, emotional, and physical needs are met. Literature is one way to talk about kids who are sitting next to you or are on the other side of the country who don't have those same experiences. This student obviously and this parent, who was able to sit and talk with her child about these things, who a year later recalled that the themes were, you know . . . Didn't recall the swearing, didn't recall the sexual fantasies, recalled the overarching themes. We have students who haven't read an entire book probably since they were in second grade, who were talking about how fabulous the book was, kids whose lives unfortunately probably mirror the protagonist's life . . .

And, it is a big topic for kids. And, it is an issue that we think needs to be explored. And, it was an optional book. It's for a lit circle about self-acceptance. But that maybe there's another . . . a better option out there. Because just because the kids can read at that level, it doesn't mean that maturity-wise they're able to.

Q: Now, thank you for sharing the e-mail that was sent to you, but for the purposes of the transcript here, can you describe the contents briefly of the e-mail that you received? This is from, again, only one parent over this one book.

A: Well, this is a person. I don't even know who it is. He equated the ability of a woman to be president and whether or not he should vote for a woman as president with my role as an assistant superintendent in this school district and the analogy of someone who comes upon a boat that has a little bit of water in the bottom and drills a hole in the boat to let the water out and continues to drill additional holes to let more water out, as of course more water's rushing in. And some man miraculously comes and says, "No, no, maybe we should stop drilling holes and plug the holes instead," and saves the day. And, who should we vote for, the man who plugs the holes or the woman who has drilled the holes? And, in his warped sense of the world, he also sent . . . Prior to my e-mail, my superintendent received an e-mail with just a shortened version of that analogy but accusing him of being a hole driller as well. But, I obviously am not . . . or women in general are not fit to be president because we obviously must be the hole drillers. There might be some warped men who also are stupid enough to drill holes with us. But, we as a gender probably are sucking them into it. So, that would be atypical . . . If I get an e-mail from a parent, it's generally related to a curricular concern or a testing question.

Q: So, and let's say you get this e-mail then. How do you deal with it? What strategies do you use, or what is that like?

A: Well, I'm not deleting it, only because I'm saving it just for posterity. Other than that, we get a lot of good laughs out of it. We shared it around the office. And you go on with your day. Exactly. It will be good for a laugh at many times in the future.

[End of Excerpt]

I shared this small excerpt of a larger transcript with my class. Take a look now at the poetry created by Jill Flansburg upon reading this excerpt. She decided to do four haiku. Haiku are generally 17-syllable Japanese poems done in three lines.

Poems

By Jill Flansburg

Parents misconstrue
The teachers, the kids, the book,
Narrow-mindedness.

Poise under pressure
Never a typical day
But I really care.

I'm damned if I do and
Damned if I don't
Too vital to quit.

Parents find fault
Intolerant of teachers
And the kids miss out.

Now, try your own poem based on the transcript above. If it is possible to work in a group, try this as a group project.

Example: Poetry Found in Text on the Web

Another example of a found data poems can be seen here. I went to the website for *The Qualitative Report* and used various statements as the data for this poem as the journal comes into its 25th year in 2015.

Celebrating the Qualitative Report

By Valerie J. Janesick

Making Sense of Qualitative Data

Transforming methodology

25 years of hard work.

Nurturing,

Mentoring,

Empowering.

We rejoice in this time and space!

(January 2015)

EXERCISE 4.6   Describing Your Role in a Research Project as Identity Poetry

Another type of poetry gaining ground in the social sciences is that of identity poetry, also known as *I poetry*. Identity poetry is a good fit for the qualitative researcher since it can be used in many places throughout a narrative report. First, it is good for identifying the role of the researcher. Second, it can be used by participants to reflect their ideas as data sets. Third, it can be used to capture the stories of your participants lives. See this example of an advance organizer for identity poetry. It is followed by a good example of identity poetry by Maggie Saturley (2014). It is common to have a final page of a dissertation proposal and the final copy of the dissertation labeled as "About the Author." Saturley wrote an I poem as her description of herself as the author.

Example: Identity Poetry Activity Guide

Where I Am From

I am from (ordinary item) _____

I am from (home adjective) _____

I am from (plant, flower) _____

I am from (family tradition) _____

I am from the (family tendency) _____

I am from (something you were told as a child) _____

I am from (religion or spiritual tradition) _____

I am from (ethnicity) _____

I am from (place of birth) _____

I am from (two food items representing your family) _____

_____

I am from stories about _____

I am from (memories you have) _____.

Example: Identity Poem

In this example, Maggie Saturley, doctoral candidate, wrote this identity poem at the end of her dissertation proposal in lieu of a paragraph about the author.

A Qualitative Look at Where I Am From . . . (Edited)

By Maggie Saturley

I am from critical friends,
From feedback carousels and sticky notes.

I am from narrative writing and stories.
I am from joining in and knowing the I.

I am from do unto others
As you would do unto me.

I'm from collecting data and making meanings
From themes and constant comparisons.

I am from its clear as mud
To reading between the lines.

. . . . am from these moments.
Lessons learned in the search for meaning.

Example: Identity Poetry in Spanish and English

See this example written by Elizabeth Visedo (2015) about her origin. Elizabeth was born and grew up in Argentina. She has traveled the world and lived on at least three continents. She completed her doctorate at the University of South Florida. She studied biliteracy.

Origen

By Elizabeth Visedo (2015)

Soy de tardes de mate amargo y bizcochitos

de la tierra del tango y el malbec

Soy de jazmín y berro

y a baldear la vereda y a regar

Pinoluz e incienso

de zarzuelas, Piazzola y Spinetta

Soy de parroquia, del estado y del mundo

del oeste, la quinta y la pileta

Soy del sur, la injusticia y el sueño

de ganar en la Davis y de River campeón

Soy de revolución y utopías

de Pichuco, Serrat y Simone de Beauvoir

de invierno confesiones y una noche en la opera

De tiros, gritos y golpes y mordazas

Soy de los pecados mortales y secretos

del incesto, el abuso y el suicidio

Soy de una dictadura militar de siete años

con miles de meses sin carnaval

Soy de la chacarera y el Rio de la Plata

la locura, el inglés y el desarraigo

las palizas de mama y las caricias de Mome

secándome las lágrimas sin retorno.

Origin

By Elizabeth Visedo (2015)

I am from the afternoons

of unsweetened "mate" tea and lard biscuits

From the land of tango and malbec

I'm from jasmines and watercress

to wash the sidewalk and water the plants

Pinesol and incense

from operettas, Piazzola and Spinetta

I'm from the Rosary parish, the state, the world

from the West country-houses with pool

I'm from the South, injustice, and the dream

to win the Davis Cup with River as champion

I am from revolution and utopias

from Pichuco, Serrat, Simone de Beauvoir

from Winter Confessions and A Night at the Opera

from gunshots, screams, coups, blows and muzzles

I am from deadly sins and secrets

from incest, abuse and suicide

I'm from a seven years long dictatorship

with thousands of months with no Carnival

I'm from "chacarera" and Rio de la Plata

madness, English and rootlessness

my mom's spanking and the neighbor's caress

wiping out my tears with no way back.

These samples of identity poetry are meant to illustrate how a researcher might use poetry to describe self-awareness and the fit for whatever research project one is involved in. It is also a way as Saturley shows, to capture a self-description.

Example: Haiku on Method

Still another way to use poetry is with haiku to capture the entire process of qualitative research. See these haiku written by Dustin De Felice (2011), which he wrote throughout the dissertation process and inserted them after his methodology chapter. He studied endangered languages in Mexico and implications for educators.

Five Haiku

By Dustin De Felice

1. My Study

My super study

Surprises, Strengths, Savvy, and

Serendipitous.

2. On Translations

English-Espanol

Hmmm, Que Hago-Which to use

I hardly know when.

3. On Terminology

My participants

Culture and Language Experts

Nahuatl or Mayan.

4. On Transcribing

Dragon voice two laps

English-Espanol My Voice

Their words their languages.

5. On Text Analysis

Text Analysis

Cyclical and Immersive

Looking for Essence.

Thus, you can see how haiku fits ways to represent the research process. In any of the poetry activities and examples, I aim to make researchers aware of the remarkable power of poetry as

1. a vehicle for data presentation

2. a process for reflecting on the research process

3. an alternative description of the role of the researcher

4. a way to capture literature in your literature review

5. an overall prompt for thinking, reflection, and understanding

Poetry is a powerful statement for qualitative researchers and reminds us of the value of the arts in the research process. As Victoria Perselli (2011) points out, poetry is an elaborate riddle that may never be solved. It is something. It is not everything. But what poetry gives us is a beautiful, provocative frame for understanding our work.

EXERCISE 4.7   The Digital, Virtual Interview and Google Groups

The amazing growth in the number of articles, books, websites, electronic mailing lists, and interviews on YouTube are indicators of the interest and growth of Internet inquiry. In terms of qualitative interviewing, the Internet affords many opportunities for interviewing without the boundaries of traveling or being physically present for an interview. On the other hand, a number of issues arise from examining data posted on the Internet. Despite the relocation to the virtual world in digital form, Internet inquiry still contains the basics of qualitative research. You will still be seeking information about lived experience and the social context. You will still need to complete your transcripts of any interview. In this exercise, there are two parts:

Part One:

Try an interview with someone you know on Skype. To use Skype, simply go to www.skype.com to create your free account and have access to video and voice capability on their system. Start with 10 minutes and see how this feels to you. Use the questions listed earlier, such as,

"What does your work mean to you?" Save the interview. Or if this is not possible, view a completed interview on YouTube. Find three major themes in the interview to discuss with a critical friend or partner in class. Write about what you learned in your reflective journal.

Part Two:

Now, go to the site groups.google.com (formerly Deja News), which is part of a cluster of groups on Google. Here, you may start a discussion about your interviewing techniques and talk about what you learned from personal online interviewing or pulling three themes out of an extant YouTube interview. You can do these things online with Google Groups:

1. Create a group.

2. Set up your group.

3. Invite people to join it.

4. Discuss online or through e-mail.

You may discuss online or in e-mail, and you can create a custom page for this. After you select your fellow group members, ask each to talk about the experience of interviewing someone online. What do you see as the similarities and differences in your real-time, face-to-face interviews?

Becoming comfortable is a must in developing your interviewing and writing habits. It is not as awkward as you might imagine. Also, visit YouTube for interviews already uploaded online. Here, you will see examples of oral history interviews and face-to-face interviews on various topics in multiple areas of study, such as gerontology, family health, nursing, education, business, and sociology to name a few.

EXERCISE 4.8 Interviewing Someone Twice

Goal:

Interview one person twice, so that you have the experience of going back for an interview. Interviews should be approximately 1 hour in length each. Be sure to allow time between interviews. Do the first transcription and then go on to the next interview.

What Does Your Work Mean to You?

Select an educator or other professional to interview about what work means to that person. The first interview should have some basic, grand-tour questions.

Interview Protocol A: First Interview

1. What does your work mean to you?

2. Talk about a typical day at work. What does it look like?

3. Tell me what you like about your job.

4. Tell me what you dislike about your job.

5. Where do you see yourself in 5 to 10 years?

6. Is there anything else you wish to tell me at this time?

7. Is there any question you have about this interview project?

You create the questions for Interview Protocol B.

Create the questions based on what you found in the first interview and to get to the goal of the interview. This should take at least 1 hour but no longer than 90 minutes per interview. Remember that people are busy, and they most likely can only give you an hour at a time. Be sure to have your original field notes so you can probe into areas of the first interview during the second interview. Be sure to record all this. Be sure to get informed consent either by signature or on the audio recording.

Write a report on the interview that includes at least the following items:

a. Describe in detail why you selected this person. Add a photo if needed.

b. Provide a list of all the questions asked in each interview and label them Interview Protocol A and Interview Protocol B.

c. Summarize the responses from both interviews in some meaningful way with precise quotations from the interview.

d. Pull out at least three themes from the interviews.

e. Tell the story of what this person's life work means to this person.

f. Include the signed consent form or a form stating that the interviewee gave consent on the digital recording, and you sign that form, too.

   g. Discuss any ethical issues that may have come up.

   h. A sample of seven to ten pages of your best transcript from the recording should be added as an appendix.

   i. Include two or more pages of your own reflections on your skills as an interviewer, as a researcher, and what you learned from this project; be sure to mention any difficulties that came up and what you would change the next time you conduct an interview.

   j. Be sure to use a minimum of five references from this term's texts.

   k. Be sure to create a title that captures your themes.

Remember that this is a narrative research paradigm, so you should write this in narrative form as if you were telling this person's story. The story is about the person's life work.

EXERCISE 4.9   Practicing an Online Interview

Goal:

To conduct an online interview using Skype.

   Because the purpose of conducting an interview is to get data, that is, to get some information from a participant about a certain topic, students born and raised in the digital era are besieging me with requests about digital interviewing. This semester, two students are trying interviews online. Because Skype is free online, open an account, and you will have video and audio capability for an interview. You may save the interview on your computer for future transcription. Use Exercise 4.7 as your guide to conduct two interviews online. In addition to the information listed there, add in your report a description of why you elected to do an interview online, what your view is about interviewing online, what the positive and negative characteristics of the interview were, and any suggestions for those considering online interviewing.

   After the experience of interviewing, creating data poems, and creating codes and categories, learners appreciate the opportunity to practice, individually and in groups, the demanding task of analyzing interview data. Members go through each other's transcripts and field notes, and they listen to the recording as often as they need to. Each group comes up with a set of major and minor categories. Remarks after this exercise often include the following:

> I was amazed at how the categories popped out of the data.

> This was harder than I thought because I forgot to take field notes during the interview, and so I really needed to know the nonverbals.

> This was much easier when I had someone with whom to check my categories. Now, I know why having an outside reader of field notes and transcripts, as suggested, is a good idea.

> This teaches me to have another interview and get more data.

> The person I interviewed taught me better questions to ask.

> As I looked over the transcripts, I realized how much I had already forgotten about the focus group. Now I know I have to transcribe everything because my memory is not what it used to be.

Through the experience of working on transcripts in the small group, members feel more confident in dealing with their mini-projects as far as analysis of data. Learners look for major themes, key words, and indexes of behavior and belief, and they make an initial list of major and minor categories. Every attempt is made to look for critical incidents, points of tension and conflict, and contradictions to help in the purposes of study. In the class situation, most students found working with a group or a partner to be helpful and illuminating.

CONDUCTING QUALITATIVE INTERVIEWS: ●
SOME RULES OF THUMB

1. Begin with a topic, a purpose and write a few big questions— basic, descriptive, grand-tour questions.

2. Establish rapport with the interviewee:

   - Establish a relaxed and open atmosphere and pace for the interview.
   - Explain clearly why you are conducting the interview.
   - Tell the interviewee about yourself.
   - Show genuine interest in the interviewee with both verbal and body language.

- Take notes if possible. Smile.
- Don't talk too much. Let the participant reveal the data.

3. Ask one of the big questions. Based on the response of the interviewee to the big question, ask additional questions to probe and to elicit more complete information. Develop your grand-tour questions for big, empty, time spaces. Revert to statements made earlier if you are worried about spaces in the interview. Relax.

4. Use both body language and verbal language to keep the interviewee talking or to let the interviewee know that you have enough information.

5. Always end in an interview with the question, "Is there anything else you would like to add at this time?"

CHAPTER SUMMARY

In most cases, interviewing is something like a duet or *pas de deux* in dance. Two people are communicating with one another and, ideally at least, understand each other whatever the context. There is a give and take in interviewing and a strong listening component. A major pitfall in interviewing is not being prepared with mechanical materials, questions, and good communication skills. (See Appendix D for additional information.) Direct experience, practice, and reflection are the strongest assets of the interviewer and the dancer. As themes and categories jump out at you from the transcripts and field notes, learn to develop models of what occurred. Models are your visual representations of what occurred and your interpretation of what occurred in the study. Today, using arts-based approaches to data presentation such as found data poems or identity poetry offer researchers new tools for approaching data representation and defining the role of the researcher. Through daily writing in your researcher reflective journal, you develop the writing habit more fully and have a road map of your thinking about inquiry and interviewing. To scan a sampler of completed interview study titles, see Appendix E.

SUGGESTED RESOURCES

Berg, B. L. (2007). *Qualitative research methods for the social sciences* (6th ed.). Boston, MA: Allyn & Bacon.

Brinkmann, S. & Kvale, S. (2015) *InterViews: Learning the craft of qualitative research interviewing* (3rd ed.). Thousand Oaks, CA: Sage.

Denzin, N. K. (1989). *Interpretive biography.* Newberry Park, CA: Sage.

Janesick, V. J. (1998). The dance of qualitative research design: Metaphor, methodolatry, and meaning. In N. Denzin & Y. Lincoln (Eds.), *Strategies of qualitative inquiry* (pp. 35–55). Thousand Oaks, CA: Sage.

Janesick, V. J. (2010). *Oral history for the qualitative researcher: Choreographing the story.* New York, NY: Guilford Press.

Janesick, V. J. (2011). *Stretching exercises for qualitative researchers* (3rd ed.). Thousand Oaks: Sage.

Kvale, S. (1996). *InterViews: An introduction to qualitative research interviewing.* Thousand Oaks, CA: Sage.

Kvale, S., & Brinkmann, S. (2009). *InterViews: Learning the Craft of Qualitative Research Interviewing* (2nd ed.). Thousand Oaks, CA: Sage.

McCracken, G. (1989). *The long interview.* Newberry Park, CA: Sage.

Merriam, S. B. (1997). *Qualitative research and case study applications in education* (Rev. ed.). San Francisco, CA: Jossey-Bass.

Mishler, E. G. (1986). *Research interviewing: Context and narrative.* Cambridge, MA: Harvard University Press.

Morgan, D. (Ed.). (1993). *Successful focus groups.* Newberry Park, CA: Sage.

Perselli, V. (2011) Painting the police station blue: The almost impossible argument for poetry in elite educational research journals. *Power and Education, 3*(1), 64–80.

Reinharz, S. (1992). *Feminist methods in social research.* New York, NY: Oxford University Press.

Roulston, K. J. (2010). *Reflective interviewing: A guide to theory and practice.* Thousand Oaks, CA: Sage.

Rubin, H. J., & Rubin, I. S. (2005). *Qualitative interviewing: The art of hearing data* (2nd ed.) Thousand Oaks, CA: Sage.

Salmons, J. E. (2010). *Online interviews in real time.* Thousand Oaks, CA: Sage.

Spradley, J. P. (1980). *Participant observation.* New York, NY: Holt, Rinehart & Winston.

Stake, R. E. (1995). *The art of the case study research.* Thousand Oaks, CA: Sage.

5

The Creative Habit

Imagination is the beginning of creation. You imagine what you desire, you will what you imagine, and at last, you create what you will.

—George Bernard Shaw

I t is said that Thomas Edison tested 10,000 substances to find and make a light bulb that would not explode. Many people asked him why so many? They asked him, "How could you fail 10,000 times?" He replied that he did not fail. He just discovered 10,000 things that simply did not work. This is a great story to keep in mind while sharpening your creative habit. In the field of dance, creativity is valued and practiced on a regular basis, thus a habit is formed. In qualitative research, it is also helpful to focus on this habit and practice creativity. This chapter contains exercises for facilitating learners to develop techniques in interpretation through the use of the imagination. In addition, these exercises are designed to assist in defining the role of the researcher. The practice of narrative writing techniques can only assist the researcher in training. Modern dance, as an art form, is characterized by a language of movement, and no one speaker makes quite the same statement. Likewise, the dancer explores new ways of moving, which include creative experiences and interpretation. Similarly, in yoga, as the practitioner begins, he or she needs to explore the postures in order to reorganize the spine and the breath. In yoga, too, one must acknowledge all the inner systems of the body in order to use the mind more fully. In working with mostly graduate students in education and human services, who have spent many years in bureaucratic settings, these are the exercises that cause the greatest disequilibrium. At the same time, they offer the practitioner the most opportunity for self-awareness. In fact, many individuals came to the realization that qualitative methods were much too demanding for them, and they would prefer to work in another paradigm. This is, of course, a creative awakening in itself. Just as everyone in dance must end up asking the question, "Do I really want to be a dancer?" the prospective qualitative researcher must ask the question, "Do I want to be a qualitative researcher?" It requires constant preparation, practice, determination, and willingness to redirect oneself if something fails. Nevertheless, as a teacher, I see these exercises as a beginning point for self-knowledge and, consequently, as valuable tools for any researcher. For the prospective qualitative researcher, these exercises help to instill an awareness of the importance of the role of the researcher. In each qualitative research project, the researcher must explain fully the role of the researcher. I require potential qualitative researchers to be able to describe and explain their own roles in their individual projects. We begin with a seemingly simple exercise, again modified from my days as a student of drawing. The exercises in this section are framed within John Dewey's notion of the development of habits of mind and the aesthetic as part of everyday experience. In Dewey's time, there was a prevailing modernistic dualism that separated the aesthetic from the world of ordinary experience. In this postmodern time, I have constructed these exercises to help the individual address this dualism and engage in ordinary experience as aesthetic experience. Be sure to write in your researcher reflective journal, describing what you did, how you completed these exercises, visual images of the exercises, and what you learned as a writer.

THE ROLE OF THE RESEARCHER AND ●
THE RESEARCHER REFLECTIVE JOURNAL

The following series of exercises are focused on developing your role as a researcher in order to understand yourself in deeper ways of knowing. In order to do that more fully, I emphasize the importance of the researcher reflective journal (see Appendix F). By putting journal writing into a historical context and understanding that there are multiple types of journal writing, the learner may be more definitive in understanding the self and the researcher as a research instrument. In conducting a dissertation study or any research, the value of keeping a substantive journal is that it may be used as a data set to complement other techniques. We begin with the most personal of exercises, that of writing your name in new ways.

EXERCISE 5.1   Variations on Writing Your Name

Purpose:

To write your name as many times and in as many ways as possible on a sheet of 8½" × 11" paper.

1. First, write your name with each hand—left hand first, then the right hand.

2. Next, write your name upside down.

3. Then, write your name diagonally, in the shape of an X.

4. Now, write your name from right to left, as many cultures do.

5. Now, write your name as you usually do.

6. Now, close your eyes and write your name.

Discuss and compare your reactions to writing your name in these varied formats. Pair up with someone in class and view each other's writing. Discuss and share your reactions.

Problem:

To liberate yourself from the usual writing of your name; to jog your multiple intelligences; to stimulate the right side of your brain.

Note: I recently took a drawing class, and the teacher used some of these variations. This reminded me of Betty Edwards's (1986) *Drawing on the Artist Within,* which was a follow-up to her renowned earlier works, *Drawing on the Right Side of the Brain* (1979) and *The New Drawing on the Right Side of the Brain* (1999). I encourage all my students to read these texts or a reasonable equivalent.

Time:

Take as much time as needed.

Activity:

Create a visual representation of one's own name.

Aim:

The purpose here is to give the person the opportunity to break away from the typical expression of writing his or her name. This is so personal an exercise and produces such confusion for some because it is the first time in a long time that they have put creativity into action. I also see this as the beginning step, a first step in recognizing the active nature of the role of the researcher. The researcher is not passive. The prospective researcher must begin to recognize his or her own investment in the research project and how critical the definition of his or her role in the project remains. This exercise generates a great deal of discussion and makes the individual learner respond to something often overlooked—the way we write our names. Overall, the goal is to sharpen awareness. Notice how you, as a learner, approach each of these phases of writing your name. Which one was most difficult?

Discussion:

1. How did you approach this exercise?
2. What was most difficult for you in each of these phases of name writing?
3. What have you learned from this?
4. What have you learned thus far about your skill as an observer? A researcher?

Evaluation:

Continue working on self-evaluation for your researcher reflective journal and portfolio.

In this second exercise, the learner progresses from the internal to the external arena by using a camera to document a familiar social setting.

EXERCISE 5.2 The Camera as an Extension of the Eye, the Eye as an Extension of the Soul

Purpose:

Take photographs of any area of campus or your workplace over a 1-hour time frame.

Problem:

To document some portions of a familiar setting.

Materials:

Individuals need a camera. Those who do not have a camera need to purchase a disposable camera, available for under $10.

Activity:

Document as many different aspects of the environment as possible with your photos. Select your five best to share with the group. If working outside a class situation, find someone with whom to discuss your work.

Of all the exercises I use with learners, this one seems to inspire the most confidence, an awareness of one's limitations and the most enthusiasm for finding out what kind of qualitative researcher one might become.

Evaluation:

Continue on self-evaluation for your journal and portfolio.

EXERCISE 5.3 Building a Collage: My Role as a Researcher

Purpose:

To design and construct a collage that represents your role as a researcher in the project you are developing for study.

Problem:

To capture your perspective on your role as accurately as possible.

Time:

2 to 3 weeks.

Activity:

Construct a collage on a piece of poster board that is a manageable size for display and discussion in class. A suggested size is 24 inches by 36 inches. Use any media you wish—printed text, photographs, magazine ads, newspaper headlines, objects, and so on.

Discussion:

1. How did you approach this activity?

2. What issues and ideas about your role as a researcher are emerging as you construct your collage?

3. What was the most challenging part of the activity for you?

Evaluation:

Continue on your self-evaluation and overall evaluation for your portfolio.

Rationale:

Students who select this activity become actively involved in representing their own feelings and ideas about their roles as researchers.

EXERCISE 5.4   Constructing a YaYa Box or Making a Quilt Patch

Purpose:

To design and construct a YaYa box. This is adapted from the field of art therapy. A YaYa box is designed to represent a person's innermost self on the inside of the box and the outward self on the outside. If you would rather make a quilt patch, the patch will represent some part of your inner self as a researcher.

Problem:

To capture yourself as you are now in terms of your current role in your research project.

Time:

Take as many weeks as you need to develop, create, and construct this, with the presentation of the box at the last class meeting.

Activity:

Find a box of any manageable size, from a cigar box to a steamer trunk. Use multimedia to build your box. The inside of the box will depict your innermost feelings, thoughts, and beliefs about who you are as you participate in your research project. The outside of the box will represent your outer self or how your participants see you. Use any objects, text, decorations, and so on that you want to convey your idea of your role as the researcher. If you select a quilt patch, use a 12-inch-by-12-inch patch with any materials of your choice.

In less than two pages, describe the contents, decorations, and meaning of your YaYa box or quilt patch to accompany the finished artwork.

Discussion:

1. How did you approach this project?

2. What issues about the role of the researcher confronted you as you began and implemented this project?

3. What was the most difficult part of this activity for you?

Evaluation:

Continue with self-evaluation and overall evaluation for your portfolio.

Rationale:

Individuals become intensely absorbed with this activity and focus on deconstructing their own roles in their research projects. The ability of learners to go deeply into reflection on their roles and their effects on research projects is evident.

These activities lead to the next, most soul-searching of activities, that of writing the researcher reflective journal.

THE QUALITATIVE RESEARCHER AND THE INTUITIVE SENSE ●

One of the amazing strengths of the qualitative researcher, the dancer, the yogi, the meditator, or the artist is the ability to use all the senses in performance. For qualitative researchers to undertake and complete the research act, we use all our senses. Sight, hearing, touch, smell, and taste often must be used to collect data. After living in the field with participants over time, the researcher also uses intuition—informed hunches, if you prefer—to plan the mode of inquiry, undertake the inquiry, and develop a way of "seeing" what is evident in the social setting. The role of the qualitative researcher demands total involvement and commitment in a way that requires, much like the artist or dancer, a total immersion of the senses in the experience. Like Dewey advises, art is the bridge between the experience of individuals and the community. So, too, the qualitative researcher is someone who must establish a bridge as a part of the community under study. The qualitative researcher takes on the implicit task of working in a given community and does not have the luxury of being distant, apart from the experience under study, or "objective." I only wish to point out that the role of the qualitative researcher is a role that embraces subjectivity in the sense that the researcher is aware of his or her own self, in tune with his or her senses, and fully conscious of what is taking place in the research project. Subjectivity is something to be acknowledged and understood. Without understanding where one is situated in the research act, it is impossible to claim consciousness and impossible to interpret one's data fully or assess our progress as researchers (see Appendix G). Meaning is constructed in the ongoing social relationship between the researcher and the participants in the study. It is no longer an option to research and run. The researcher is connected to the participants in a most profound way, and that is how trust is established. This trust then allows for greater access to sources and ensures involvement from participants, which enables them to tell their respective stories. Those of us who have conducted long-term qualitative studies know that participants want their voices to be heard and do not want to be abandoned after the research project. My field, education, has a long history of researchers who come into a school or other educational setting, collect data, and flee. Thankfully, this is changing in terms of researchers' sensitivity to maintaining contact, partnertships, and a relationship with participants in their studies in order to maintain that sense of community that is part of any qualitative research project. This relationship remains as part of the research context throughout a significant period of time well beyond the end of data collection. This is one of the checks and balances in the system. Time in the field is at least to be matched by time in analysis. There really is no such thing as speedy qualitative research. Time is required in qualitative research projects to complete the research act.

As I mentioned earlier, the senses are used in an intelligent way. Although sight and hearing are obvious senses employed in doing observations and interviews, the other senses may be used while conducting research at various sites. For example, the researcher may need to interview a participant at a restaurant or coffee shop. Once, while interviewing a blind and deaf research project participant, I had to sign into the person's hand, thus using touch as part of using the senses for research. Beyond this, however, all researchers use a sixth sense, an intuitive sense, to follow through on hunches that emerge from observing and interviewing in a particular social context over time. Researchers ought to have the opportunity in their training and in practice to sharpen their intuitive skills, which often open up avenues of data previously unknown or hidden. In exercises that I give my students to become better listeners and better observers, I often see the prospective researcher refine some of those intuitive skills so needed in research and life. The next six exercises are designed for practicing the use of all your senses.

EXERCISE 5.5   Writing About Your Favorite Vegetable

Incorporating Sight, Touch, Smell, Sound, and Taste

In this exercise, select your favorite vegetable. Hold it in your hand to feel its texture. Smell this vegetable. Now write two pages describing this vegetable. Recall how it tastes or taste it. Write another page just about its taste. Next, write another page about your favorite meal incorporating this vegetable. Now, construct a metaphor about this vegetable, and write about that for another page. Find a partner in class or at home to read your description. Ask for feedback, and rewrite your narrative on this, your favorite vegetable. Now, write your thoughts in the reflective journal about what you learned from this exercise. Can you tie this to your role as a researcher?

SERENDIPITY ●

So, too, the qualitative researcher often stumbles onto something in the course of a research project that leads to a rich course of inquiry and was unplanned in the original design. In other words, one builds in a type of latent flexibility that enables the researcher to find, through serendipity, a tremendous amount of meaningful data for a fuller picture of the study. The qualitative researcher should expect to uncover some information through informed hunches, intuition, and serendipitous occurrences that, in turn, will lead to a richer and more powerful explanation of the setting, context, and participants in any given study. The qualitative researcher is in touch with all of his or her senses, including the intuitive sense, or informed hunches, based on key incidents and data from the research project. Furthermore, the qualitative researcher may expect the unexpected. For the qualitative researcher, the role becomes expanded in that the number of options for coming upon new data is enlarged because one can always count on serendipity, contradictions, and surprises in everyday life, the true domain of the qualitative researcher. Furthermore, the qualitative researcher describes and explains these occurrences as part of the discussion of the research process and the researcher's role.

Analysis of data, like the dancer moving across the floor with floor exercises, consists of the actual *doing* of the work. For the researcher in progress, the researcher sifts through mounds of data; looks for emerging themes, ideas, issues, conflicts, and tension; and checks back with participants to verify the accuracy of these points in the journey. After the researcher has sifted through the data transcripts, field notes, and other documents, the good analyst uses the following guide to move on to reporting and interpreting data. (See Appendixes H and I.)

INTUITION, CREATIVITY, AND COMPASSION IN RESEARCH ●

The lunatic, the lover, and the poet

Are of imagination all compact . . .

The poet's eye, in fine frenzy rolling,

Doth glance from heaven to earth, from earth to heaven;

And as imagination bodies forth

The forms of things unknown, the poet's pen

Turns them to shapes and gives to airy nothing

A local habitation and a name.

—William Shakespeare

A Midsummer Night's Dream (5.1)

Here, I would like to discuss the nature of intuition and creativity as key components of qualitative research projects. By discussing intuition and creativity, I hope to initiate a conversation that may illuminate how we view the role of the qualitative researcher and how we may better explain that role. Also, I add the notion of compassion to this configuration. To be aware of the context you have placed yourself in during the research process, compassion is need to identify with the lived experience of your participants. I will once again use the metaphor of dance, and in this case, I see intuition, creativity, and compassion as a triangle of inspiration. In dance, whatever the number of dancers in a piece, the idea is that they move as one. They are totally connected to the final product, whatever the meaningful movement is to be and however it is to be articulated through choreography. For our purposes here, I define *intuition* as immediate apprehension or cognition. Intuition is a way of knowing about the world through insight and exercising one's imagination. Compassion is used here in the true Zen sense, that is, having the ability to feel what another person is feeling and if it is suffering, to have deep sympathy, empathy, and a strong desire to alleviate suffering. Likewise, I define creativity in its generic sense, that is, having the sense or quality of being created rather than imitated. In other words, I am trying to shift the conversation about qualitative research methodology and design from the linear approach to method and design to an understanding of the intuitive, the creative, and compassionate.

Doctoral students often discuss with me the ways in which intuition has manifested itself in their research projects. They often want to go further in exploring how they came to probe in interviews, how they decided to go back to social settings on given days, or how they revisited their interview transcripts. This is the phenomenon we seek, the act of using intuition, creativity, and compassion (see Appendix J). Historically, over the past 50 years, we have been writing and thinking a great deal about the design of qualitative research projects and about technique. Although design and technique are critical, I want to shift this conversation to go beyond technique. I would like to pause and look to writers from art, science, literature, and dance to make my key points.

I begin with the words of the Chinese master painter and teacher Lu Ch'ai, from the 1701 classic on painting, *The Tao of Painting:*

> Some get great value on method, while others pride them-
> selves on dispensing with method. To be without method is
> deplorable, but to depend on method entirely is worse. You
> must first learn to observe the rules faithfully; afterwards
> modify them according to your intelligence and capacity.
> The end of all method is to have no method. (Chuan, 1963,
> p. 17)

Although Lu Ch'ai codified these remarks and the entire text in the 18th century, it is actually a formal text put together from material spanning the previous 11 centuries. The advice is relevant here to the work of the qualitative researcher. Have we not found, as we teach our classes, that learners begin with an almost slavish adherence to rules? Have we not seen, in the many methods texts, advice on how to do observations, interviews, journal writing, archival retrieval of evidence, and the like? This advice, almost prescriptive in nature to assist beginners, must be extended to include rules of thumb or information on technique, much as choreographers, stage directors, yogis, and artists do. In the case of dance, for example, mastering the rules of technique is critical but only a beginning. The dancer continues to practice those techniques daily, which eventually allows him or her to modify and interrupt movement and technique. The result is a creative act. The creative act relies on the dancer's intuition as much as physical technique, endurance, and stamina. It also relies on the dancer's ability to empathize with the character performed through the dance. This is similar to the qualitative researcher who needs to have empathy and compassion in order to capture the lived experience of the participants in the study.

Likewise, the qualitative researcher may benefit from exercising creativity by being awake to the intuitive inclinations ever present in fieldwork. In thinking about and investigating what has been written about intuition and creativity, I turn now to analyzing some current writing as well as reviewing work that touches on intuition, creativity, and in many cases, compassion. In addition, the role of the qualitative researcher is of critical importance because the researcher is the research instrument. If we can help describe how we use our intuition, creativity, and compassion in our research projects, all of us benefit. In fact, most doctoral students in the social and behavioral sciences fully explain their particular roles in their research projects in their dissertations in a section on methodology and may revisit their roles in a later chapter. For those who might be using this book outside a class setting, these basics also apply. Like the artist who uses paint and brushes or the dancer who uses movement, the qualitative researcher uses many techniques as tools to ultimately tell a story. For us, words and the power of the narrative are essential. By understanding how we use our creativity, we may widen our vocabularies to understand the role of the qualitative researcher.

I want to address some of the key points in Mihaly Csikszentmihalyi's (1996) work as reported in his major text, *Creativity: Flow and the Psychology of Discovery and Invention.* Csikszentmihalyi was awarded a grant from the Spencer Foundation to study creativity as a lifelong process. In beginning the project, Csikszentmihalyi found no systematic studies of living, creative individuals aside from biographies and autobiographies. He ventured to design a four-year interview and observation study of 91 creative individuals in the fields of literature, art, physics, and biology (although, I am sorry to say, no one from dance or yoga). Csikszentmihalyi found three ways to look at creativity:

1. The first way to approach creativity is the way we normally do in ordinary conversation. Here, we refer to those who express unusual thoughts, are interesting and stimulating, and are bright people with quick minds as brilliant. These are people with curious and original minds.

2. A second view—personal creativity—refers to people who experience the world in novel and original ways. They make important discoveries, but only they know of the discoveries.

3. The third view of creativity refers to individuals who have changed our culture in some way. For example, Michelangelo, Leonardo da Vinci, Albert Einstein, Steve Jobs, Martin Scorsese, Arthur Miller, Martha Graham, Pablo Picasso, Salvador Dali, Charles Dickens, Leonard Bernstein, Dale Chihuly, and Virginia Woolf would fall into this category. Viewing creativity in this way, the individual must publicize in some form the idea that makes a shift or change in culture. Likewise, the qualitative researcher must publish or at least disseminate his or her findings from a study.

What Csikszentmihalyi found as major themes are those that qualitative researchers often discuss, describe, and explain. Creative people, he pointed out, are constantly surprised and always find new ways of looking at a given problem. They are remarkably curious people. He labeled their ability *problem finding*. I would go a step further and say that good qualitative researchers are indeed problem finders, but they are also problem posers. In any given study, a new way of looking at a setting can also be a way of posing and constructing something new. In fact, qualitative researchers are often coresearchers with the participants in a given study, and the participants open up new ways of looking at the social setting. Furthermore, he found that creative individuals exhibited curiosity and interest in their worlds *not limited to their content expertise*. They often read both outside and inside their own field. Of course, they were all content experts in various fields, such as literature, physics, biology, and music, and were curious about moving forward in their fields. In addition, they were curious about the world around them and how that related to their worlds, their fields of expertise, and their lives. So too qualitative researchers need this type of curiosity. Read widely and read often in fields other than our own field.

Threads of continuity from childhood to later life were another valuable finding of Csikszentmihalyi's 1996 study. Some followed convoluted and unpredictable routes to where they stood. Yet most, such as Linus Pauling, always knew they were the artist or scientist in the making. Pauling worked in his father's drugstore as a child, which sparked his interest in chemistry. Likewise, Frank Offner, the famed electrical engineer and inventor, recalled wanting to fix things as a child and he tried to figure out how mechanical objects worked. Offner went on to make many discoveries. He developed transistorized measuring devices, the differential amplifier, and medical instrumentation. He figured out how to make the measurements with an electrocardiogram, electroencephalogram, and the electromyogram. Some of his greatest inventions involved a stylus moving across a drum. So, there was a very long thread of continuity in his case. Marty Scorsese mentions regularly in interviews the first time he saw a motion picture, he knew he was going to make films. This continuity is critical in continuing the creative process.

Another example of continuity can be found in C. Vann Woodward's interest in the history of the South:

> The place I grew up was important. The environment and the time following the Civil War and Reconstruction. . . . It is the defeated who really think about a war, not the victors. (Csikszentmihalyi, 1996, p. 216)

For Woodward, again, the interest in his work began early in childhood. Likewise, Ellen Lanyon, the painter, described her first feeling of destiny and creativity related to her grandfather's death. Her maternal grandfather, also an artist in the medium of painting, came to the United States from Yorkshire, England, for the World's Columbian Exposition of 1893 in Chicago. She always knew that she would follow in her grandfather's footsteps. Similarly, the meditation teacher models compassion and initiates stillness, breathing exercises, body awareness exercises and stretching, prior to the actual practice of chanting and mantra based meditation in order to come closer to compassion. This is often done through writing about it in a meditation journal. What these creative individuals show us can help us, as qualitative researchers, to dig deeply into our roles and go further in explaining the beginnings of our interest in the work we do. This can help illuminate more clearly the role of the researcher in qualitative research projects.

At this point, you may be wondering about the lessons we might learn from this regarding intuition, creativity, and compassion. The triangle of intuition, creativity, and compassion seem almost as one. Like yoga, body, and mind are one. The word *yoga* means "joined together," in this case mind and body. Like the Zen practitioner, quietude, contemplation, compassion, and serenity offer a platform for developing our thinking, writing, creativity, and research habits. They embolden our discoveries and questions, whether in art, music, literature, the sciences, or everyday life. Intuition is connected to creativity, for intuition is the seed, so to speak, of the creative act. Qualitative researchers spend a great deal of time and energy inquiring into social settings and the meanings of the actors' lives in those settings. If we take the time to carve out some space to understand the place of intuition, creativity, and compassion in our work, we may present a more complete, holistic, and authentic study of our own roles as storytellers and artist-scientists. For qualitative researchers, the story is paramount. And nothing is so important to the story as the words we use, which should glow with creativity and compassion. A good way to document the story is for you as the qualitative researcher to keep the story going and writing in your researcher reflective journal.

● THE RESEARCHER REFLECTIVE JOURNAL AS CREATIVE ACT

In working with prospective qualitative researchers, one goal is to inspire my students to keep a researcher reflective journal in order to use that as a data set in the dissertation or thesis and in subsequent projects. It is a solid habit of mind that can enrich any field of study. Along with the interview transcripts, documents from the study, and photos, now the learner adds sections of the researcher reflective journal. They read *At a Journal Workshop: Writing to Access the Power of the Unconscious and Evoke Creative Ability* by Ira Progoff (1992). This text offers an extremely sophisticated and challenging approach to deepening one's self-awareness through journal writing. In my view and Progoff's, deepening self-awareness helps to sharpen one's reflections, writing, thinking, and ability to communicate. Thus, for the qualitative researcher, the meditative focus of journal writing can only help to refine the researcher as a research instrument. The ideal situation would be to work through every component of the text, which I see as a lifelong task. Because we are limited in our class to only 16 weeks together, I have adapted some of Progoff's ideas into a workable routine for my students and myself. Progoff writes about journalizing as a *life history log*. The following framework is adapted to make the student a better researcher.

Introducing the Researcher Reflective Journal

The reader may remember that field note writing, journal writing, and descriptive vignettes in general have been part of the exercises described in this text. I have always been struck by the power and place of writing in my career as an educator. In fact, most of my life consists of writing, reading other people's writing, editing, and rewriting, and evaluating the writing of myself or others. What is ironic to me is that in research programs of doctoral students, so little emphasis is placed on writing as a pedagogical tool and as a preeminent focus of research dissemination. Without narrative and poetic writing, where would the field be? In my classes in research, students often express amazement at the amount of reading and writing required to be a good researcher, yet months or years later, they express gratitude for having that opportunity to realize that writing is a chief component of qualitative research. Earlier in this text, I introduced the notion of the *dialogue journal* based on the Progoff model. That was for the purpose of the researcher coming to an awareness of self. Now, we turn to the researcher reflective journal during the research process to go further and come to an awareness of how your participants think, feel, and behave.

Furthermore, writing that is accompanied by reflection on that writing often leads to new questions about the research act, the study being reported, and questions in general about society, social justice, and responsibility. When learners reflect on this within the framework of their research, they often remark on a feeling of empowerment. When individuals keep journals of their own thoughts on the research process, or interactive journals with the participants in their studies, or write letters to me or other researchers, they discover and articulate their own theories about their research practices.

What results is a kind of active learning from one another so that power is decentered and the research process is demystified. In addition, writing is one of the acts of democratization of the research process. Writing engages, educates, and inspires, which can only be helpful in trying to understand what qualitative researchers do in their respective research projects.

On the Importance of Journal Writing for the Qualitative Researcher

A journal may be used as a qualitative research technique in long-term qualitative studies. For qualitative researchers, the act of journal writing may be incorporated into the research process to provide a data set of the researcher's reflections on the research act. Participants in qualitative studies may also use journals to refine ideas, beliefs, and their own responses to the research in progress. Finally, journal writing between participants and researcher may offer the qualitative researcher yet another opportunity for triangulation of data sets at multiple levels. Journal writing and blogging for that matter might be used for member checking, that is, checking back with members of the study for meaning and accuracy. Journal writing has a long and reliable history in the arts and humanities, and qualitative researchers may learn a great deal from this. It is not by accident that artists, writers, musicians, dancers, therapists, physicians, poets, architects, saints, chefs, scientists, and educators use journal writing in their lives. In virtually every field, one can find exemplars who have kept detailed and lengthy journals regarding their everyday lives and their beliefs, hopes, and dreams. I see journal writing as a powerful heuristic tool and research technique and will discuss reasons for using journals within qualitative research projects in order to do the following:

1. Refine the understanding of the role of the researcher through reflection and writing, much as an artist might do

2. Refine the understanding of the responses of participants in the study, much as a physician or health care worker might do

3. Use a journal as an interactive tool of communication between the researcher and participants in the study

4. View journal writing as a type of connoisseurship by which individuals become connoisseurs of their own thinking and reflection patterns and, indeed, their own understanding of their work as qualitative researchers

The notion of a comprehensive reflective journal to address the researcher's self is critical in qualitative work because of the fact that the researcher is the research instrument. In reviewing the literature in this area, journal writing, although an ancient technique, is only now being used and talked about as a serious component in qualitative research projects. I have always seen journal writing as a major source of data. It is a data set that contains the researcher's reflection on the role of the researcher, for example. It is a great vehicle for coming to terms with exactly what one is doing as the qualitative researcher. Often, qualitative researchers are criticized for not being precise about what they do. I offer journal writing as one technique to accomplish the description and explanation of the researcher's role in the project. Of course this means including sections of the journal in your data presentation and possibly a sampler for your appendix to your research project. You will model for future researchers how you used the researcher reflective journal. Qualitative researchers may use a reflective journal to write about problems or ethical issues that come up on a regular basis in any given study. Examples of problems include representation of interviews and field notes, co-construction of meaning with participants in the project who also keep journals, and issues related to the interpretation of each other's data. Often, we qualitative researchers are positioned outside the very people and situations about which we write. Journal writing personalizes representation in a way that forces the researcher to confront issues of how a story from a person's life becomes a public text, which in turn tells a story. Furthermore, how are we to make sense of this story?

Basically, the art of journal writing and subsequent interpretations of journal writing produce meaning and understanding that are shaped by genre, the narrative form used, and personal cultural and paradigmatic conventions of the writer, who is also the researcher and participant. As Progoff (1992) points out, journal writing is ultimately a way of getting feedback from ourselves about ourselves and our world. It enables us to experience in a full and open-ended way the movement of our lives as a whole and the meaning that follows from reflecting on that life.

Issues to be considered by the qualitative researcher include movement from the field to the text to the final, public research report and problems of interpretation, meaning, and representation.

Interactive journal writing between researcher and participants is another way of understanding a given study. I have written earlier about journal writing (1999) and then wrote of the lengthy history of journal writing. All periods of history have benefited from journal writing. After all, journals are texts that record dreams, hopes, visions, fantasies, feelings, and innermost thoughts. Today, one can look to the amazing work of Edward Robb Ellis (1995). Ellis was a diary writer who kept a journal from 1927 to 1995. He was born in 1911 and kept a journal for 67 years, or more than 24,000 days. His descriptions provide amazing coverage of the events he lived through personally, but he also describes societal changes.

Yet, literary and historical figures are not the only journal writers. The field of psychology has long made use of journal writing as a therapeutic aid. The cathartic function of journal writing has been widely recommended by many schools of therapy. Therapists view the journal as an attempt to bring order to one's experience and a sense of coherence to one's life. Behaviorists, cognitive therapists, and Jungian analysts have used journals in the process of therapy. The journal is seen as a natural outgrowth of the clinical situation in which the client speaks to the self. Most recently, Progoff (1992) has written of an intensive journal. Progoff developed a set of techniques that provides a structure for keeping a journal and a springboard for development. As a therapist himself, he has conducted workshops and trained a network of individuals to do workshops on keeping an intensive journal for unlocking one's creativity and coming to terms with one's self. The intensive journal method is a reflective, in-depth process of writing, speaking what is written, and in some cases, sharing what is written with others. Feedback is an operative principle for the Progoff method. The individual needs to draw upon inner resources to arrive at the understanding of the whole person. The journal is a tool to reopen the possibilities of learning and living. Progoff advocates the following:

1. Make regular entries in the journal in the form of dialogue with one's self.

2. Maintain the journal as an intensive psychological workbook in order to record all encounters of one's existence.

3. Attempt some type of sharing of this growth through journal writing with others.

The method makes use of a special, bound notebook or computer file divided into definite categories that include the following: a dream journal in dialogue form, stepping stones in your life, dialogues with people, events, work, and the body. The writer is asked to reflect, free-associate, meditate, and imagine what relates to immediate experience. Currently, one only has to walk through the display aisles of the major bookstores or online offerings through Amazon to see the many examples of recently published journals. Recently, I found the following:

- The journal of an Afghani war survivor
- The Andy Warhol journals
- The journals of Sylvia Plath
- *The Diary of Anaïs Nin*
- *Water Cooler Diaries: Women Across America Share Their Day at Work*
- The journal of Lewis Carroll
- The journal of a surgeon
- The journal of a peace corps volunteer

The point is that this genre is alive and well, and qualitative researchers should not be afraid of trying to keep journals. In fact, journal writing is so prevalent now that one only has to surf the Internet to see thousands of journal resources, examples, and personal histories online. For example, there is an online course on journal writing offered by Via Creativa, a website entirely devoted to Progoff's Intensive Journal Workshop, chat rooms on journal writing, exemplars of diaries and journal writing, and literally thousands of resources. In general, the common thread that unites all of these resources on the Internet is the agreement that journal writing is a way of getting in touch with yourself in terms of reflection, catharsis, remembrance, creation, exploration, problem solving, problem posing, and personal growth. I see all of these as part of the research process. In addition, the new site, Penzu at www.penzu.com offers users a digital journal space with their own password, utterly private, and a way for digital natives to become involved in journal writing. For qualitative researchers, journal writing offers a way to document the researcher's role, triangulate data by entering the journal itself as a data set, and use the journal with participants in the study as a communicative act.

Why Journal Writing?

Students and colleagues have often asked me why they should invest time in journal writing. To this, I can only reply that journal writing allows one to reflect—to dig deeper, if you will—into the heart of the words, beliefs, and behaviors we describe. It allows one to reflect on the recordings and interview transcripts from our research endeavors. If participants also keep journals, it offers a way to triangulate data and pursue interpretations in a dialogical manner. It is a type of member check of one's own thinking done on paper. The clarity of writing down one's thoughts will allow for stepping into one's inner mind and reaching further into interpretations of the behaviors, beliefs, and words we write. Not everyone finds it easy to keep up with the demands of journal writing. The discipline and desire involved nearly outweigh some individuals' abilities or time. On the other hand, can this not be an option for all who are interested in becoming better researchers, writers, thinkers, and scholars? How does one set time apart for journal writing? I recall the teacher who said she had only 20 minutes after school to write in her journal, and that was that. Then, she ultimately decided she needed to keep a journal at home as well, because once she started to write, she found that she was staying at school and writing for at least an hour each day. She got up an hour earlier than anyone in her house and started writing in the early morning hours, a technique advocated by many writers. Many writers of journals have directly or indirectly stated how journal writing can assist one in developing creativity. The focus and energy demanded of one who writes a journal can be instructive for qualitative researchers. See Tristine Rainer's *The New Diary* (1978) for her categories below:

1. **Travelers.** People who keep a written record during a special time, such as a vacation or a trip

2. **Pilgrims.** People who want to discover who they really are

3. **Creators.** People who write to sketch out ideas and inventions in art or science

4. **Apologists.** People who write to justify something they have done and plead their case before all who read the journal

5. **Confessors.** People who conduct ritual unburdenings with the promise of secrecy or anonymity

6. **Prisoners.** People who must live their lives in prisons or who may be invalids, and as a result, must live their lives through keeping a journal

In general, any writer might be a combination of any of these categories, but this might be useful as a tool to understand different approaches to keeping a journal. Progoff (1992) gives numerous examples of individuals who fall into these categories to illustrate the importance of keeping a journal. In fact, he got interested in writing his book because he himself has kept a journal for more than 30 years. I share that interest with him.

Rainer's book contains superb examples of journal writing. I agree with her use of the terms *journal* and *diary* interchangeably. She describes seven techniques for journal writing, some very similar to Progoff's techniques. Her list is one that qualitative researchers may recognize as being used regularly in the arts and humanities.

Rainer's Seven Techniques

1. **Lists.** This technique allows for a person to write lists of activities, such as things to do, things that upset a person, things that are problematic, and so forth. It allows a writer to capture the pace of his or her activities and can be a good beginning for a journal writer who may go back and fill in the story in narrative form regarding all of the entries on the list.

2. **Portraits.** This allows the writer to describe a person or any number of people. The portrait is never really finished for the qualitative researcher. It evolves and takes on a life of its own throughout the project, and the writer may add to and subtract from it as the work takes shape.

3. **Maps of Consciousness.** This technique is borrowed from the arts, and it involves actually drawing a map of what one is thinking. Rainer advocates using stick figures, lines, or shapeless blobs. It is a way to free up one's thoughts and put them to paper in another format.

4. **Guided Imagery.** This technique is borrowed from the field of psychology, which advises that daydreaming images allow for an individual to start writing about any given topic.

5. **Altered Point of View.** In this technique, the writer takes a different perspective on any given activity. For the qualitative researcher, for example, one might write about something in an observation or interview from another person's viewpoint, not the researcher's viewpoint. Many beginning researchers find it hard to write in the first person, and they talk about their projects in a third-person voice. It is a way of looking at something

from the outside. For Rainer, looking from the outside might aid in getting to the inside of a topic.

6. **Unsent Letters.** Obviously, this is about writing a letter to someone without any intention of showing it to that person. In a research situation, the researcher may write to one of the participants in the study, for example.

7. **Dialogues.** This is the technique Progoff suggests, and many writers use this effectively.

As I finish this section, the major ideas I want to punctuate have to do with journal writing as a technique used in the arts that resonates with the qualitative researcher. Writing down what we think and feel helps in the journey to improve our research practice, for example. Some of the personal examples used in the body of this text may serve to illustrate the individual writer's thinking processes and the willingness to analyze, rethink, and go deeper into a critical stance about one's life and work. Progoff calls this the *scope of personal renewal*. Others call it *reflection*. Still others, myself included, see journal writing as a tangible way to evaluate our experiences, improve and clarify our thinking, and become better writers and scholars.

The researcher reflective journal, used while conducting qualitative research projects, helps the researcher with the following:

1. Helps to focus the study

2. Helps set the groundwork for analysis and interpretation

3. Serves as a tool for revisiting notes and transcripts

4. Serves as a tool to awaken the imagination

5. Helps to keep the written record of thoughts, feelings, and facts

6. May incorporate art forms, poetry, and possibly digital content if done on the Web

We are talking about examining our own thoughts, beliefs, and behaviors. Many will say that helps only the writer. Still, if that were the only outcome of writing a journal, I would say that this continuing self-reflection is a first, vital step in modeling this for our students. Journal writing is a powerful research technique for the researcher and the participants in a given study. The definitions of the roles of the researcher and participants in a study are clarified through the reflection and the writing process involved in journal writing. Because the researcher is the research instrument, keeping a journal is another of those checks and balances during the entire course of a qualitative research project. Likewise, keeping a journal during the course of a research project is a way to practice interdisciplinary triangulation. In order to get students to begin this project, I suggest the following exercise.

An Activity to Enrich Your Researcher Reflective Journal

Think about the points listed here before you begin this activity.

- Examining the familiar
- Observing the details
- Exploring positions
- Investigating issues
- Revealing current thoughts
- Reflecting your own direction

1. Write one sentence that indicates something you already know about journal writing.
2. Write one sentence that indicates what you would like to know about journal writing.

This gets things started. Next, we have volunteers read to the class their first sentence and then their second sentence. Then, we begin a journal writing exercise. The next set of exercises are designed to get you to write in your journal.

EXERCISE 5.6   Your Journey

Position yourself in this present moment. Describe your journey to this class or book. How did you come to this class or to this book today? This program? What prompted you to select this area of study? What were your obstacles? Expectations? Write about yourself and your goals. How can this class make you a better researcher?

As you can see, this inspires quite a bit of writing. Next, we pair up and read to one another for 30 minutes. When we return to the larger group, volunteers read sections of their first journal entries. Learners are delighted that many in the group have similar interests and backgrounds. Many are inspired to write more. But overall, everyone writes and rewrites. In the next class meeting, we continue to save 15 minutes per class for journal writing.

At the end of each session, I ask all to do the following:

Please write three things that you learned about journal writing today.

This keeps learners focused on writing, writing, writing. In fact, students tell me that they run home and continue to write in their journals. For many, it is a liberating activity. (See Appendix F for multiple examples of journal writing.)

● FUTURE DIRECTIONS

In speculating on the future of this useful technique of journal writing, I think that researchers in training may benefit from the practice of journal writing as a qualitative research technique for the following reasons:

1. Journal writing allows the writer to be more reflective.

2. Journal writing offers the writer an opportunity to write without interruption and to be totally focused on the point at hand.

3. Journal writing is a technique well used in the arts and humanities that may offer social science researchers an opportunity to cross borders, so to speak.

4. Journal writing allows for deepening knowledge.

5. Journal writing allows participants in a research project an active voice.

6. Journal writing may allow researchers and participants the opportunity to write cooperatively and interactively as needed.

7. Journal writing provides an additional data set to outline, describe, and explain the exact role of the researcher in any given project.

In concluding this section, I recall these words for thought:

There was so much to write. He had seen the world change; not just the events; although he had seen many of them and watched the people, but he had seen the subtler change and he could remember how the people were at different times. He had been in it and he had watched it and it was his duty to write of it.

—Ernest Hemingway

The Snows of Kilimanjaro (1995)

EXERCISE 5.7   Reflective Journal Writing Practice in Dialogue Form

Purpose:

To keep a journal in dialogue form over the length of the semester. Set aside a minimum of 15 minutes each day for writing.

Problem:

The individual records mini-dialogues with the self in the present, focusing on the following areas:

People

Focus on dialogues with key people in your own life: best friends, lovers, partners. What have you discovered about the person you are today as a result of these dialogues?

Work or Projects

Focus on a dialogue about significant projects or work that take up a great deal of your energy. Which projects succeeded? Which failed? What have you discovered about yourself as a result of these projects?

The Body

Focus on your view of your own body. How have you cared for it? How do you treat it today? Are there moments in your life history where you mistreated your body? What have you discovered about yourself as a result of awareness of your body?

Society

Focus on your relationship to social groups. Of which groups are you a member? How do you describe your own ethnic and racial identity? Are you aware of your political beliefs? Are you reconsidering how you relate to groups? What have you discovered about yourself as a result of awareness of your relationship to society?

Major Life Event(s)

Focus on one or more life events that have had a profound effect on the person you are today. What have you discovered from reflecting on this?

For many learners, keeping a journal is a new experience, and by reading about journal writing and doing it as an activity, learners begin to reflect more deeply on their roles as researchers and as human beings. The journal is kept throughout the class to show evidence of one's progress on the journey of developing as a qualitative researcher. It is an opportunity to think in a new way. In addition to keeping a journal, the student is asked to include some poetry indicative of or using one of the techniques practiced in class.

EXERCISE 5.8   Haiku and Any Form of Poetry on the Role of the Researcher

Purpose:

To write a poem in any style, including haiku, about the role of the researcher or one that reflects some skill in describing an object, place, person, or setting.

Problem:

To capture the essence of the individual's role in a particular study undertaken during the semester or as part of a larger project.

Activity:

The student is introduced to haiku, which is 17-syllable Japanese poetry in its classic form with a 5–7–5 pattern, or five syllables in Line 1, seven in Line 2, and five in Line 3. Also introduced is the 14- to 17-syllable form. Haiku is the poetic form most like qualitative work because it takes its imagery from careful observations. Many complain that they are unable to write poetry, so I give them some of my own samples of haiku as well as other students' work. Amazingly, they seem to feel exhilarated after seeing that they are, indeed, able to do this. Recently, students took up writing poetry on their own about doing their dissertation projects. So, I expanded this exercise to include any form of poetry. The point is to capture in another idiom—poetry—something of what occurred in the study, either about the role of the researcher or the participants in the study. Here are some examples.

Poems Written While Writing the Dissertation
By Ruth Slotnick (2010)

Poem 1: Uncovering

Draped in nuances

where lines blur

suddenly become clear

revealed in utterances

where truth arises

the themes emerge

and transformation ensues

A balance is restored

life deepens; enriches as

possibilities unfold

This is a process

no number can reveal

what shadows conceal—

stirred out of dormancy

waiting to be told

This is our passion

Our destiny

Poem 2: When Analysis Eludes (on Writing the Dissertation)

Foggy place

Burry space

Clarity desired

Tired and mired

Not a number

Nuances asunder

Unable to unscramble

Barbs and bramble

Unpuzzled daily

Though today, not gaily

Start over, retract

Intuition out of whack

Emerge, emerge!!

Frustration, purge

Constructing lines

Weave symbol and sign

Poem 3: Analysis Breakthrough

Rummaging

Repeatedly

Revisiting

Rhythms

Revising

Realities

Reasoning

Representations

Reframing

Results

EXERCISE 5.9   Framed Photograph and Narrative Writing Exercise

Purpose:

These two exercises combine description and narrative writing. Describe a framed photograph of a familiar person. Then, pair up with someone and exchange photographs, and each of you describes the other person's selected framed photograph. Then, write about your partner's photo as though you were a reporter telling that person's story.

Problem:

1. Individuals think about and use time to describe the framed photograph they themselves bring to class.

2. Next, they pair off and exchange their own framed photographs with their partners. After receiving the partner's photograph, each describes the partner's photograph.

3. Partners stop to share and discuss their descriptions. Each group of two has two descriptions to review and find differences and similarities. This is designed to prepare learners for analysis of data exercises later.

4. Next, everyone stops to write about this as if they were reporters trying to tell a person's story. This writing entry is of course to be considered for the researcher reflective journal.

Time:

At least 15 minutes for each of the two descriptions; at least an additional 15 minutes for discussion; at least 30 minutes for writing and rewriting.

Activity:

This activity serves to sharpen awareness of the role of the researcher by working with a familiar artifact, a framed photograph of someone dear to the learner. At the same time, it extends and reviews observation expertise by moving to the description of an unfamiliar photograph. By pairing off, learners have the opportunity to practice communicating with another researcher about something in common, which is how to approach both descriptions and how to compare and contrast descriptions, thus establishing a collaborative habit. This is a precursor to the next round of exercises, which include practice in interviewing individuals and analyzing interview data. In addition, the writing exercise continues the habit of writing and, beyond that, writing for the researcher reflective journal.

Although, strictly speaking, this exercise forces the individual to observe and could fit in the observation cycle, this activity allows for a transition to interviewing and analysis of data and focuses on discovery of the role of the researcher and writing in the reflective journal.

Discussion:

Following the exercise, individuals are asked as a group to respond to the following questions:

1. How did you approach the first part of the activity? The second part?

2. What differences did you find in your own thinking as you approached each description?

3. What was the most challenging part of the exercise for you?

4. Would you read a sample of your description?

5. Could you write in your researcher reflective journals on this experience?

Rationale:

This exercise again is part of the practice of disciplined inquiry designed to make the researcher more reflective, establish and strengthen writing habits, and encourage collaboration. Reflection on the actual mechanics of approaching the description of the photographs is the first part of the activity. In the second part, individuals are forced to reflect on their own roles as researchers. By discussing this with other people, members see similarities and differences as part of the scope of disciplined inquiry. The habit of writing in the researcher reflective journal and contributing to the portfolio is enhanced. Creativity is the underlying theme in all these exercises. Creativity is a habit that is practiced and learned.

EXERCISE 5.10   Writing Timeline Exercise

Goal:

Prepare a writing timeline that reflects your entire history as a writer. Think of the very first thing you wrote. Was it a letter to Santa Claus? Was it your first paragraph? Was it a poem or verse? Begin charting your life as a writer. How did you develop as a writer? Did you evolve developmentally? Where are you today as a writer? What kind of writer are you today? After this, write at least two paragraphs describing yourself as a writer. Insert all this in your researcher reflective journal.

See this example of a timeline by Maggie Saturley (2013), followed by a narrative timeline by Jose Sanchez (2014).

My Writing Timeline
By Maggie Saturley

Part One: Three Years old—Letter to Santa

K–6th grade—Letters to friends

Part Two: Jr. High School—Short Stories

Sr. High School—Poetry and Short Stories

Part Three: College—Poetry and Speech Writing

Part Four: Adulthood and Graduate Studies

Poetry, Journaling, and Scholarly Articles

My three adjectives: *Playful, expressive, authentic*: That's the me you should see in my poetry.

My writing today: The type of writing that best identifies me today is poetry. I find a sense of personal freedom when I write poetry. Though I write well in other genres, I feel poetry best represents me as a writer. Unlike many forms of writing, there is no need for me to follow grammatical rules when I compose poetry. I am not constrained by the elements of style Strunk and White promote. Poetry encourages my creative nature. I enjoy combining unlike words into unique pairs to inspire imaginative writing; *lavender fog*, *serious moonlight*, and *kaleidoscope corners* are a few of my favorite phrases.

Poetry writing is fun for me. I'm like a child at FAO Swartz in New York City playing with words like new toys, rearranging and stacking them, running from display to display touching the furry softness of their existence. I share secrets with my poetic muse just as I did my childhood best friend. We toss hot potato words back and forth burning our fingertips when we hold on too long. I encourage rhythm and rhyme to join meter and cadence in a word dance with my pen. But there on the page, they do not remain. I speak my poetry to awaken the midnight silence of paper dreams.

My Writing Timeline History (Class Activity)

By Jose Sanchez

In my attempt to recall my earliest experiences with writing, a few salient memories come to mind. First of all, I remember learning to write my name. I recall that I was doing my best to write down my name correctly, painstakingly striving to perfectly form each letter. I vividly remember comparing my work with a classmate and even recall that my name was correctly written except for the letter *E* which included multiple horizontal lines instead of the standard three. After all, being able to write my name was my first written form of self-expression. Those four letters along with the remaining letters for my last name symbolically represented my name and ultimately me to some degree.

My next most salient memory brought me to my fifth-grade English class where, as a fervent reader of the Ann Landers advice column, I volunteered to be "Dear Anonymous" for our classroom newspaper. Although our readership consisted solely of our classmates and, of course, the teacher, I enjoyed the opportunity to give advice to my classmates. However, this experience also served to be my first experience with peer feedback, which resulted in harsh feedback from other students. As unusual as it may seem, I actually still vividly remember the question that was posed to Dear Anonymous and my response. A student needed advice on a poignant issue that many of us at that age likely experienced. The concerned student asked, "My little brother bothers me all the time and he gives me a headache, what should I do?" Drawing on my years of reading my favorite advice column, I mustered my best Ann Landers-like response, tersely advising the student to "swallow two aspirins, and call me in the morning." Once the issue was "published," a classmate ridiculed the wording of my response and suggested a better choice of words would have been "take two aspirins." Although seemingly trivial, this negative feedback made me much more self-conscious about publicly sharing my writing. Many years later, I ended checking the Web with the search terms "swallow two aspirins" and realized that although my choice of words was not incorrect after all.

I also recall one particular journal writing assignment in high school. I clearly remember the informal feedback I received from my English teacher in my freshman year in high school. She semi-jokingly commented on my paper by comparing it to that of another student's work. She mentioned that the other student always wrote about positive aspects of his life while my writing was the complete opposite, pointing out that I often wrote about my experiences in a negative light.

I remember that my experiences were really not that negative, but I did not enjoy sharing personal aspects of my life. Unusually, I enjoyed the teacher's feedback, as my attempts to be somewhat dark and negative in my writing were noticed and were therefore successful. I muddled through the rest of my high school years not placing much importance on any subject, and eventually graduated.

I joined the Air Force shortly after that and soon regretted my prior lackadaisical attitude towards high school. By the time I reached my new duty station in Sacramento, California, I realized that I needed to be more serious about my education. I enrolled in American River Community College and started off taking a U.S. history course, since I had always enjoyed the subject. I felt that everything was going well in the course, until I had to complete the final project—an essay about one of the topics we had discussed during the semester. I was rudely awakened when I received my final grade. The history teacher, who also taught English classes, explained that my low grade was due to my poorly written final paper. At first I was in denial, but shortly after that I decided to focus on my writing skills by taking the necessary classes at the community college. Although my college experience started off on the wrong track, I eventually got back on track as I gradually started to improve my academic writing.

At first, I was not very happy about my history teacher's criticism of my final written assignment, but I now realize how much of a favor he really did for me. He was brutally honest with his feedback and after a bit of introspection on my part, I realized that I would have to address my deficiencies in writing if I were to continue with my college education. After taking a few classes, I was transferred to Italy, where I immediately enrolled in a conversational Italian course, but other than the Italian course my college education was in a sort of "pause" mode. I was subsequently reassigned to multiple duty stations, by choice, and eventually had the opportunity to become an Airborne Linguist, which necessitated that I work a variety of duty shifts, making it even more difficult to continue my studies. I eventually enrolled in a class again, but could not remain in the class due to the demanding work schedule. Although my formal college education was in a virtual standstill, as an Airborne Linguist I had the opportunity to further develop my writing.

I was eventually selected to become an Airborne Analyst, which among other things, required that I write intelligence summaries. I completed a course that was designed to teach how to write intelligence reports. Essentially, this new form of writing that I was learning was very similar to journalistic news reports, with a focus on the essential elements of information (EEIs). The EEIs related to the "who, what, when, where and how" of the event that was being reported. After several years of this, I was transferred to the Defense Language Institute Foreign Language Center in Monterey, California, where I knew things would be different.

By the time I arrived in Monterey, I was approaching the end of my Air Force career. With respect to my college education, I had accumulated quite a few credits with all of the college and military courses I had completed over the years, but was still short of a few to earn my associates degree. Since my work schedule in Monterey would be more stable, I enrolled at the Monterey Peninsula College where I continued working towards completing my education. Eventually, I completed both an associate's and bachelor's degree. Later experiences included perfecting my writing skills during my master's degree studies program, which provided me with the opportunity to take a Spanish language creative writing class. During that time frame, I even had the opportunity to translate English language articles into Spanish for a newspaper in California.

Eventually, my master's program culminated in the presentation of my portfolio which included a position paper clearly delineating my philosophy towards teaching foreign languages. In light of what I have outlined above, as well as many other experiences I have not mentioned, I now consider myself to be an expressive writer. My favorite type of writing includes any narrative which allows me to inject my personal insight, which oftentimes could feature my sometimes overly dry sense of humor. Such writing does not always correspond to academic writing in school or in professional academic journals, although I personally think there is room to highlight certain points by using humor or perhaps irony to some degree. I believe that my best writing is when I feel free to express myself with no inhibitions or perceived restrictions. Three adjectives which would best describe me as a writer would include **expressive, creative,** and **descriptive.**

Recap of the Timeline

1. Began as a writer with writing my name

2. Wrote advice column in fifth grade

3. High school journal writing assignment with negative feedback

4. Community college history essay with negative feedback

5. Writing reports for the Air Force

6. Completed associate's, bachelor's, and master's degrees

7. Translated English into Spanish articles for a newspaper in California

8. Currently a narrative writer: expressive, creative, and descriptive working on my doctorate in second language acquisition.

Discussion:

Following the exercise, individuals are asked as a group to respond to the following questions:

1. How did you approach the first part of the activity? The second part?

2. What differences did you find in your own thinking as you approached each description?

3. What was the most challenging part of the exercise for you?

4. Would you read a sample of your description?

5. Could you write in your researcher reflective journals on this experience?

Rationale:

This exercise again is part of the practice of disciplined inquiry designed to make the researcher more reflective, establish and strengthen writing habits, and encourage collaboration. Reflection on the recollection of the points in life which identify you as a writer, sparks a new awareness in the researcher. In the second part, finding three adjectives to describe oneself solely as a writer, extends awareness and consciousness of the importance of writing in qualitative research projects. By discussing this with peers, members see similarities and differences as part of the scope of disciplined inquiry. The habit of writing in the researcher reflective journal and contributing to the portfolio is enhanced. Creativity is the underlying theme in all these exercises. Creativity is a habit that is practiced and learned.

CHAPTER SUMMARY

Because the researcher is the research instrument in a qualitative research project and that creativity, intuition, and compassion are part of the role of the qualitative researcher, these exercises have been designed to sharpen one's creative habit and awareness of the role of the researcher. Many writers throughout history have described creativity and intuition and here I traced this to the 17th-century text, *The Mustard Seed Garden Manual of Painting,* which was part of a larger work, *The Tao of Painting,* by Lu Ch'ai. Nearly everything written by the Chinese master painters was aimed not just at the technique of painting but also at the painter's spiritual resources in order to express the spirit, or *chi,* the breath of Tao. The chi is looked upon as an underlying harmony. Similarly in Zen philosophy, the practitioner goes inward to find those creative spaces to develop an awareness of the universe. So too in dance, the spirit of the dance must emerge as part of movement. These exercises are akin to the chi meaning of painting, Zen inwardness to develop compassion and serenity, and the spirit of the dancer's movement. In order to stretch, the qualitative researcher must be able to articulate creativity and the role of the researcher as the underlying harmony or spirit of the study. The qualitative researcher is always dealing with lived experience and must be awake to and for that experience. By acknowledging and articulating the complexity of need for creativity, defining the role of the researcher, and keeping a reflective journal, we are now able to begin the next cycle of exercises in the next series, the analysis cycle.

SUGGESTED RESOURCES

Berg, B. L. (2007). *Qualitative research methods for the social sciences* (6th ed.). Boston, MA: Allyn & Bacon.

Chuan, C. T. Y. H. (1963). *The mustard seed garden manual of painting.* Princeton, NJ: Princeton University Press.

Dali, S. (1986). *The secret life of Salvador Dali.* Wantagh, NY: Geneva Graphics for Dasa Edicions.

Edwards, B. (1979). *Drawing on the right side of the brain.* Los Angeles, CA: J. P. Tarcher.

Ellis, E. R. (1995). *A diary of the century: Tales from America's greatest diarist.* New York, NY: Kodansha International.

Gelb, M. J. (1998). *How to think like Leonardo da Vinci: Seven steps to genius every day.* New York, NY: Dell.

Goldberg, N. (2005). *Writing down the bones: Freeing the writer within.* Boston, MA: Shambala.

Hemingway, E. (1995). *The snows of Kilimanjaro.* New York, NY: Scribner.

Janesick, V. J. (2001). Intuition and creativity: A pas de deux for the qualitative researcher. *Qualitative Inquiry, 7*(5), 531–540.

Kohler Reissman, C. (2008). *Narrative methods for the human sciences.* Thousand Oaks, CA: Sage.

Leavy, P. (2015). *Method meets art: Method meets art* (2nd ed.). New York, NY: Guilford Press.

Mallon, T. (1995). *A book of one's own: People and their diaries.* St. Paul, MN: Hungry Mind Press.

Noddings, N., & Shore, P. J. (1984). *Awakening the inner eye: Intuition in education.* New York, NY: Teachers College Press.

Osho. (1999). *Creativity: Unleashing the forces within.* New York, NY: St. Martin's Press.

Progoff, I. (1992). *At a journal workshop: Writing to access the power of the unconscious and evoke creative ability.* New York, NY: J. P. Tarcher.

Rainer, T. (1978). *The new diary.* Los Angeles, CA: J. P. Tarcher.

Richardson, L. (1995). Writing-stories: Co-authoring "The Sea Monster," a writing story. *Qualitative Inquiry, 1*(2), 189–220.

Stuhlman, G. (Ed.). (1976). *The diary of Anaïs Nin, 1955–1966.* New York, NY: Harcourt Brace Jovanovich.

Tharp, T. (2003). *The creative habit: Learn it and use it for life.* New York, NY: Simon & Schuster.

6

The Analysis Habit

Logic can take us from A to B. Imagination can take us everywhere.

—Albert Einstein

Returning to the dance metaphor, if these exercises represent the stretching in a dance class, analysis of data and interpretation and representation of data, and writing the narrative represent the floor exercises and performance stages of dance. After completing the series of exercises in observation, interviews, and the role of the researcher, learners have stretched a bit. They stretch even further with exercises to develop the creative habit. They've had a taste of some aspects of data analysis through study of interview transcripts and field notes. Working either alone or in groups, learners have practiced developing categories from the data, looking for points of tension and conflict, and in general, focusing on making sense of the data over the time period of a semester of study. As Harry F. Wolcott in *The Art of Fieldwork* (1995) pointed out, there is a difference between analysis and interpretation. In order for prospective researchers to realize their interpretation skills, it is important to think about the use of intuition in research just as it is used in choreography, or yoga or meditation. In dance, the critique after the end of a performance is like our analysis of the data. Likewise in yoga, feedback from the yoga teacher enables us to understand our bodies, mind, and self. The meditation teacher relies on you the student of meditation to keep track of your self-knowledge in the meditation journal.

The role of the qualitative researcher in research projects is often determined by the researcher's stance and intent. Similarly, choreographers create dances with the knowledge of where they fit in the history of dance. In addition, the roles of the researcher, like the dancer and choreographer, and the Zen practitioner and yogi, are ones where our history makes us aware and alive. We seek to be mindful, in order to understand ourselves and the social world. In other words, we embrace complications, surprises, chaos, and are open to serendipity. We acknowledge impermanence, non-self, and nirvana. At the same time, as researchers, we work within the frame of a mindful plan of inquiry, adhere to the high standards of qualitative inquiry, and look for ways to complement and extend the description and explanation of the social worlds we study and contribute to our various disciplines. Qualitative researchers do not accept the misconception that more methods mean a better or richer analysis. Rather, the rationale for using selected methods is what counts. The qualitative researcher wants to tell a story in the best possible configuration.

THE QUALITATIVE RESEARCHER AS ● CONTEMPLATIVE AND MINDFUL

The qualitative researcher is like the person who meditates. If you take a Zen view of the importance of reflection and quietude, you begin to open up to endless possibilities in the qualitative research project. In today's world, it is easy to spot the student who has a hard time disengaging from digital devices. Where is the solitude and stillness in this world? When appropriate in research projects, the qualitative researcher relies on many possible sources of data and uses a variety of methods in the process, including but not limited to observation, participant observation, interviews, documents, the researcher's personal reflections, and so on. From the conceptualization of the research project to its completion, the researcher needs to continually reflect and redirect processes and practices just like someone perfecting their yoga and meditation practice. It is usually the case that the qualitative researcher wants to understand the situation under study and must decide if the stance is taken from the inside or outside, as participant or observer, or as some combination with varying degrees of both, and whether or not the researcher will approach the project holistically. Like the yogi, the qualitative researcher must identify a point of view. For example, I study hatha yoga and Zen meditation practices. I work to integrate mindfulness into my research practice. I participate in thought and action. The qualitative researcher uses primary sources either as an insider and participant or as an outsider. In any event, each of us has to declare and describe our points of view, our theoretical frames, and our beliefs about the topic we are researching. Most often, this is done in the description of the role of the researcher. To truly know and describe your role, a Zen-like approach may come in handy. By working for total awareness of the impermanence, the non-self aspects of research, and nirvana, in knowing ourselves, we can reach a solid description of our role. Qualitative researchers early on in the narrative of the project most often put forth a thick description of their role as the researcher. This should include the researcher's beliefs about the content of the study, the entire process of the study including number and length of interviews, and over what period of time. Finally, if any ethical issues arise in the study, these should be described.

● CHECKPOINTS FOR DATA ANALYSIS, REPORTING, AND INTERPRETATION

1. **Look for empirical assertions** supported by the data. Look at what the participants said in the transcripts to find those meaning units.

2. **Use narrative vignettes and exact quotations from participants** to support your assertions. In this case, more is more. Convince your reader of your argument with evidence from transcripts, observations, reflective journals, and any other documentary evidence.

3. **Scan all other reports, documents, letters, journal entries, demographic data**, and so on. Use direct references. Connect these to your analysis and interpretation. In this work, the data need to be accessed and shown to your readers. To convince your reader of the meaning and interpretation of your study, use data from multiple sources such as your interview transcript, your field notes, your journal, the participants writing, and site documents.

4. **Include interpretive commentary** related to the data because data simply do not speak for themselves. In other words, lead your reader to your themes.

5. **Include a theoretical discussion**, and relate your data to the theory that guided the study. Give your readers a hint of what will be included in your model of what occurred in the study.

6. **Situate yourself in the study**, describe fully your role as a researcher, and describe the entire context of the study. This entails a thorough description of your values and beliefs about the study, your theoretical frame for the study and exactly what techniques were used. Describe how many interviews, over what time period, the length of interviews, and how the interviews were transcribed. Next, set the context for the study. Describe the setting and persons involved. Use demographic statistics to round out your description when needed. For example, if you are studying a music teacher, describe her school setting within the context of her district and also situate specific problems music teachers face.

7. **State clearly any and all ethical issues** that arose in the study. What these checkpoints do is allow your reader to experience the study and its social context and setting.

8. **Have a peer reviewer, outside reader, or auditor review your transcripts** and look at your preliminary and final categories. To verify this, design a simple form for your peer reviewer stating that the person reviewed transcripts, notes, and the final write-up of the research and that there is a fit with the data. (See Appendix K.)

9. **Write in your researcher reflective journal** all the thoughts you can possibly write about regarding your beautiful data.

10. **Work for saturation and sustainability of your data**. This means that you get to your goal in the project by saturating in the interview data, the relevant documents, your research reflective journal, and any other artifacts in the study, like photographs, for example. You will know the moment you get to your goal. There is no formula for that.

The range of evidence should be used to support your assertions and view the work in progress throughout the entire history of the inquiry. A good description of what you learned from your pilot study is always a good place to start the description of the project. See this example of a class project by Lisa Piazza who conducted a life history of a librarian for a class project. Here she introduces the context of the study.

A Life Portrait: One Research Librarian's Métier as a Call to Service (Edited)

By Lisa Piazza

And so I love this university. . . . I've loved it because it has given me the opportunity to really serve. I'm a very service-oriented person. I was raised Catholic and um we were taught to give back . . . and I never wanted a profession where I felt compromised ethically and being a librarian . . . I've always felt through librarianship, I serve not only students but the community and the larger world.

—Canny (pseudonym), September 15, 2014

Introduction: Setting the Stage

The American Library Association (ALA) enumerates eleven core values of librarianship on its website (www.ala.org) including access, confidentiality/privacy, democracy, diversity, education and lifelong learning, intellectual freedom, preservation, the public good, professionalism, social responsibility, and service. While the individual selected for this interview project eloquently exemplifies all of these values in her dual roles as both an academic research librarian and library administrator, it is the value of service that underscores her *raison d'*être, particularly in the context of her work.

I first met Canny (a pseudonym) approximately three years ago when I began working as an administrator in the Office for Undergraduate Research (OUR), located on the second floor of the library. As I remember it, on my first day at work Canny came into my office to formally introduce herself and to welcome me to the library. We immediately connected as we both share a great deal of passion and excitement for our work, and work best in a collaborative environment. Through the years, Canny and I have worked on numerous projects to support student success and Canny has contributed her time (and money) to OUR projects including the endowment of a scholarship associated with the OUR annual research colloquium. Thus, when I first discovered that one of the assignments for this course would be an interview project, Canny immediately came to mind. I selected Canny for this interview because I wanted to learn more about her professional trajectory and how she successfully manages all of the heavy demands her work requires. I also admire the values of academic librarianship and wanted to learn more about how these values manifest in the day-to-day work of a librarian. Thus, I came into this project with a strong desire to capture the many elements that constitute Canny's work situation. During the course of this examination, I have discovered a great deal about Canny as an individual and as a professional and learning about her work has in turn taught me much about myself as a novice qualitative researcher.

Canny has been employed with the university since 2005. In her position, she serves the role of both academic research librarian and library administrator. Her role as a librarian involves among many other things teaching, training, faculty and patron support, and the development of library programming. As an administrator, she oversees all academic services including units such as interlibrary loan, special and digital collections, and the new digital media space. She manages staff in all of these areas and she also directly manages approximately 60% of the faculty librarians. In addition to management duties, Canny sits on numerous committees on behalf of the library and develops key library programming including the campus Common Reading program. As this brief overview of Canny's job duties indicates, the scope of her responsibilities is very broad and covers a variety of library functions.

My Position as a Qualitative Researcher: The Frameworks That Guide This Study

As a qualitative researcher I am thoroughly aware of the philosophical assumptions that guide the qualitative enterprise. I have reflected on each of the five assumptions outlined by John W. Creswell in *Qualitative Inquiry and Research Design: Choosing Among Five Approaches* (2007), and below, I present a brief overview of these assumptions in order to establish my position in relation to the research project. I hold the opinion that individuals subscribe to many "ways of being." Reality is highly subjective and varied and it is the responsibility of the researcher to illuminate the varied perspectives of participants in order to give voice

(Continued)

(Continued)

to their stories. In this project, I rely heavily on the words and ideas of the participant, and I use her words as much as possible to tell "her" story. From an epistemological perspective, I approached this research project as a reciprocal endeavor in the hopes that I would learn from Canny and Canny would perhaps learn from me. To facilitate this reciprocity, I communicated with Canny often throughout the process about the aims of the project, the interview questions, and other details. I wanted to make certain that Canny understood that I was genuinely interested in her story and not simply going through the motions of completing a required course assignment. Building a relationship of trust with Canny was critical to the project and ethically appropriate. I also acknowledge that research (mirroring circumstances in life) carries a certain degree of biases and value judgments. Thus, I assert that I am coming to this project from a particular position, one that involves my various statuses as a student, woman, and education professional. I understand that what I observe and "do" as a researcher is influenced by who I am and my epistemological and ontological beliefs. It is my responsibility as the researcher to fully disclose and work to transform possible biases into learning opportunities. Regarding the rhetorical assumption, as I continue to grow as a qualitative researcher, I aim to improve and nurture my unique writing style. Through this narrative I endeavor to paint a portrait of Canny that is both engaging and informative and one that respects Canny's story and what she can teach us about ourselves. Lastly, through a comprehensive discussion of the research design and methods, I attempt to clearly explicate and illustrate the "process" of research.

In addition to particular assumptions I hold as a researcher, I also possess a particular worldview that informs my research. I believe that *reality is constructed through local human interaction* (Jones, Torres, & Arminio, 2006, p. 5). Moreover, I believe that this interaction engenders learning and understanding, and provides a certain amount of agency with respect to the participant. However, I also acknowledge that the construction of meaning occurs in a social, historical and cultural context. For this project, my primary aim was to understand the participant as fully as possible, in her own words. More specifically, I sought to understand what (and how) her work "means" to her. I sought to make connections between the various views, opinions, and beliefs she shared with me during our conversations, and I sought to understand the context of her views. Finally, through the course of the research process, a "pattern of meanings" emerged, which helped me to construct, interpret and "re-story" Canny's narrative.

Lisa goes on to describe her methods used in the study, including interviews, notes following the interviews, keeping a researcher reflective journal and various site documents. She lists here the interview protocols.

The following protocols were used for each interview:

Interview Protocol A

1. What does your work mean to you?

2. Talk about a typical day at work. What does it look like?

3. Tell me what you like about your job.

4. Tell me what you dislike about your job.

5. Where do you see yourself in 5 to 10 years?

Interview Protocol B

1. At several points during the first interview, you mentioned that you do not have time to "go deep" in your position as an administrator. Can you please describe what you mean by this and also explain how the work environment would be different if you did have time to "go deep"? During the first interview you mentioned that you had several excellent mentors early in your career, one of whom died of AIDS. Can you talk about what each of these individuals taught you about librarianship?

2. Previously, you discussed the idea of dysfunctional libraries. You also described being "poorly managed" within these dysfunctional environments. Can you describe how

(Continued)

(Continued)

    you were treated as a librarian in these environments and provide examples of how you were poorly managed?

3. How did this experience shape who you are as a librarian and administrator?

4. During the last interview, you described how you were charged with moving the reference section to make room for students and student services and how the librarians resented this move. Can you explain how you managed this as an administrator and what you learned from this episode?

5. What is your recommendation for young librarians entering the profession? How do you suggest they balance all of the challenges of their work?

6. If you had to choose an image to stand for your work, what would it be?

7. If you had to choose a color that represents your work, what would it be?

If Time Permits, Additional Back-Up Questions

1. Can you provide additional information about the work you did in Mexico and the work you did in collaboration with Mexican librarians in the United States?

2. How has working with library professionals in other countries and from other nationalities shaped who you are as a librarian and administrator?

Data Analysis

My approach to the data analysis process represents a combination of techniques and methods put forth by Creswell (2007), Valerie Janesick (2004), Herbert J. Rubin and Irene S. Rubin (2005), and Johnny Saldaña (2013). However, I was determined to discover my own personal analysis process, and I describe my individual process and approach in further detail below. I began the data analysis process with what Saldaña (2013) refers to as *decoding* the data, or analyzing and reflecting on the data to determine meaning. I also utilized the process of *encoding* the data, which involved coding and labeling the text (Saldana, 2013). Further, my initial coding involved a combination of descriptive codes, in which I attempted to use one word to describe a particular passage, and I also used In Vivo coding, the method of extracting certain words used by the participant. To begin the final analysis process I read through each transcript twice. The goal of the first reading was to become familiar with the participant's story. During the first reading, I also attempted to locate patterns in the data. For instance, as I read through the transcripts for the first time, I noticed that certain words and phrases emerged from the data and were repeated by the participant in both interviews. Rubin and Rubin (2005) refer to this phase as the *recognition* phase of the analysis. As I read through the transcripts for a second time, I highlighted certain data, sections, and words that began to form patterns and the highlighted data represented the initial emergence of the participant's narrative. Next, I began to code the data.

Lisa coded the data by sifting through the written transcripts and notes and finding key phrases that popped out and assigning a word for that code, then a family of codes as a category and then themes from the data. She goes on to explain:

I repeated this process with the data from interview two. As I completed the second phase of the analysis process, I began to refine the codes (Rubin & Rubin, 2005) in order to identify emerging themes. A careful analysis of the data revealed three themes, including work as service, identity, and life. These themes appear in Figure 6.1.

In addition to the themes, as I analyzed the data and the participant's story began to "emerge," I observed three epiphanies in Canny's story. Briefly, Creswell (2007) describes epiphanies as *turning points* in the participant's story, which are sometimes repeated in this process with the data from interview two. As I completed the second phase of the analysis process, I began to refine the codes (Rubin & Rubin, 2005) in order to identify emerging themes. A careful analysis of the data revealed three themes, including work as service, identity and life. These themes appear below.

(Continued)

(Continued)

Figure 6.1 Themes in the Librarian Study

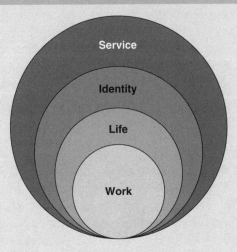

The three epiphanies that emerged include Canny's early training and the influence of key mentors and how her early career experiences shaped her current role as both an academic librarian and administrator; her experience with dysfunctional libraries and subsequent move to Florida to "escape" these environments; and how she sees her current position as the "right fit" for her skill set and values. Each of these moments represent turning points in Canny's personal life and professional trajectory. For example, Canny's values as an individual and a professional have been shaped and influenced by her mentors. In addition, her experience in dysfunctional libraries forced her to quit the profession for a time and reassess her life and career. Finally, Canny views her position at USF as the "right fit." For her, USF is like "home," she is comfortable in her position and passionate about the work she is doing as both an academic librarian and administrator. The three epiphanies described here are illustrated in Figure 6.2.

Figure 6.2 Three Epiphanies

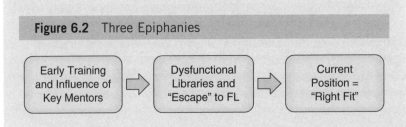

Finally, as part of the data analysis process, as I listened to the audio recordings of each transcript, and later as I began to code the data, I recorded key terms that emerged from the interviews. I created a word cloud from this list to visualize the terms and help identify additional connections and patterns. Figure 6.3 illustrates many of the terms Canny used to describe what work means to her.

Figure 6.3   Word Cloud of Initial Codes

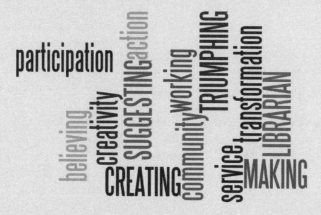

I would like to discuss one last point regarding my analysis process. As mentioned previously, I believe that qualitative inquiry, specifically narrative inquiry, involves the notion of asymmetry, or the ability to discover in the data what Janesick (2004) describes as the points of conflict, tensions, or contradictions. Thus, as I analyzed the data, I attempted to observe certain anomalies that could provide the basis for rich, thick description or unexpected moments. A primary instance of asymmetry in this project involved Canny's description of her experience in dysfunctional libraries. Though we did not spend a great deal of time discussing this point during the first interview, after the interview, as I listened to the audio recording and read the transcript this detail became increasingly intriguing to me and I had the intuition that further exploration of this detail during interview two might help me to understand Canny's story and yield additional breadth and depth in the final narrative. In fact, as will be revealed below, this detail and experience was critical to Canny's trajectory and as she explained in interview two, this negative experience influenced her in various ways both in terms

(Continued)

(Continued)

of her personal growth and values system and her professional development.

A Portrait of Canny: On a Train in Guatemala

> I was on a train in Guatemala when I decided to look at librarianship.
>
> —Canny, September 15, 2014

Canny's story involves three key narrative "moments" that build a portrait of her work–life trajectory and correspond to the three epiphanies described above. The three moments include Canny's early training and the influence of key mentors and how her early career experiences shaped her current role as both an academic librarian and administrator; her experience with dysfunctional libraries and subsequent move to Florida to "escape" dysfunctional library environments; and how she sees her current position as the "right fit" for her skill set and values.

Canny's story begins on a train in Guatemala. During the first interview, Canny explained that following the completion of her undergraduate degree in international studies, she was undecided regarding her future profession. She explained

> I'm kind of the old school you know, my life is my job, yeah, it's that kind of thing . . . I was at a turning point and I was trying to decide what I wanted to do and I was on a train in Guatemala when I decided to look at librarianship. I was um, I was an international studies major, I learned Spanish. I was a double major and I didn't . . . I had a lot of problems working with the government because I didn't want to toe the government line . . . I was a radical left-wing student . . . But I loved to serve and so I was on a train in Guatemala and these two librarians were on there and they asked me they said well what are you going to do? And I said, well, I didn't know and I was thinking maybe a law degree . . . and they said well have you ever thought of being a librarian, and I was like oh I don't want to shelve books because you

know I had done that as a student, and they were like we're administrators we don't shelve books. And they said "You should check into it" and it stuck in my head and I thought to myself if I can go get a librarian degree and I can be in academia and I could serve all these people and I don't have to teach and I can serve students and serve these faculty.

It was at this point in her life, the transition from undergraduate to graduate school, and one that marks the first major "epiphany" identified in this study that Canny's conception of work began to emerge as a tripartite idea of work as intimately intertwined with life, identity, and service. As she explained, she was initially trained in corporate librarianship but decided early on that she did not want to remain in that field. As she indicated, *I realized that I just didn't want to work for clients . . . and there really wasn't enough teaching in it.* During the second interview, Canny revealed additional details regarding her early training in librarianship and three key individuals (mentors) who shaped her beliefs about the values of librarianship (and life) and the type of library administrator she endeavored to become. From Ben W., she learned how a talented administrator has the potential to "fix" a broken library and raise up staff to achieve their potential. Ben also introduced her to the concept of *servant leadership*.

Lisa then explains the various epiphanies supported by the lengthy extracts from the interview transcripts and adds a follow-up question:

As a follow up to this discussion, I asked Canny to share three words that describe who she is as a librarian and three words that define her as an administrator. Canny shared the following with me:

Canny: I think I am a **direct communicator**; I don't . . . I try not to sit on things; I try not to just hush up you know but I try to be direct in my communication, um, I try to be **forward thinking**, and I try to **create a supportive environment** for everyone's work.

LMP: And then as a librarian?

(Continued)

(Continued)

Canny: As a librarian I like to, I like to think of myself as **tenacious**, in terms of finding information. I think, um, I like to, I like to see, um, when I work with students, I like to **work holistically** in terms of understanding where they, what their ultimate goals are—you know so I can kind of feed into that instead of just this one piece of it, um, and also as a librarian I think I like, um, gosh, um, . . . (long pause) (thinks out loud in a low voice) let's see, tenacious, holistic in terms of my support, um, and, um, (another long pause) and actually, yeah, and then just **working with the students to see where they are, you know**. It doesn't, if I suggest a course of action or a set of resources or whatever and if that really doesn't work for where they are, it's not gonna work at all.

Clearly, the ways in which Canny conceptualizes her roles as a librarian and an administrator stand in sharp contrast to the characteristics she described in relation to the environment of dysfunctional libraries. As Canny explained to me, she has worked hard to distance herself from the petty selfishness that permeates dysfunctional environments.

I Went Into the Profession of Librarianship to Serve

The prominent theme that runs through Canny's story of work is the notion of service. As aforementioned, Canny's work centers on three key themes: work as a part of her identity, work as a prominent component of her life, and work as service to others. Thus, Canny's work is intimately entwined with who she is as an individual. In other words, for Canny, there is no separation between life and work, one serves the other and is supplemented and supported by the other. The strongest component of this tripartite idea is the element of service. For Canny, service is intimately linked to identity and intertwined with her life. When asked the question, *What does your work mean to you?* during the first interview, Canny responded without hesitation:

I can start out by saying it [work] is a central, central part of my life. It's a central part of my identity, as a person. It's how I feel like I give to the world. Um, my life and my energy has been focused on my career, and um, my work here, this is the first really place I have felt—I've worked here since 2005— where I felt like this is my home . . . and so I love this university . . . I've loved it because it's given me the opportunity to really serve.

In addition, during the first interview, Canny provided numerous examples of how her work as both a librarian and an administrator centers on a service-oriented mindset and the notion that her work is intimately connected to her identity and to her life.

Lisa goes on with several direct quotations pertaining to service as a major overriding finding and them and then explains her role.

My Role as the Researcher

Janesick (2011) uses the metaphor of dance to explore the ways in which intuition and creativity figure prominently in a researcher's conception of their "role" in the research enterprise. As a trained art historian and artist, I wholeheartedly embrace her argument. I strongly believe that good qualitative research is only possible if one is willing to explore and exploit one's creativity and intuition. In my view, the creative use of words to generate thick, rich narrative represent the "currency" of good qualitative research. Moreover, the ability to assemble words into a convincing and engaging narrative is an artistic one and one that requires the abandonment of symmetry, formulas, or dictated prescriptions. On the contrary, good qualitative research invites asymmetry, and the ability to "see" and observe in creative, nonformulaic ways. It likewise involves the ability to utilize one's intuition to pursue fruitful lines of inquiry.

I found that the research process required me to problem solve as I worked through the various phases of the research activity. For example, the transcription of both interviews totaled over 50 pages. How would I decide where to begin the analysis process? What data would I include in the final report? What data would be omitted? Clearly, such questions involve intuition and creativity and more importantly the ability to "work the problem" and

(Continued)

(Continued)

adapt as necessary. Working through these questions also helped me learn about who I am as a qualitative researcher and the type of researcher I aspire to become in the future. For instance, during the course of this assignment, I learned that my background and training in the arts have provided a good foundation for becoming a good qualitative "storyteller" in the future; however, I am aware that my ability to improve is contingent on my willingness to write often and to become more reflective about my process. I strongly believe that practicing these skills will allow me to exploit my creative and intuitive potential in the future.

Finally, as the research "instrument," I am aware that the role of the researcher is both complex and thoroughly rewarding. I hold the opinion that my role as a researcher is one that must be reciprocal in relation to the participant. While it is my responsibility to present a compelling narrative about the participant it is equally if not more important to ensure that the story is accurate and respects the participant's views and story. It is also important that the participant is fully involved in the research process, and that she understands that the qualitative research process is designed to give "voice" to her story rather than reduce her to an aggregate group. This is perhaps the most important lesson I have learned during the course of this project.

Personal Reflection on Research Process

After each interview, I spent several hours in quiet contemplation reflecting on the experience, my performance during each session, and I recorded possible strategies to improve my technique and style. The text below includes excerpts from my reflections after each interview. The first reflection focuses on my experience conducting my first qualitative interview. The second reflection centers on my perceived faults as a research instrument, and specific skills and other items that I feel require additional development. Each reflection includes a surprise detail or event that emerged from the interview sessions and an assessment of how I handled each.

Reflections on Interview One

I am writing this reflection several hours after the interview. The primary goal of this reflection is to carefully review and consider the details of today's interview, what I learned and what I need to improve regarding my interview skills. The participant was on time and enthusiastic about sharing her story. The interview took place at my place of work in an empty office. Before the interview, I made sure to tidy up the space and clean the table and chairs to make the sparse room as welcoming and comfortable as possible. This was a good spot for the interview as it was quiet and familiar to both of us. After a brief discussion about how busy we both are at the moment, she said that she had just come from a very boring financial meeting and was happy to get out of it. I thanked her for agreeing to be interviewed and explained that I would be using three different recording devices to record the interview. I also explained the assignment and the reasons why I selected her to participate in the research project. I explained the consent process.

Before the interview, I was nervous and unsure about how I would handle the interview, and if I would ask the right follow up questions; however, as we started the discussion I felt very comfortable and intuitively followed up on specific points I thought could benefit from further elaboration. I was very conscious about interrupting the participant during her responses and I wanted to be sure not to lead the conversation where I wanted it to go but where she wanted it to go. I must admit that I was very nervous about the equipment during the entire interview. I checked and double-checked the equipment the day before the interview, the morning of the interview, and an hour before the interview (my obsessive personality at work). In any case, I felt that at certain times during the interview, I was much too preoccupied with looking at the recorders.

After I asked my last question today, I asked the participant if there was anything else she wanted to add. These final moments were some of the most intriguing parts of the interview. I shall return to the ideas and themes shared during these moments in interview two. One final reflection, and this is of a more personal nature. I am not sure I handled this correctly, but it was an awkward moment and caught me off guard I suppose. The last question, *Where do you see yourself in 5 to 10 years?* was awkward for the participant because she is battling illness at the moment and might not be around in 5 or 10 years. While I was aware that she was having health issues, I did not know the severity and gravity of

(Continued)

(Continued)

the situation. I have not listened to the audio yet but after the interview, I had the sense that she may have wanted to share this part of her story with me. I did not realize this in the moment, but now that I am reflecting on that part of the interview, I have a sense that this was perhaps the case. The lesson here: I need to hone my listening skills. I also need to do a better job with reading the emotions and feelings of the participant.

Lisa then goes on to reflect on the next interview and closes with the following:

Concluding Thoughts

People say, "Oh, what did you do with a library career ? . . . You are stuck in a library." I say no. I've worked in other countries, I've worked for corporate, I've worked for universities, I've lived in three states . . . I make really good money and I love what I do, you know, and so it's just great!

—Canny, September 15, 2014.

Qualitative research is not simply learning about a topic, but also learning what is important to those being studied.

—Rubin and Rubin

When I first read this statement by Rubin and Rubin (2005) before engaging in this research project, I was inspired by the comment but did not completely grasp the full "meaning" of the passage. After completing my first qualitative research project, I now comprehend the significance and sentiment of these words. The participants with whom we interact through the research process are not "topics," but rather, they are individuals with feelings, opinions, and emotions. One cannot really understand this until one has engaged in the qualitative research process. Through the research process, participants unselfishly share their stories, both the good and the bad bits, so that we can learn from their stories and hopefully make a contribution to the field in our own small way. Thus, qualitative research is about trust and relationship building. Moreover, it is about understanding and agency, and it is about reciprocity and learning. Canny has taught me what it means to have passion in life regardless of your profession and to be committed to others and to serve with compassion

However, perhaps the most valuable lesson I have learned as a result of this research project is that I am a committed qualitative researcher. The way I think, the way I process information, and the way I value the words and stories of individuals over a preference for formulas and statistics has helped me realize the kind of researcher I endeavor to become in the future. While I have a long way to go and lots of areas in which to improve, this project has allowed me to discover my passion and this has been an extraordinary and rewarding journey indeed.

VARIOUS APPROACHES TO ANALYSIS AND INTERPRETATION OF DATA

To start your analysis process it is a good idea to return to your purpose of the study, your questions that guide the study, your theoretical frame that guides your study, and of course the literature on qualitative research methods which inspired you in the first place. Return to your transcripts over and over again (see Appendix L). Now turn your attention to these four approaches to data analysis from Rubin and Rubin (2005, 2013), Saldaña (2013), Elizabeth Visedo (2013), and Gary Padgett (2012). They illustrate how individual researchers eventually create their approach to data analysis and at the same time share basic principles.

Example: Rubin & Rubin (2005, 2013)
Moving Toward Data Analysis

Action	Purpose
Recognize:	Find the concepts, topics, and words in the interviews or documents.
Examine:	Clarify what is meant by these concepts topics, and words. Synthesize in order to form a narrative.

(Continued)

(Continued)

Action	Purpose
Code or Name:	Find a label or signifier to designate these concepts, topics, and words. Then rename families of the concepts and topics.
Sort:	Group them once again and sift through them to find nuance and overall unity.
Synthesize:	Put the concepts, topics, and identifiers into themes and connect these to your research questions.

Another solid approach to making sense of data is that of Saldaña (2013) who advises the researcher to do an initial set of codes, look for families of codes which then become categories, and look for families of categories which then become themes. He goes further and suggests making theoretical statements from those themes as part of theory building. This is in a nutshell the basic thematic analysis most of us have used. And another fine example is Visedo's (2013) explanation of her data analysis process. She studied biliteracy of Spanish/English speakers and their personal histories in education. She devised this system for her study after combining both Rubin and Rubin, and Saldaña's principles. She added the frame of praxis to add the meaning layer to her analysis.

Data Collection:	Autobiographies online through blogs, e-journals, artifacts, electronic portfolios, and interviews online
Analysis:	Total immersion in the data, meticulous reading of texts; organizing data into emerging patterns; data coding by highlighting, color coding, and comments; audits by critical friend; finding patterns, identifying themes
Triangulation:	Member checks, negative theme analysis, final themes
Praxis:	Find the meaning in the study.

Another way to look at data analysis is Padgett's (2012) analysis of content in American history textbooks regarding the American Indian. He used the five values configured below to analyze the five most often-used history textbooks in high schools in Hillsborough County, Florida, in terms of their depiction of American Indians. The

Five Values were developed in conjunction with American Indians and represent what were identified as common American Indian values. As such, the data is analyzed and organized from an indigenous perspective (see Figure 6.4).

Figure 6.4 Visual Schema of Data Analysis and Interpretation

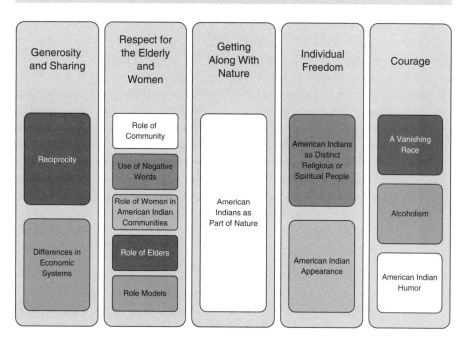

In each of these four approaches to data analysis and interpretation, we find common processes. These include the following:

Find Your Codes, Categories, and Themes

One important thing to recall is that there is no one way or no one formula to do qualitative analysis. These four examples of approaches to analysis are helpful for any qualitative researcher. The Visedo (2013) example is timely since she used technology throughout the study and used Skype interviewing as a key data collection technique. She downloaded and transcribed the interviews with the updated software available. Padgett (2012) used the well-known techniques of an existing model, the Five Values, to guide his analysis and interpretation of the data through Rubin and Rubin's (2011) suggestions for approaching analysis. These three are congruent with Saldaña's (2009) approach to data analysis. Once you immerse yourself in the data and find your focus, finding codes, categories, and themes emerge organically. Put time into this and it gets you to interpretation.

Interpret Your Study

You already have immersed yourself in the content knowledge and research in your discipline. So too, you have immersed yourself in the content area of qualitative research, conducted a pilot study, and are ready to begin making sense of your data in all its forms. In effect, you see ordinary things in a new and extraordinary way. Thus, once you decide on which approach to analysis suits your study, then following the standard checks and balances in the method is a wise way to proceed. Interpreting the data after a presentation of major and minor categories of the findings is a chief responsibility of the researcher. Because qualitative work relies on grounding the theory in the data, researchers usually develop a model of what occurred in the study. This model may be represented in visual terms with drawings and graphs or in verbal terms as you have just read in the Piazza study. Now see this example of Slotnick's thought process as she reflects on how to approach analysis.

Example of Thinking Through an Analysis and Interpretation

By Ruth Slotnick

July, 2009: Analysis

How much of the data corpus should be coded?

Some believe all data should be coded to locate the nuanced patterns; others believe that only the salient points should be coded, that most of the data can be excluded, leaving the quarter of the data to be analyzed. Saldaña (2009) calls this "the primary half for intensive data analysis" (p. 15). He concludes by saying that, no matter which side you ascribe to, make sure your data is quality. Code trivial data as nonapplicable or N/A (p. 15). He talks about "metadata activities" as codes that come about from field notes, observations, and analytical memos.

Also, Saldaña recommends graphic summaries (p. 16). For analysis, he suggests dividing the text up into units according to the changing of topics. This will make analysis easier in ATLAS-ti. I will use topic and subtopic breaks as recommended. I will reformat all the transcribed texts to read this way. Saldaña calls these unit divisions.

So my system of analysis is this:

1. Listen and make corrections to transcriptions. Although my transcriptionist has done a fairly good job of catching the text as spoken, she does not transcribe some of the nuanced expressions used, so I have filled in what was missed, for example, the sound of laughter, when appropriate. The transcripts with my corrections and additions are saved in an interview file.

2. Send file to interviewee for member check.

3. Make any changes to the document post member check.

4. Delete any extraneous talk (regarding the digital recorder and final good-byes) as well as other irrelevant text, such as extra ums or repeated words as a sentence is being formed; "I . . . I thought I might . . . I thought I might be doing the wrong thing" would look like "I think I might be doing the wrong thing." The digital recording will help me determine if there is hesitation in the voice of the interviewee. This will be noted in parentheses. This becomes the draft from which I will code.

5. The next step is to start summarizing the interview text as recommended by Rubin and Rubin (2005), summarizing each passage with a few words and looking for themes, concepts, events, and topical markers.

6. While the document is still single spaced, break texts into topics and subtopics. Saldaña (2009) calls them stanzas that help to format the text and reveal meaning and intent otherwise lost in long paragraphs of text (p. 16). Breaking the text into stanzas is also key to make coding in qualitative software easier to compile and analyze.

(Continued)

(Continued)

7. Use a left-flush margin, leaving a two-inch, right-hand margin for pencil coding.

8. Precoding: With digital recording, field notes, and the researcher's reflective journal, I will begin my precoding. Precoding is where I am circling, underlining, bolding text. These are also called "codable moments" (see Saldaña, p. 16).

9. Preliminary jotting: The goal is to have all the tangible pieces related to each case available for consideration as the analysis commences.

10. Primary coding: This is the first round of identifying codes.

11. Secondary coding: In this stage, I'm building categories.

12. Third round: Then, I'm finalizing categories and cases.

September 6, 2009: Analysis

What am I hearing? What am I not hearing?

What assumptions am I making or are my interviewees making?

What is being downplayed or overplayed?

What policies and practices enhance or increase the chance of access and student success?

What are external pressures? Internal conflicts?

Developed a case study matrix. Further developed into three cases.

September 9, 2009: Analysis

I am developing a proximity matrix. Let's see what differences I find! I think these will either be responses that are more subtle or that indicate a general lack of familiarity or brevity with the state policy. I created instead a policy proximity continuum using *policy expert* as the closest description and *technocrat* as slightly further away.

September 10, 2009: Analysis

I created continuum for all three cases. Then I met with Valerie, my methodologist. She was happy with my progress. We came up with suggestions for the subcategories for close and distant on the proximity continuum. I went home and reworked this continuum. Then, I started to work on the next category: perceptions of under-represented students, differentiated and undifferentiated.

Thus it is evident that there is no one way to do data analysis. However, the tried-and-true method of anthropologists, sociologists, historians, and critics is helpful here:

1. Pour through your written and audio data.

2. Select themes and codes based on frequency, distribution, and meaning to the participant.

3. Read the transcripts over and over again. After you get a transcript, it is good to read it a few times or more per week as you move into the analysis and interpretation phase.

4. Write everything down that you are thinking of, and write about what this means.

5. Use your imagination (see Appendix M).

The data tell you something, but data does not speak for itself. You the researcher need to interpret that data. Your job is to find out what the data are saying to you. Now, you constantly compare and contrast what you are finding and come up with some interpretation of all that you compared: themes, meaning units, words, and categories about the themes. Also, as you look for repetition and constant recurring statements, you know you have a grip on what the participant is telling you. Next, you need to interpret these data. Make a visual diagram or figure representing your data and what you found. In addition, the range of ethical issues encountered in a study should be part of its analysis and interpretation. Qualitative researchers should include a section on ethical issues that arose in the study in any of their reports and especially in the dissertation.

● ETHICS AND THE QUALITATIVE RESEARCHER

If the qualitative researcher can be assured of serendipity and contradictions, he or she can also be assured of ethical issues. In conversations about works in progress, dissertations, and class projects, learners need a forum for discussing the ethical issues that arise in any given field setting. To prepare for discussing these everyday moments of fieldwork, learners have an opportunity to discuss and react to actual cases of ethical dilemmas that previous students have encountered. To warm up the group in discussing ethical issues, learners assemble in groups and choose one of the following actual cases for discussion. Think of these two exercises as stretching your thinking about ethics and fieldwork.

● TRUE STORIES: SAMPLE ETHICAL DILEMMAS

Discussion Exercises

The Case of "Just Delete That Data"

Recently, a doctoral student was conducting recorded interviews for a study that was designed to describe and explain the quality of a federally funded music and arts camp for the handicapped, with a particular focus on teacher effectiveness. The seven teachers were teaching music, art, piano, voice, and composition. The student conducted interviews with all of the teachers over a six-month period and observed in the seven classrooms. He also transcribed all the recordings and found that one teacher was totally neglecting his work as an instructor. Not only that, all of the other instructors knew that one of their group was doing this and that he was basically unqualified, rude to students, and arbitrary in his assessments. The researcher showed these data to the director at a member-check discussion; the director was also one of the teachers. In the discussion, the director revealed that he hired that teacher and could not accept the results of student evaluations or the comments from other instructors. The teacher in question was an old friend. Furthermore, the director asked the researcher to delete all comments referring to that teacher in case the data jeopardized funding for the next summer.

Questions for Discussion of the Case

1. How would you handle this?

2. What is the role of the researcher in this case?

3. What ethical issues are raised in this case?

4. What would you change, if anything, in this situation?

"I Said That, But Now I Want It Erased"

As you know, anything can happen in the social world. That is why we enjoy this type of research. Recently, a doctoral student got incredibly rich data recorded from a nurse educator who was onto something like the Enron fiasco. The nurse educator read the transcripts, signed that she read them, and after the study was completed, returned to the researcher and said that she would like to delete some of the things she said because she was fearful of repercussions from her supervisor. The researcher was now faced with a decision to (a) recast what was said in a way that would be less threatening, (b) delete the information entirely, or (c) leave everything as it was.

What would you do in this instance?

Of course, there are endless examples of ethical questions in qualitative research studies; these two cases offer some examples for discussion. Actual examples each semester provide grist for the forum, and by using group members to share viewpoints, prospective researchers at least begin to grapple with ethical issues and write descriptions of these issues in their reports. Likewise, doctoral students need to write about and include ethical questions that arose in their studies as part of the ongoing explication of all components of qualitative work. In dissertations, writers often include the ethical questions in the Methodology section under Role of the Researcher or in an appendix, as needed, depending on the nature of the ethical issue (see Table 6.1).

ATTRIBUTES OF THE QUALITATIVE RESEARCHER ●

Notice that many beginning qualitative researchers often remark about the difficulty in doing a qualitative research project. They are often amazed at the significant and in-depth time and energy commitment required to complete and sustain the project. Consequently, a forum is needed to discuss, with a reflective posture, exactly the qualities needed to complete such a project. Over the past 30 years, students have engaged with me in such discussions, and so we offer this list of qualities that may be helpful for new researchers.

Table 6.1 Schema of a Section of a Literature Review by Ruth Slotnick

Transfer Literature Integrating Policy Implementation Theories				
Year	Author(s)	Policy Implementation Researchers Cited	Topic of Study	Focus on Underrepresented College Students?
1974	Knoell, D., & McIntyre, C.	Dror, E., & Wildavsky, A.	Planning Community Colleges	Yes
1985	Richardson, R. C.	Wildavsky, A.	Baccalaureate for Urban Minorities	Yes
1989	Richardson, R. C.	Wildavsky, A.	Minority Achievement	Yes
2000	Schaffer, L. J.*	Bardach, E., Dye, T., Sabatier, P., & Yanow, D.	Implementing Transfer Policies	None
2008	Gonzalez, J. M.*	Elmore, R. F., Hill, H. C., Lipsky, M., Mazmanmian, D., Pressman, J., Sabatier, P., Wildavsky, A., & Yanow, D.	Academic Tracking Systems	None

Attributes Needed to Conduct and Complete a Qualitative Project

1. A high tolerance for ambiguity

2. A strong determination to fully complete the study

3. A willingness to change plans and directions as needed

4. Resourcefulness and patience

5. Compassion, passion, and integrity

6. Willingness to commit to time in the field and equal time in analysis

7. Ability to trust and question others

8. Ability to know one's self

9. Authentic and strong curiosity

10. Above-average writing ability

11. Ability to focus and not allow distractions

12. Discipline to write every day

13. Diligence

14. Above-average faith in people and appreciation for their circumstances

15. Voracious reading in one's field and other fields

Although this list is not meant to be exhaustive, these qualities emerge in nearly every discussion of this nature. In fact, above-average writing ability is critical in terms of representing data, analyzing it, and interpreting it. The qualitative researcher must be an excellent writer. Of course, many tools are out there for all qualitative researchers, including many resources on the Internet. We also must interact with the Institutional Review Boards, IRBs.

QUALITATIVE RESEARCHERS INTERACTING ●
WITH INSTITUTIONAL REVIEW BOARDS, IRBs

Over the past three decades, qualitative researchers have been dealing with a number of serious issues when interacting with their respective IRBs. Most often issues arise with the following:

1. Informed consent

2. How we use language

3. Coresearchers in a project

4. The use of blogs and social media

In terms of values, the issue of informed consent is at the heart of the matter. Likewise, the issue of how language is used and how data are represented is addressed. Furthermore, the issue of coresearchers in a project uncovers various subtextual ethical issues imposed upon qualitative researchers. Most recently, some IRBs have been concerned about the use of blogs in research and the use of social media sites. We simply must be watchful as qualitative researchers in applying for approval from respective IRBs. At the same time, a hopeful message can be gained from qualitative researchers taking an active part in membership on IRBs. As blogs, electronic mailing lists, and social media grow, more education is needed for IRB members and researchers alike about the ethical implications of Web-based research.

Over the years, I have become increasingly interested in the problems arising for qualitative researchers, particularly doctoral students, when the IRB applications are open for review. In recent years, the types of questions asked of qualitative researchers, the ethical issues imbedded in these questions, and the burden put upon the shoulders of the researchers involved make this an issue for consideration. Qualitative researchers are successful when they construct a dialogue between themselves and IRB members. I also encourage qualitative researchers to gain membership on these boards. As a former member and co-chair of an IRB, it was clear that some IRB members possessed the following qualities:

- had little knowledge of the procedures, theory, history, or work of qualitative researchers;

- had little interaction personally with qualitative researchers;

- were requiring a standard for qualitative researchers unlike that of other researchers; or

- had never thought about including qualitative researchers on the board itself.

This makes me think we need to be more active in IRBs. Why should we become members? Because we advance our field, build bridges with those who may not know of our approaches to research, and elevate the level of discourse about research. In effect, we open windows to view many other approaches to research. We also uncover all sorts of ethical issues, because *one size does not fit all* in qualitative research. I want to emphasize here that we must continue to educate IRB members about the theory that guides us and the practice to which we are committed. Persistence and membership pays off.

CHAPTER SUMMARY

Perhaps the most difficult challenge for beginning and intermediate qualitative researchers is the analysis and interpretation of data and dealing with the IRB. However, this can become nearly effortless through some of the suggestions made in this section, such as the following:

1. Keep a journal and write every day.

2. Don't be afraid of ethical issues that pop up. Instead, write about those issues. Analyze and interpret them.

3. Rely on your intuition and imagination. That is something every researcher needs to do. Check out the many books on creativity and great scientists, writers, and artists. All of them trust their intuitions. Develop your curiosity as fully as possible.

4. Get educated about your IRB boards. Learn their language and follow up as needed. Treat work with the IRB as an innovation and even get on the board!

5. Find your passion. Do not write someone else's study with data so moldy that even the original collectors of the data forgot where the data were stashed or what it meant.

6. Become a member of the IRB.

7. Find a peer who will read your work and vice versa.

8. Know yourself.

Obviously, a lot of this is common sense, but if we look to the arts, especially in dance and yoga, we can learn a lot about the process. All dancers practice, practice, practice—continually. All students of yoga do as well. I think that, to the extent that you exercise your mind as well as your body, you can only be sharper in your analytical and interpretive skills. The exercises in this book are geared toward practicing each habit of the qualitative researcher.

Analysis and interpretation of the data in any given research project must include a clear description of unintended moments in the research; intuitive, informed hunches; ethical concerns and issues; and a serious description of the researcher's role in the entire history of the project. Analysis of data is very much like the dancer's floor exercises. Floor exercises follow stretching exercises in dance warm-ups. After floor exercises, the dancer's next step is performance of a given dance. Interpretation of data by the researcher is like the dancer's act of performance. It can occur only after long-term practice and work. The normal checks and balances system in qualitative research work includes a reasonable, long-term commitment to the research practice at hand and relies on the stability embedded in a long-term activity.

Likewise, the study of dance relies on stretching and floor exercises before moving into the realm of performance. The exercises described in this book rely heavily on the arts and humanities for their inspiration. Observation exercises, interview exercises, role of the researcher exercises, writing exercises, evaluation exercises, and discussion of ethical issues exercises all provide an opportunity for learners to stretch. These exercises were designed to allow individuals to stretch from one point to another in a focused pattern of practice to educate and inspire them to become better qualitative researchers. By using activities from the arts, like drawing, photography, and dramatic art, individuals may discover new ways of thinking and opening the mind. By relentless writing activities, such as journal writing, description of beliefs and behaviors, letter writing, and self-evaluation, learners widen their repertoire of research skills. Likewise, physical and mental construction of collages, YaYa boxes, wreaths, quilts, posters, and so on also expand our notions of how we can become sharper at research skills in the field by sharpening our senses. The researcher is the research instrument in qualitative research and must be ready to become physically sharper at observation and interview skills. This is like the dancer who relies on his or her body, which is the instrument with which the story of the dance is told. As Martha Graham put so well, using words to this effect, the body is the instrument through which life is lived and which tells the story of the dance. For those of us who pursue qualitative research questions and design qualitative research studies, I hope that the exercises and resources in this book provide ways to approach developing a stronger body and mind for completing qualitative research projects. Before we move to the next chapter on technology, here are some final exercises to spark your creativity as a researcher.

EXERCISE 6.1   Design and Create a Cover for Your Researcher Reflective Journal

Goal:

Now that you have kept a researcher reflective journal while using this book, design and create a cover that represents you. What kind of research instrument are you? How would you like to represent all that you learned doing these exercises? Use any photographs, products, and artifacts that best describe you as the research instrument, you as the qualitative researcher. Make categories of your journal as needed.

Insert all your reflections and any of your completed exercises. Make a dedication in the front of the journal to someone who you think would appreciate this. At the end, make a list of at least three goals for you to work on in the future in terms of developing as a qualitative researcher.

EXERCISE 6.2   Describe Your Favorite Meal

Goal:

Describe fully a favorite meal you recently enjoyed. Write about the setting where this meal took place. What was the context of the meal? Who was present at the meal? Describe the people present at the meal. Describe the smells and tastes, the colors, and textures of the meal.

Who prepared the meal? When might you repeat eating a meal like this? Now write a short piece for your favorite newsletter about this meal.

EXERCISE 6.3   Writing About Change in Yourself in Any Five-Year Period

Goal:

Darwin wrote that it is not the strongest of the species that survives. It is not the most intelligent who survives. Rather, it is the one most responsive to change. Think about any five-year period in your life where you totally changed. Name that period of time. Describe fully that period and how you changed. Write something about your willingness to change and relate this to your research habit of writing and analysis. Write three adjectives about yourself during that five-year time period. Develop this in your researcher reflective journal.

7

The Technology Habit

New technology is common. New thinking is rare.

—Sir Peter Blake

The technology habit is one to formulate early in your career as a qualitative researcher. Qualitative researchers regularly encounter points of potential technology use in a qualitative study. When we collect data through interviewing and collect documents as data, technology can assist our work. When we create our analysis and interpretation system, we may save ourselves hours of work simply by using the free software and applications available to us. Dustin De Felice and Valerie Janesick (2014) suggest a marriage of the minds and practice for qualitative researchers and technology usage. Furthermore, by establishing the habit of using technology throughout the entire qualitative research process, qualitative researchers are well on the way to understanding and becoming technology experts. There are a number of applications and software packages available as alternatives to costly prepackaged software. These applications and software packages can assist the researcher in making the overall process less cumbersome and more efficient while ensuring the complexity of the meaning of the lived experience of our participants remains in place.

For instance, interview tools (e.g., audio recorders, virtual voice-over-Internet protocols, and audio editors) provide methods of recording, editing, and working with interview text that is secure, transferable, and permanent. During the transcription process, additional tools allow for more efficient and safe renderings of recorded text through the combination of the transcription, voice recognition, and word processing software. Finally, the use of a common office programs like Excel and Microsoft Word, and Apple applications can assist in rendering strikingly beautiful renderings in tables and figures. Quite often, these technology tools also create additional opportunities for helping the researcher interpret the text. We may see something new in the data just by using technology. There is no need to fear technology. You are still using your own brain to analyze data. The researcher will always be the key analyst and interpreter of data. Software alone cannot replace us yet. It is noteworthy that technology changes so rapidly so that by the time this book is on the market, even more effective new software will have been discovered.

Much of qualitative research requires multiple interviews, multiple rereading of collected text, and multiple interactions with the text. Thus, the process of collecting, creating, and analyzing through these possible tools preserves the essence of the qualitative process and gives the researcher the opportunity to expend time and resources in creating an analysis and interpretation of a study with a small number of participants as well as a larger number of participants.

BENEFITS FOR SMALL-SCALE STUDIES USING TECHNOLOGY ●

For many of us working with a smaller pool of participants, costly qualitative software programs often provide little benefit when weighed against other less expensive and more common tools. Know that a number of free, low-cost or otherwise common software programs or applications are available to all of us (see Figure 7.1). For example, De Felice (2012) studied disappearing languages, Nahuatl and Mayan, from the perspective of native teachers of those languages. In his dissertation project, he was able to use technology effectively throughout the project. In this chapter, I will refer to this study as an example of how technology was used in the entire research project from start to finish. Consequently, this may allay some fears of technology and may strengthen your resolve to use technology in any of your qualitative research projects. I would like to describe technology usage from the beginning to the end of that study to illustrate the merits of technology use for any qualitative researcher. Finally, I end this chapter with a listing of suggested digital resources to improve qualitative research projects.

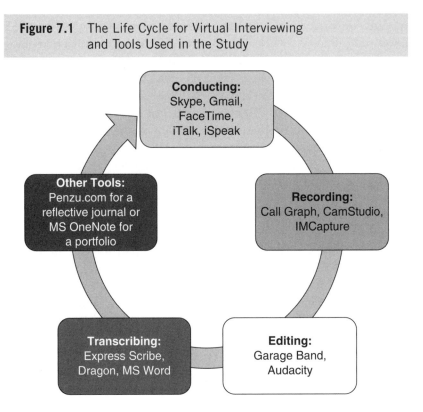

Figure 7.1   The Life Cycle for Virtual Interviewing and Tools Used in the Study

● THE CONTEXT

In De Felice (2012), the study focused on indigenous educators and their experiences teaching online. These educators from Mexico were tasked with teaching, studying, and integrating technology within an online environment for a predominantly U.S. audience through distance learning platforms. We worked with participants who were in their early or late 20s from the following settings where an indigenous language (Yucatec Maya or Nahuatl) or culture was the subject of instruction through either synchronous (real time) or asynchronous (anytime) tools.

As this research study was firmly situated in a qualitative tradition, we collected various texts and we analyzed each of them in order to have diverse perspectives that enriched the possible interpretations of the phenomenon under investigation. In order to demonstrate and explain the tools we used, we discuss the ways we collected three types of texts: interviewing via Skype, participants' reflective comments from writing prompts, and site documents provided in English and Spanish. The first type of data collected was interview data through Skype, followed by immediate transcription of each interview through free software.

THE POWER OF SKYPE INTERVIEWING ●

As we were not in the same geographic region as our participants, we needed to develop a set of procedures for working long distance. We begin with those interviewing procedures through Skype, our recording through Call Graph, and our use of voice recognition software to create the transcripts. As De Felice (2012) conducted the interviews through Skype and recorded them using an outside program called Call Graph, he also kept a researcher reflective journal of his own thoughts. Call Graph would immediately begin recording (see Figure 7.2 for Skype, Call Graph, and the recording message).

Note that in many interviews, the video option in Skype was used for convenience. However, please realize that there were a number of times when the connection quality was so unreliable or poor that interviews were completed using audio only. By removing the video feed, the quality of the recording would always improve. At some later date and as technology improves on a regular basis in real time, this complication may someday be resolved.

Figure 7.2   Skype and Call Graph Screenshot

We chose to use Skype instead of other possibilities, such as land-line interviews, or other voice-over-Internet protocol services, for two reasons. First, the Nahuatl-speaking participants were already using this program in their daily lives. Second, the program was available at no cost to its users. We would later learn that the Mayan participants were also familiar with the program and their university supervisor maintained an account. Some of these participants would choose to complete their interviews on campus and, often times, they would use their supervisor's account and her office.

There were a number of features that also made Skype a powerful tool for completing the interviews. While the program offers audio and video capabilities, it also has a chat function embedded in the program. This chat function is available whether or not a user was connected by a call. In other words, the chat worked much like an instant messenger service. Take advantage of this feature to share consent forms, inter-view questions, and other notes with all of the participants. The par-ticipants welcomed this feature.

Above and beyond the advantages in Skype for the participants, Skype also had a number of add-ons available that we investigated for recording purposes. Finding a program with recording capabilities was crucial for this study. The free program, Call Graph, can be synchro-nized to work with Skype. Call Graph was also useful because upon completion of the Skype call, Call Graph would send the completed recording as an MP3 file directly to the computer desktop in a folder. How easy is that? Finally and obviously, if a researcher cannot get to the site because of cost and geographic location, Skype is an effective and efficient tool.

● NEXT STEPS: EDITING THROUGH AUDACITY

The next step upon receipt of the file, is opening it using Audacity, a free program, to complete some minor editing tasks. Use Audacity to edit files to remove any sections of the recording that are not relevant to the research in hand as well as to fix any problems that occurred with the Skype call (see Figure 7.3). Many times, a call would be inter-rupted because of issues with either Skype or the Internet. Do not panic if this happens. Simply piece together those conversations into one whole conversation. Additionally, Audacity is good for cutting the conversation into manageable chunks of about 10 to 15 minutes in length. This step assisted us in the transcription process because the chunking of the audio file made it easier to work through interviews over a long period time.

Figure 7.3   Audacity Screenshot

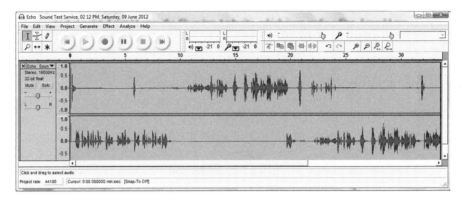

TRANSCRIPTION WITH EXPRESS SCRIBE,   ●
DRAGON, ITALK, ISPEAK, AND MS WORD

With the completed audio file exported out of Audacity as an MP3 file, it is nearly effortless to import that file into the Express Scribe transcription program. Two different options within the Express Scribe program were utilized. Initially, after becoming more experienced with Express Scribe, it is easier to use the transcription function directly within Express Scribe and then to copy and paste sections from within Express Scribe about every 10 to 15 minutes. I would copy and paste those sections into Microsoft Word and save it as an additional backup for the work. As wonderful as technology is in our lives, always back up your files at regular intervals.

One feature from within Express Scribe that allows efficient and complete transcriptions is the fact that it enabled the user to slow down

Figure 7.4   Express Scribe Screenshot

the speed of the file (see Figure 7.4). By slowing the speed down to about 45%, transcriptions become less of a problem both in time and effort.

● VOICE RECOGNITION SOFTWARE

We are very fortunate to work in a research context of continual upgrades for voice recognition software and applications. The question becomes should we try and use it or not? Will this help with our transcription processes? De Felice (2014) began using voice recognition software a few years before his dissertation project and found it to be an incredible resource and time-saver when transcribing. He used Dragon NaturallySpeaking 11.5 during his dissertation study. The current version is 13. Since he was working with files that contained both English and Spanish, he purchased the Dragon program in both languages. He installed the English version on one laptop and the Spanish version on another. This is how we learned that the software itself does not have reciprocal capabilities in a bilingual context.

Dragon software is a useful transcription tool which uses the so-called parrot method. The researcher listens to the interview in the headset and speaks back what is heard into either Microsoft Word or Express Scribe. This software only recognizes one voice, your voice as the researcher, hence the parrot method. You may start out slowly but, in the end, find that you can transcribe around 150 words a minute. Doing your own transcriptions allows for an intimate connection to the research project as you live, eat, and breathe your transcriptions. You become intimately connected to your data, which later enables you to analyze and interpret that data more fluidly.

Other software available on the Mac system through Apple software is that of iTalk or iSpeak. These are constantly upgraded on your devices. For example, these applications for the iPad or iPhone provide you the researcher with voice to text capability. Just as in the Dragon software described above, the iTalk and iSpeak software provide the text as it is spoken without punctuation, headings, and so on. You later go back and make the text readable.

● RESEARCHER REFLECTIVE PORTFOLIOS

During the process of working through the text and the research process, we recommend maintaining a reflective portfolio. This portfolio can be a space to evaluate the work externally and internally. Janesick

(2011) noted that portfolios have been used in classrooms to provide evidence for ongoing learning, for record keeping and for showcasing the work done by students. In this particular study, we incorporated the researcher's reflective journal as a centerpiece of a researcher portfolio that we assembled electronically to include various sections that documented our journey through the research process. Based on the long history of journaling writing in various fields and endeavors (Janesick, 1998), we built on this tradition through the incorporation of new technology tools that allowed us to go beyond the written word. We explored this portfolio more fully in the next section because it became an integral part of the research process while providing a space to develop as a researcher and to analyze the ongoing thought process. Lastly, we detail how this portfolio became an invaluable space where we were able to record the overall progress with this research project in a safe space. These types of researcher reflective portfolios are perfect vehicles for developing ideas, continuing one's growth as a writer-researcher and encouraging creative uses of language, visuals, and poetry. For instance, we put together and used the researcher reflective portfolio as a text source where we could write about experiences, feelings, interpretations, and intuitions throughout the research process. This portfolio may serve to document the role of the researcher, as a triangulation of perspectives from the research process and, when possible, as a connection between the participants and the researcher. Because these portfolios are best served by an open-ended format, the researcher is then able to interact with any issue or topic in a creative and safe virtual context. Within this electronic portfolio, there can be simple text-based entries as well as multimedia files embedded throughout.

EXCEL AS A TEXT/DATA ANALYSIS TOOL ●

Throughout the research process, one tool can serve to house all of the collected and created text: Excel as a text analysis assistive tool. After much trial and error, we decided this analysis tool was the right fit for this dissertation work. We hasten to note that each qualitative work is unique and the description we provide may not be suitable for every project. In any case, we outline the steps we took to convert text sources into files ready for importation into a spreadsheet. This conversion process is an important step in making the files render properly (or as desired) in the spreadsheet program, which is what we chose to use for our analysis.

Of course, the decision to use Excel as a data analysis tool has a number of ramifications for qualitative research that may require additional modifications or revisits to procedures in place. We recommend the following procedures for using Excel as a data analysis tool. Upon completion of each interview transcriptions, send them back to the participants and asked them to review the file. In De Felice (2012), sharing files was challenging. He sent the files as attachments and asked participants to work with an attached MS Word document. In a number of instances, he did not receive any response from some of the participants. After talking through the process with participants, he found out that sending the files as attachments was limiting access for participants. Many of them were accessing the files at Internet cafés or on their university Web server. At times, these locations have pop-up blockers or other systems in place that restrict access to attachments. As such, we recommend revising procedures regularly to include sending most files as text within the body of the e-mails rather than as attachments. After participants finished reviewing the transcripts and making any changes they felt necessary, those transcripts were ready for importation into Excel. Try to avoid any common formatting problems. We recommend formatting each document so that each line of text has a participant's name followed by a colon marking each meaning unit or utterance the person made.

● ANALYSIS STRATEGIES FROM MS WORD TO MS EXCEL

To ensure the transcription material renders properly in Excel, the researcher must reread the entire transcription in order to check for any identifying information that needs to be removed or modified for ethical reasons. This information can be items like names of institutions or universities, names of specific towns and cities, and names of individuals, among other types of identifying information.

We recommend choosing delimited text rather than a fixed width (see Figure 7.5). This limits the text that goes into cells based on a specific chosen symbol (in this case, a comma).

Finally, choose text for the data format because Excel needs to understand that imported text is text rather than equations, dates, time, and so on (see Figure 7.6).

Once these steps are completed, the text will appear in the appropriate columns throughout the Excel spreadsheet. We developed these guidelines in conjunction with the work of Daniel Meyer and Leanne Avery (2009) where they lay out a number of procedures

Figure 7.5   File Type Choice Screenshot. The preview window provided a chance to review the original text file.

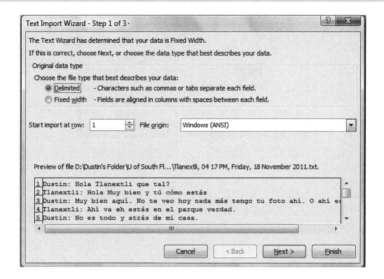

Figure 7.6   Text Formatting Screenshot

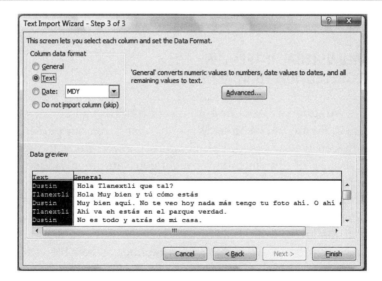

and considerations for the use of Excel as a qualitative data analysis platform (see Figure 7.7).

We completed all of the steps for the interview files, writing prompts, and the artifacts collected from the educators. These files

Figure 7.7 Final Import Step Screenshot Into the Spreadsheet

were also imported in separate worksheets within the final Excel spreadsheet. We did maintain one shared worksheet where the final textural-structural descriptions for all the participants were shared. Please note that once you find your rhythm, you will decide based on your reading of the literature, your pilot study and your preferences, which type of analysis to use as a guide. What worked for us was using Saldaña's (2009) approach. Using Saldaña's *Focused Coding*, we developed categories to help see the common set of features that were present within the documents under study.

● OVERALL VIRTUAL INTERVIEW: FROM COLLECTION TO ANALYSIS

In short, we summarize our procedures for conducting interviews long distance in Figure 7.8. We used Skype to initially call our participants. Once the call was accepted, Call Graph began recording the session. Upon receipt of the recorded conversion (audio-only), we used Audacity as an audio editor to clean up and segment the file. Through the parrot method, we used Dragon along with Express Scribe to complete the final transcription document.

Since we utilized technology to help us with more than just the interviewing process, we summarize a number of possible tech tools for the overall qualitative research process in Figure 7.9. There are a multiple of tools available to conduct an interview long distance. We list three in the first column: Skype, Google Voice and Video Chat, and FaceTime. As handheld devices continue to proliferate, these choices will continue to expand. For recording these sessions, we recommend

Figure 7.8 Overall Tools for Qualitative Interviews

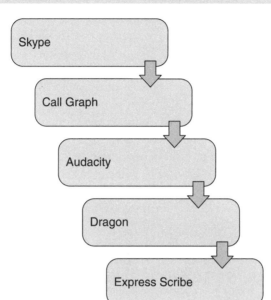

Call Graph when using Skype and CamStudio or IMCapture for other devices. We utilize Audacity for editing our audio files and it is available as a free download for PC and Mac users. Depending on the available computer platform, GarageBand works for Mac users while Movie Maker works for Windows users. As we described in this article, we used a combination of tools to complete the transcriptions that

Figure 7.9 Overall Technology Tools

included MS Word, Express Scribe, and Dragon voice recognition software. Lastly, we outlined steps for using Excel as a data analysis tool, though there are other options available like QDA Miner and NVivo.

Thus, we believe that the qualitative researcher can benefit from the use of technology during numerous points in the process. The tools will most likely change as the technology advances, but many of the principles we outlined can transfer to other tools. In fact, it is possible today to bypass the use of costly software for most of the process we covered through the use of various applications. Technology is the friend of the qualitative researcher and we think of our work here as developmental in terms of the technology habit. It is a good thing to use what is available at no cost to you the researcher. Costly prepackaged software can only go so far. In the end you have to use your own system. We like to view these technology tools as guides.

● ELECTRONIC MAILING LISTS, WEBSITES, JOURNALS, AND SOFTWARE OPTIONS

We now navigate in the electronic age with resources at our fingertips at the touch of a keypad. Qualitative researchers are able to access quite a bit of information about techniques, design, issues, and problems. Qualitative research electronic mailing lists, discussion groups, message boards, software tools, and electronic and regular journals are numerous and easily accessible to all. In fact, the sites are so numerous that listed here are only a sample of some of the regularly visited sites. A search of the World Wide Web, WWW, and Web2.0 sites will result in thousands of results. In addition, social media sites such as Facebook and Twitter offer a platform for digital practice.

Electronic Mailing Lists and Resources

Qual Page: http://www.qualitativeresearch.uga.edu/QualPage

Center for Collaborative Action Research: http://cadres.pepperdine.edu/ccar/define.html

Phenomenology Online: http://www.Phenomenologyonline.com

Saint Louis University: Qualitative Research Committee: http://www.slu.edu/organizations/qrc/QRCweblinks.html

ATLAS.ti: http://forum.atlasti.com/showthread.php?t=2188

Grounded Theory Institute: http://www.groundedtheory.com

International Institute for Qualitative Methodology: http://www.iiqm.ualberta.ca

International Congress of Qualitative Inquiry: http://icqi.org

Many professional organizations have, within their subgroups, numerous electronic mailing lists devoted to several approaches to qualitative research as well. Get to know your professional group's offerings. Helpful websites for writing qualitative dissertations, proposals for funded research, and to help new professors in the field include

Academic Ladder: http://academicladder.com

This site provides networking options and writing services for new professors and teachers new to qualitative methods.

The Dissertation Doctor: http://dissertationdoctor.com

This site helps students with brainstorming for topics for study, demonstrates how to do literature reviews, and allows for blogging with peers, along with many other positive resources.

Journals Dedicated to Publishing Qualitative Research

The International Journal of Qualitative Studies in Education (QSE)

Qualitative Inquiry (QI)

The Qualitative Report (TQR online)

International Review of Qualitative Research (IRQR)

International Journal of Qualitative Methods (IJQM online)

Software

Literally, nearly every year, new software packages become available or an existing package is improved. The list below includes some of the top-selling software packages that some students have found useful. Each of the first four on this list has had decades to test, assess, and reinvent aspects of the software. The fifth on this list is relatively new to the field but particularly helpful for its features.

ATLAS-ti

Ethnograph

NVivo

MAXQDA

Transana

Transana is the latest software for qualitative researchers. Developed at the Wisconsin Center for Education Research, Transana is similar to the others programs and integrates video, auditory, and still-image data and allows for real-time collaboration. This factor is particularly appealing to digital natives, those students who grew up with technology since childhood. According to the website (http://www.transana.org/), it allows "researchers to analyze and manage data in very sophisticated ways" and include tools to "transcribe video and audio files (in a wide variety of ways useful for different analytic purposes)." It can analyze audio and video and create "Clips," categorizing them into groups by theme and key words; manage your audio, visual, still images file, and clips. Transana's Professional version allows you to "create and manipulate multiple simultaneous transcripts to analyze different analytic layers within your data." The Multi-user version supports collaboration with colleagues. Where video is an important part of their methodology, many in educational research find Transana a useful tool.

Dedoose (Research made easy): http://www.dedoose.com

Dedoose is a site that goes beyond the software package and offers numerous resources for qualitative researchers for a monthly fee. On the home page, you will find pricing, videos that educate about each component of the research process, analysis software, tips for coding, and frequently asked questions. You have help through the analysis process continually. It is a valuable professional addition to the qualitative research community and all of these enhance our history.

Comprehensive Listing of Resources: http://www.nova.edu/ssss/QR/qualres.html

On the website for the e-journal *The Qualitative Report* you will find a healthy set of listings for resources for the qualitative researcher.

There you will find examples from all disciplines in terms of websites, journals, books, individual papers, and abstracts all designed to assist the qualitative researcher.

AQUAD7 Free Software

AQUAD 7 is a software package for the analysis of qualitative data and is available for download since January 1, 2013, as free, open-source software in accordance with the conditions of the GNU General Public License v.3. The actual version 7.2 of the software AQUAD 7 permits analysis of qualitative data

- by interpretation within the framework of the coding paradigm,
- by Boolean minimization to identify types, and
- by successively generating hypotheses about text segments and testing them according to the method of sequence analysis in the approach of objective hermeneutics.

The version 7.2 of AQUAD 7 contains an interface with the open-source statistical package R to simplify combined qualitative-quantitative analyses for those projects that give equal time to both qualitative and quantitative data. (See the main menu of AQUAD 7 for options) You may also develop your own scripts.

With AQUAD 7, you can process the following types of data:

- Any kind of texts (transcriptions of interviews, letters, documents, etc.)
- Audio files (interview recordings)
- Video files (recordings of observations)
- Pictures and other graphic material (photos, drawings, etc.)

More information is available from www.aquad.de/en; above all, a detailed list of analytic options and sample files and the manual are ready for free download. Go to http://www.aquad.de/en/infosandfeatures/.

Penzu: https://penzu.com

Penzu is a digital journal writing space. You may store mounds of pages of data, and this is password protected.

Digital Storytelling Resources for the Qualitative Researcher

Since qualitative researchers rely on telling the story of their participants, the following sampler of storytelling sites can be added to your qualitative research methods tool box.

DigiTales: http://www.digitales.us

This site introduces the viewer to digital storytelling in multiple formats and catalogues many such stories. By inclusion of voices, there is a social justice component to many of the life histories, oral histories, and biographies.

Center for Digital Storytelling: http://storycenter.org

This center is dedicated to the art of personal storytelling. The center offers workshops, programs, and ad services all focused on capturing personal voice and facilitating teaching methods. Their motto is *listen deeply, tell stories.*

Stories for Change: http://storiesforchange.net

Stories for Change is an unique online community for digital storytelling, whose members advocate for social change through stories. It is a wealth of information and offers many models and exemplary storytelling. They offer resources and a curriculum and to use this site you need to open an account to upload your digital stories.

Center for Studies in Oral Tradition: http://www.oraltradition.org

The Center for Studies in Oral Tradition began in 1986 with the approval of the Board of Curators (University of Missouri) and "stands as a national and international focus for interdisciplinary research and scholarship on the world's oral traditions." This group mission is to create communication links among specialists in various fields and disciplines "to foster conversations and exchanges about oral tradition that would not otherwise take place."

EXERCISE 7.1   Conducting and Transcribing a Skype Interview Using Express Scribe for Transcription

Goal:

Now that you have a sense of how technology may be used in qualitative research projects, prepare five grand-tour questions as an interview protocol and interview someone in another country as a pilot test for yourself to learn digital interviewing. Prior to that, download Express Scribe software to assist you in transcription. Transcribe your interview. Make a list of at least three goals for you to work on in the future in terms of developing your technology habit.

EXERCISE 7.2 Create a Word Cloud Using Wordle and One With Tagxedo

Goal:

Visit the following sites: http://www.wordle.net/create and http://www.tagxedo.net/create

Next, choose your colors and designs for displaying words associated with technology and some of the software titles, freeware, or techniques you might use in your qualitative study.

Create a word cloud at each site. Display and share it with at least one of your peers. Now write about this in your researcher reflective journal.

EXERCISE 7.3 Create a Glog, a Poster Online Through Glogster

Goal:

Learn to navigate the Glogster site at http://edu.glogster.com/?ref=com. This site allows you to create your own poster for a small fee. It is creative and intuitive and allows you to build a visual online poster with wallpaper, photographs, video links, and your choice of graphics. Here, you may mix texts such as excerpts from your own files, from around the Web, audio, video, clip art, and photos and include zoom effects. On the site, there are many examples of completed glogs to view and see how they operate.

After you create your glog, share with a peer and discuss each other's technology usage.

Next, write about this in your researcher reflective journal.

Discussion:

Following these exercises, individuals are asked as a group to respond to the following questions:

1. How did you approach each of these activities?
2. What differences did you find in your thinking as you approached each task?
3. What was the most challenging part of these exercises for you?
4. Did you read a sample of your description to someone in class? How did they respond?

5. Did you write in your researcher reflective journals on this experience? What were the highlights?

Rationale:

These exercises are part of the practice of technology usage as a regular part of the qualitative researcher's toolkit. They are designed to make the researcher more reflective, establish and strengthen technology habits, and encourage collaboration. Reflection on the actual mechanics of approaching the description of using various types of technology can only assist in awareness of the value of technology and hopefully will inspire curiosity about technology. Individuals are forced to reflect on their own use of technology. By discussing this with other people, members see similarities and differences as part of the scope of disciplined inquiry. The habit of writing in the researcher reflective journal and contributing to the portfolio is enhanced. Technology is the underlying theme in all these exercises. Using technology is a habit that is practiced and learned.

CHAPTER SUMMARY

We have at our fingertips literally and figuratively every possible technological invention for improving our work. Express Scribe, for example can make doing transcriptions a joy rather than a big headache. Assorted websites, electronic mailing lists, blogs, and professional technology services offer researchers in training and skilled researchers a wide repertoire of opportunities. It is in the best interest of qualitative researchers to practice and learn about those techniques, the software, and the freeware that can make the research process smoother. We can save time and energy by learning and practicing good technological habits. The amount of electronic mailing lists, blogs, discussion boards, social media offerings, and software continues to change daily in some cases. What is mentioned here may be outdated quickly so this is a caution for readers. Furthermore, many of our students and new researchers already come into the process as digital natives. Those who are digital immigrants, so to speak, need to be updated on technology if for no other reason than to inspire the next generation of researchers. At every stage of the qualitative research process, technology can be used effectively. Now is the time to work on the technology habit. The list of resources on the Web and in books is plentiful.

Appendixes

Appendix A

Sample Letter to Participants

Note that the purpose of the research is included in your letter; the time commitment, procedures and that the data will only be used for educational purposes.

Dear _____,

I am a doctoral candidate in the Department of Educational Leadership and Organizational Change at Roosevelt University in Chicago, Illinois. I am pursuing my dissertation topic on educational leader perspectives on integrating technology into the undergraduate general education curriculum. The purpose of the study is to describe and explain selected deans', technology directors', and faculty members' perspectives on instructional technology use in the undergraduate general education curriculum. Your participation is requested because of your past and current work as an educational leader at an institution that has integrated technology in the undergraduate general education curriculum.

Participating in the study will require approximately two 1-hour, in-depth interviews. The interviews will, with your permission, be recorded and transcribed. To maintain confidentiality, you will not be identified by name on the recording. I or a professional typist will be transcribing the recordings. An outside reader will read the transcriptions of the recording; however, they will be able to identify the technology directors and assistant deans only as technology director A or assistant dean B. The recordings will be kept in a safe in my house. Each participant will be offered a copy of the recording as well as a copy of the transcription. The participants and I will be the only ones with access to the recordings after transcription. Once the recordings are transcribed, a master recording will be made from the originals, and they will be erased. The master recording will remain in my possession and will be destroyed three years after publication of the dissertation. A comparable amount of time will be required for conducting observations by shadowing you in a variety of situations related to your role as technology director or assistant dean. Interviews and observations will be arranged at the college at your convenience. The tentative schedule calls for one interview in February 2002, one interview in March 2002, and an observation in April 2002.

In addition, you may be asked to share relevant artifacts and documents. Your name, the name of the college, and any other information gathered in this study will remain confidential and will only be used for educational purposes. I appreciate your thoughtful consideration of my request. I look forward to your participation in the study.

Sincerely,
Carolyn N. Stevenson

Appendix B

Sample Consent Form Recently Accepted by the Institutional Review Board (IRB)

This study involves interviewing _____ about _____ and is therefore research.

1. The purpose of this study is _____.

2. The study is expected to last from _____ to _____.

3. The number of people to be interviewed is _____.

4. The procedure of the research involves asking participants about their views on _____.

5. The interviews will be one hour each in length, and each participant will be interviewed twice. The audio recordings will be protected in my home and will be kept for two years.

6. There are no foreseeable risks to the participants, and they may leave the study at any time.

7. Possible benefits are educational, that is, to contribute to the body of knowledge about _____.

8. Members may choose to be completely anonymous, and all names will be changed for reasons of confidentiality. This information will only be known to me and the chair of my dissertation committee.

9. For questions about the research contact me _____ at _____.

10. Participation in this study is totally voluntary. Refusal to participate will not result in penalty or loss of benefits.

11. There is no cost to you to participate in the study.

12. The [name your university] Institutional Review Board, IRB, may be contacted at _____. This IRB may request to see my research records of the study.

I, _____ *[print your name here]* agree to participate in this study with _____. I realize this information will be used for educational purposes. I understand I may withdraw at any time. I understand the intent of this study.

Signed _____ Date _____

Appendix C

*Sample Interview Protocols
From a Completed Study*

By Daryl Ward (2014)

- ## INTERVIEW PROTOCOL 1

The Life Story Interview (adapted from Dan P. McAdams, 2008)

Introduction

This is an interview about the story of your life. As a social scientist, I am interested in hearing your story, including parts of the past as you remember them and the future as you imagine it. The story is selective; it does not include everything that has ever happened to you. Instead, I will ask you to focus on a few key things in your life—a few key scenes, characters, and ideas. There are no right or wrong answers to my questions. Instead, your task is simply to tell me about some of the most important things that have happened in your life and how you imagine your life developing in the future.

A. Life Chapters

Please begin by thinking about your life as a teacher as if it were a book or novel. Imagine that the book has a table of contents containing the titles of the main chapters in the story. To begin here, please describe very briefly what the main chapters in the book might be. Please give each chapter a title, tell me just a little bit about what each chapter is about, and say a word or two about how we get from one chapter to the next. As a storyteller here, what you want to do is to give me an overall plot summary of your story, going chapter by chapter.

B. Key Scenes in Your Life Story as a Teacher

Now that you have described the overall plot outline for your teaching life, I would like you to focus in on a few key scenes that stand out in the story. Consider a key scene to be a moment in your teaching story that stands out for a particular reason—perhaps because it was especially good or bad, particularly vivid, important, or memorable. Below are some prompts for you to consider as key scenes:

1. **High Point.** Please describe a scene, episode, or moment in your career that stands out as an especially positive experience. This might be the high-point scene of your entire life, or else an especially happy, joyous, exciting, or wonderful moment in the story. Please describe this high-point scene in detail. What happened, when and where, who was involved, and what were you thinking and feeling?

2. **Low Point.** The second scene is the opposite of the first. Thinking back over your teaching career, please identify a scene that stands out as a low point. Even though this event is unpleasant, I would appreciate your providing as much detail as you can about it. What happened in the event, where and when, who was involved, and what were you thinking and feeling?

3. **Turning Point.** In looking back over your professional life, it may be possible to identify certain key moments that stand out as turning points—episodes that marked an important change in you or your life story. Please identify a particular episode that you now see as a turning point in your career. If you cannot identify a key turning point that stands out clearly, please describe some event in your teaching life wherein you went through an important change of some kind.

4. **Childhood Memories.** Describe any childhood memories (positive or negative) you can recall about schooling. Think of specific events (fieldtrips, dances), locations (schools), and people (students, teachers). What makes them particularly memorable for you?

Now, we're going to talk about the future.

C. Future Script

1. **The Next Chapter.** Your life story includes key chapters and scenes from your past, as you have described them, and it

also includes how you see or imagine your future. Please describe what you see (or would like to see) as the next chapter in your career.

2. **Life Project.** Do you have a project in life? A life project is something that you have been working on and plan to work on in the future chapters of your life story. The project might involve your family or your work life, or it might be a hobby, avocation, or pastime. How does this project have the potential to impact you as an educator?

D. Challenges

This next section considers the various challenges, struggles, and problems you have encountered in your professional life.

1. **Teaching Challenge.** Looking back over your teaching life, please identify and describe what you now consider to be the greatest single challenge you have faced. What is or was the challenge or problem? How did the challenge or problem develop? What is the significance of this challenge or problem in your teaching life story?

2. **Failure, Regret.** Everybody experiences failure and regrets in life, even for the happiest and luckiest lives. Looking back over your teaching career, can you identify and describe the greatest failure or regret you have experienced? How have you coped with this failure or regret? What effect has this failure or regret had on you and your professional life story?

E. Personal Ideology

Now, I would like to ask a few questions about your fundamental beliefs and values and about teaching and learning. Please give some thought to each of these questions and prompts.

1. What do you feel is the most important aspect of the teacher's role?

2. What is your overarching philosophy of education in general? What is its purpose? Do you feel you have helped or hindered that purpose throughout your career?

F. Reflection

Thank you for this interview. I have just one more question for you. Many of the stories you have told me are about experiences that stand out from the day-to-day experiences. I'm wondering if you might reflect for one last moment about what this interview, here today, has been like for you. What were your thoughts and feelings during the interview? How do you think this interview has affected you? Do you have any other comments about the interview process?

INTERVIEW PROTOCOL 2 ●

Co-Participant Interview Protocol

Please consider thoughtfully the following questions or reflection statements:

1. Think back on your time and experiences in Nina's class—with little introspection (in other words, quickly and responsively), think of three words you would use to describe her teaching and your experiences.

2. Is there a particularly memorable story or event that you recall that happened in Nina's class or was a direct result of an interaction with her? What stories have "stuck with you" these years after leaving her tutelage?

3. Reflecting back on your time as a teacher, can you think of any lessons or pedagogical precepts you learned from Nina? Were there any particularly meaningful examples she set for you in terms of dealing with students?

4. As an administrator, reflect back on how and what Nina taught you. In retrospection, are there any skills or practices you would recommend to other teachers that you recall her employing? How would you describe her as a teacher from an educational leader's perspective?

5. Is there anything else you'd like to add to your recollections of your time spent in Nina's classes?

Appendix D

Qualitative Research Methods:
Sample Syllabus

This syllabus is a recent example of what might be covered in a second qualitative research methods course. I created this syllabus over time and each rotation I update the book selection and readings.

● THEME

> Perhaps the greatest of all pedagogical fallacies is the notion that a person learns only the particular thing he is studying at the time.
>
> —John Dewey, 1967

● COURSE DESCRIPTION

This course deepens the understanding of qualitative research methods, design, data collection, analysis, and interpretation through the focus on selection of qualitative research approaches. Participants will **analyze and interpret observations, documents, and interview data, as well as learn techniques** to enable this. This course **deepens the understanding of qualitative research methods, design, data collection, and analysis. Multiple analysis strategies will be studied. Use of digital cameras and video** recorders will be a central technique practiced this semester. Ethical issues in fieldwork and the role of the researcher will be key topics for discussion and writing. Students will identify the **theoretical framework that guides their work** and potentially their dissertation project.

In this course you will be expected to

- Complete all readings and in-class assignments
- Master and deepen library research and archival skills
- Deepen your practice of interview and observation skills
- Identify your theoretical framework such as phenomenology, critical theory, interpretive interactionism, chaos theory, feminist theory, social constructionism, constructivism
- Identify which of the qualitative approach suits you such as ethnography, bounded case studies, autoethnography, oral history, life history, portraiture, and so on. Continue practice in writing analytical vignettes based on field work, particularly in terms of multiple case analyses
- Discuss in small groups and the groups as a whole, problems related to fieldwork including ethical issues which arise in research
- Continue the study of major writers in the field and learn how to read research articles as a reflective, critical, active agent, and public intellectual. Read, write, discuss, and reflect upon key issues in qualitative case research methods including issues of race, class and gender, issues of practice like locating oneself ideologically, purposeful sampling, and ethical issues in fieldwork.

INSTRUCTIONAL METHODS

1. Small group discussion and group work
2. Computer lab and library work
3. Projects in and out of the classroom
4. Some guest speakers to be announced
5. Some lecture, demonstration, discussion, mini-lectures as needed
6. Documentary film and follow up discussion
7. New techniques for transcribing interviews

EQUIPMENT NEEDED

It is helpful to have a **digital voice recorder for interviews**: any MP3 player or iPod with appropriate attachments, or **iPad application,**

iTalk, or **iSpeak.** The cost of a digital recorder is minimal. Many students buy their equipment at a major discount store. Make life easier for yourself by using a digital voice recorder. In the event you do a qualitative dissertation and need transcriptions done, today's transcribers prefer and charge less for digital interviews that can be sent to the transcriber via e-mail. It is optional, but a digital **camera or a combo digital camera and video recorder** are also quite helpful. This type unit also plugs into the TV monitor, so you can see your interview or observation at any time in class or at home.

Optional foot pedal system for those doing their own transcripts. Olympus makes a device and you need to weigh that against the going rate for transcriptions in the open market. Currently a one-hour interview transcribed from a digital voice recorder is around $110.

Professional Transcriptions:

> Check transcription rates at this transcription center, which is in Los Angeles, California: http://www.productiontranscripts.com

Copy Editor:

> You may need a copy editor for the final reading of your proposal and your final copy for the final defense.

> This site offers services for APA editing and consultancies at fair market value rates: http://myapaeditor.weebly.com/.

Check your local area for copy editors for dissertation work.

For data analysis and representation of text check out this site for graphics, video creation, and so on:

> www.animoto.com

For use of photography as a qualitative technique go to:

> http://www.photovoice.org

Comprehensive List of Mobile Apps for Qualitative Research:

> http://www.mrmw.net/news-blogs/295-a-quick-review-of-mobile-apps-for-qualitative-research

Here is another site for free software:

> http://www.umass.edu/qdap/

Dissertation Support Sites: Here you may want to join a writing group to get you through the dissertation process and you may also find a coach for a monthly fee.

http://www.dissertationdoctor.com

http://www.academicladder.com

Required reading in common: Note that many books are available in the library and, in addition, as an e-book in the library. Thus there is no cost for reading e-books through the library site or taking books out of the library.

PACE YOURSELF. ESSENTIALLY, YOU READ A BOOK A MONTH AND AT LEAST ONE OR TWO ARTICLES PER MONTH.

SELECT ONE OF THESE FIRST TWO BOOKS AS YOUR MAJOR TEXT:

1. *Qualitative Inquiry and Research Design: Choosing Among Five Approaches* (3rd ed.) by John W. Creswell (Thousand Oaks, CA: Sage, 2013).

OR

2. *Qualitative Research: The Essential Guide to Theory and Practice* by Maggi Savin-Baden and Claire Howell Major (New York, NY: Routledge, 2013).

WE ALL ALSO READ TOGETHER:

The Coding Manual for Qualitative Researchers by Johnny Saldaña (Thousand Oaks, CA: Sage, 2010).

"Stretching" Exercises for Qualitative Researchers (3rd ed.) by Valerie J. Janesick (Thousand Oaks, CA: Sage, 2011).

If you are using interviewing as your major technique in the dissertation data collection process this book is **highly recommended**:

Qualitative interviewing the art of hearing data (3rd ed.) by Herbert J. Rubin and Irene S. Rubin (Thousand Oaks, CA: Sage, 2012).

REQUIRED: SELECT ONE OF THESE OPTIONAL TEXTS for your reading, reporting to the class, and future use. These are completed studies or methods supplements. Upon reading the text, have a one-page handout for class members or an online copy describing the pertinent information:

Title, author, publisher, number of pages in the book, cost of the book, main ideas, lessons learned about the content and methods used

Would you recommend this book or not? Explain.

To report to the class, use any media of your choice. SELECT ONE:

These represent methods and completed qualitative projects.

An Anthopologist on Mars by Oliver Sacks (New York, NY: Knopf, 1995) (Or any book by Oliver Sacks).

Animal, Vegetable, Miracle by Barbara Kingsolver (New York, NY: HarperCollins, 2007).

The Art and Science of Portraiture by Sara Lawrence-Lightfoot and Jessica Hoffmann Davis (San Francisco, CA: Jossey-Bass, 1997).

Detroit: An American Autopsy by Charlie LeDuff (New York, NY: Penguin, 2014).

The Good, the Bad and the Data: Shane the Lone Ethnographer's Guide to Qualitative Data Analysis by Sally Campbell Galman (Walnut Creek, CA: Left Coast Press, 2013).

Digital Tools for Qualitative Research by Trena Paulus, Jessica Nina Lester, and Paul Dempster (Thousand Oaks, CA: Sage, 2014).

The Immortal Life of Henrietta Lacks by Rebecca Skloot (New York, NY: Broadway Books, 2001).

Interpretive Autoethnography (2nd ed.) by Norman K. Denzin (Thousand Oaks, CA: Sage, 2014).

Lives in Context: The Art of Life History Research by Ardra L. Cole and Gary J. Knowles (Walnut Creek, CA: Alta Mira Press, 2001).

Living autobiographically: How we create identity in narrative by Paul John Eakin (Ithaca, NY: Cornell University Press, 2008).

Musicophilia: Tales of Music and the Brain by Oliver Sacks (New York, NY: Knopf, 2007).

On writing by Stephen King (New York, NY: Scribner, 2000).

Open: An Autobiography by Andre Agassi (New York, NY: Vintage Books, 2009).

Oral History for the Qualitative Researcher: Choreographing the Story by Valerie J. Janesick (New York, NY: Guilford Press, 2010).

Playbuilding as Qualitative Research: A Participatory Arts-Based Approach by Joe Norris (Walnut Creek, CA: Left Coast Press, 2009).

Qualitative Content Analysis in Practice by Margrit Schreier (Thousand Oaks, CA: Sage, 2012).

The Qualitative Dissertation (2nd ed.) by Maria Piantanida and Noreen B. Gorman (Thousand Oaks, CA: Corwin, 2009).

Qualitative Research: Studying How Things Work by Robert E. Stake (New York, NY: Guilford Press, 2010).

Researching Lived Experience: Human Science for an Action Sensitive Pedagogy by Max Van Manen (Albany: SUNY Press, 1990).

Reviewing Qualitative Research in the Social Sciences by Audrey A. Trainor and Elizabeth Graue (New York, NY: Routledge, 2013).

Writing Down the Bones: Freeing the Writer Within by Natalie Goldberg (Boston, MA: Shambala Press, 2005).

Recommendations:

All class members go to AERA's site for information on this professional organization:

http://www.aera.net/Default.aspx?id=777

Also check the qualitative methods blogging if you like.

There are key journals in hard text and online journals which focus on qualitative inquiry. There are numerous Web resources and transcription services.

Check out the e-journal *The Qualitative Report* online: Sign up for free delivery of the journal and also the weekly newsletter at the same site. You will receive extra credit for being on the list for both the newsletter and the journal:

http://www.nova.edu/ssss/QR/index.html

Electronic Resources: A comprehensive listing can be found at

http://www.nova.edu/ssss/QR/web.html

CRITICAL TASKS/DEMONSTRATIONS OF LEARNING   ●

There will be FOUR CRITICAL TASKS/DEMONSTRATIONS OF LEARNING. Three of them graded with a letter grade and percentage. The fourth is graded as Pass/Fail.

1. FIRST CRITICAL TASK/DEMONSTRATION OF LEARNING: *TAKE-HOME EXAM* due _____. You will receive the questions two weeks before the due date.

2. SECOND CRITICAL TASK/DEMONSTRATION OF LEARNING: *REFLECTION* on your role as a qualitative researcher; five to seven pages due _____.

3. THIRD CRITICAL TASK/DEMONSTRATION OF LEARNING: *INTERVIEW PROJECT* and report—25-page minimum, unlimited pages as maximum. If you have recently, within the past year but preferably within two semesters, completed two interviews and have the transcripts from a previous class, you may

rework those transcripts and find at least two NEW ways to explain the data and construct two models to explain the data. <u>Due no later than the final date of class at 5:00 PM.</u>

4. FOURTH CRITICAL TASK/DEMONSTRATION OF LEARNING: There will be a report to the class on a book of your choice in any media format: powerpoint-style slide presentation; online on YouTube, Glogster, or PosterMyWall; or verbally with one-page handout.

This is graded Pass/Fail. We will begin presentations _____.

Book report on your selected exemplar of a study completed with handout OR powerpoint-style presentation reporting on the book you selected to read as an example of a completed study, highlighting the methodology, to be presented in class. Or if you have a better media technique such as a movie, or a poem or a play, for example, feel free to teach through that media.

There will be **three in-class assignments,** including observation exercises and an interview exercises, with Pass/Fail grading during some of our class time.

Each class member must pass the following tasks at the proficiency level:

A. Participant observation exercise including field notes, thick description, preliminary informed hunches, and what would you do next for

   *observation of a social setting or a person (in-class activity)

B. Interview and preliminary data analysis of same for

   *interview of a person you know or a stranger (in-class activity)

C. Practice with digital photography (as needed)

D. Document review and analysis (as needed)

E. Writing in the researcher reflective journal. (See the site www.penzu.com for doing your journal electronically.)

Attendance, class participation, and field work is 20% of your grade.

GRADING ●

1. Students must inform the instructor before the due date if an assignment will not be ready on time. Students who are absent must find someone to take notes and pick up any in-class hand-outs for them. Recall that each Saturday is basically worth three classes of real semester time.

2. Students must inform the instructor before class when and if they will be late or absent from any class. Each project is worth:

% Mastery	Grade
100–95	A
94–90	A–
89–86	B+
85–80	B
79–70	C

Standard rules of etiquette apply in class. Thus, it is advised that all cell phones, pagers, and other distracters be turned off out of respect for the learners in the class. Refrain from offensive language and bullying.

TOPICS AND SCHEDULE: SUBJECT TO CHANGE ●

We will discuss specific pages and chapters for assignments as needed. Pace yourself in your reading time and completion. Build yourself a good library of methods texts and articles.

Class Meeting and Topic	Assignment
1. Intro to class, each other, syllabus, in-class observations	Begin Text 1
2. Questions for research, in-class observation activity	Continue Text 1
3. Nonparticipant/observation/ interviewing, documents, library strategies, obs. activity continued, introduction to technology usage	Complete Text 1; begin Text 2

(Continued)

(Continued)

Class Meeting and Topic	Assignment
4. Analyzing interview data, category development, first assignment due, interview activity, in-class narrative methods	Continue Text 2
5–9. Document analysis and archival techniques, computer-assisted data analysis, Interview Activity 2; finding your theoretical frame and locating yourself	Begin Interview Text 3
10–15. Qualities of the qualitative, second assignment due, multimethod descriptive validity	Complete Interview Text 3 Continue next readings Complete all readings Self-selected text reporting

● CRITICAL TASK/DEMONSTRATION OF LEARNING: INTERVIEW PROJECT ASSIGNMENT

Due: On the final class night at 5:00 PM.

Reminder: This project cannot be handed in late.

Living with and making sense of transcripts: Developing a model of what you learned in your mini-study. Describe the setting in all its richness, describe the person being interviewed with as much of their history as possible.

For this assignment construct a model of what occurred. In narrative form, tell the story of the individual's views and list the initial categories that emerged from the data, then the shortened list of actual categories that helped you to develop your model. Be creative and use good graphics. Add photos as needed to lead the reader through the report. Be sure to use direct quotations from the transcripts. **Be sure to use at five references from our texts.**

Project: Interview one person, twice, so that you have the experience of going back for an interview. Interviews should be at approximately one hour in length each. The topic of the interview is (suggested) "What does your work mean to you?" Transcribe the first interview. Required.

Note: If you are at the point that you are focused on your dissertation study, you may wish to do a **pilot** study interviewing a potential member of your study. In which case, let's make a contract for this.

If you already have two transcripts from this project in your previous qualitative class, your assignment will be to review more deeply your transcripts and find another way to interpret your data including

A. A new set of themes and a new visual model

B. A description of your process

C. Relevant references

D. Any related appendixes of your choice

WHAT DOES YOUR WORK MEAN TO YOU? ●

Select an educator or other professional to interview about what work means to that person. The first interview should have some basic grand-tour questions such as the following:

Interview Protocol A: First Interview

1. What does your work mean to you?

2. Talk about a typical day at work. What does it look like?

3. Tell me what you like about your job.

4. Tell me what you dislike about your job.

5. Where do you see yourself in 5 to 10 years?

Interview Protocol B

You create the questions based on what you found in the first interview and to get to the goal of the interview.

This should take at least an hour but no longer than 90 minutes, per interview. Remember that people are busy and they most likely can only give you an hour at a time. Aim for each interview to take an hour of time. Be sure to take field notes so you can probe into areas of this first interview during the second interview. Be sure to record all this. Be sure to get informed consent. Use the sample consent form that is in the book *"Stretching" Exercises.*

Due on last class: A paper or report—25-page minimum, any number of pages—which includes at least the following:

A. Describe in detail why you selected this person.

B. Describe the context, the setting, and the person interviewed in full.

C. Describe briefly your theoretical frame that guides the study.

D. Provide a list of all the questions asked in each interview and label them Interview Protocol A, Interview Protocol B.

E. Summarize the responses from both interviews in some meaningful way with precise quotations from the interview.

F. Pull out at least **three themes** from the interviews and create a **visual model** of these themes and any sub themes

G. Tell the story of what this person's life work means to this person.

H. Include the signed consent form.

I. Discuss any ethical issues which may have come up.

J. Add a sample of 10 pages of your best transcript from the recording as an appendix.

K. Describe your role as the researcher. Explain your values and beliefs and specify how you conducted this mini interview study.

L. Finally, **include at least three pages** or more of your own reflections on your skills as an interviewer, as a researcher, and what you learned from this project; be sure to mention any difficulties that came up, what you would change the next time you conducted an interview.

M. Be sure to use references from our texts this term.

N. Be sure to create a title that captures your themes.

Answer the following questions:

O. What difficulties did you encounter in the field setting?

P. What would you do differently if you were to return?

Q. What did you learn about yourself as a researcher?

R. If you had all the time and money in the world, what would you like to do next or differently?

Remember that this is a narrative research paradigm, so you should write this in narrative form as if you were telling this person's story. The story is about the person's life work.

Critical Task/Demonstration of Learning: Take-home exam.

Due _____.

Critical Task/ Demonstration of Learning Critique:

Five to seven pages. Critique of your own skills as a researcher: your observational skills, interview skills, reflective journal writing skills, narrative writing skills. Due on final class day at 5:00 PM.

Critical Task/Demonstration of Learning:

Book report on your self-selected book in any media format presenting to the class. Presentations will begin in November and continue until completed. These may be individual or in a group if you select the same book.

For your slide presentation, video, or verbal presentation, imagine you are teaching the class about this book. What are the main ideas content-wise and what qualitative techniques are evidenced throughout the book? In other words, what is this case exactly? Use your imagination and creativity to display your knowledge base. List the information about the book: title, author, publication date, publisher, number of pages, and cost.

WRITING RUBRIC   ●

Each item is worth 20 points.

_____ 1. Creates an organizing structure establishes context and relevance; introduces the purpose of the project.

_____ 2. Selects and summarizes key ideas to establish context appropriate to audience by using tools such as precise language, descriptive language, and authoritative voice. Establishes an interpretive claim or assertion. Uses an organizational structure that allows for a progression of ideas to develop.

_____ 3. Skillfully selects and summarizes key ideas to establish context appropriate to audience by using tools such as precise language, descriptive language, and authoritative voice: analysis of relevant experiences, thoughts, constructed knowledge.

_____ 4. Demonstrates awareness of content of a given text and clearly connects it to appropriate theoretical constructs showing deep understanding and thoughtfulness. Uses appropriate references to the text.

_____ 5. Demonstrates facility with language, APA style, and correct use of grammar. Uses correct paragraph development. Writing contains references to and understanding of any or all of the texts in class and contains correct grammar, spelling, punctuation, sentence construction, and paragraph construction. Note all paragraphs must have a minimum of three sentences. Writing is submitted, typed, double-spaced. The requirements of the assignment are met.

● PLAGIARISM

Copying someone else's work is a very serious offense and can bring about a student's removal from the program and the university. You plagiarize when, intentionally or not, you use someone else's words or ideas without giving them credit. Quotation marks should be used whenever you are using the exact words of another author. Square brackets and ellipses should be used to indicate any words that are deleted from the original material. Summarizing a passage from another source or rearranging the order of a sentence or sentences is *paraphrasing*. Every time you paraphrase the work of another author, you should give credit to the author by citing. If you are using someone else's ideas, you must give them credit as early as possible in your text. In this course, if you are found guilty of plagiarism, you may receive an F (failure) in this course and be dropped from the program.

● ETIQUETTE AND NETIQUETTE

Be respectful of your classmates. Not all students may share your views, so listen carefully and respond in a way that permits difference of opinion to exist. All class etiquette standards apply. Put into practice Paulo Freire's respect for one another. If you insult someone in class, be sure to apologize before you leave class. Please no side bar conversation in the back or while someone is speaking. It is extremely rude. And remember **this is your reference group for your career lifespan**.

Netiquette is etiquette on the Web and on Blackboard. All standard etiquette applies as well as the following:

1. Do not send any information out under another person's name. Use your own name only.

2. When you send an e-mail, begin with a courteous salutation such as *Good morning, Good afternoon,* or *Dear Jane Doe.* Likewise, end your e-mail with a sign off and your name. For example, *Thanks,* (your name) or *Best wishes* or *Warm regards,* for example. It is confusing for some to receive an e-mail without identification.

3. Remember that e-mail is forever. Think before you write.

4. Avoid naming a person in your e-mails, for example, *Jane Doe said such and such.* Instead depersonalize it with something like, *a person who had responsibility once said X.*

5. Also, if you insult your class members or the professor or both, please be sure to make amends with an apology.

● ATTENDANCE AND LATENESS POLICY

Regular attendance and on-time arrival in each class is expected. It is, however, the responsibility of the student to discuss with the instructor in advance the reason for an absence. The student must call or e-mail the instructor ahead of time if an absence is necessary. It is the student's responsibility to arrange with a fellow student to get copies of handouts, notes, and adjustments in assignments. Absences or chronic tardiness may have an adverse effect on a student's grade. Only one absence is allowed, but the student must still write a minimum of one page of reflections on the assigned reading for the class which has been missed. A second absence will result in a lower final grade. To make up a missed class, please write a three to six page reflection on the readings for that day you missed.

MISCELLANEOUS: ACCOUNT REQUIRED

RefWorks: http://www.refworks.com/

Ref Works is a research management system designed to help you organize your research, simplify references storage, and keep abstracts and articles for further use in your research. If your university library subscribes to this system, it is free for you.

OR

EndNote: http://endnote.com/

EndNote is a research management system that charges fair market value fees.

EACH CLASS MEMBER MUST BE A MEMBER OF A PROFESSIONAL ORGANIZATION FOR PROFESSIONAL DEVELOPMENT.

By student request, this is added to my syllabus for your future work.

● WHAT EVERY DISSERTATION PROPOSAL SHOULD CONTAIN

Here is a sample checklist of items for each chapter that you may use as a guide. Of course, depending on your purpose and questions, not all items are appropriate. This is to be a guide, not a slavish recipe, for you as you clarify your research agenda.

CHAPTER ONE: The Problem, Purpose, Theory Which Guides the Study (8–10 pages depending on purpose, content, etc., of the designed study)

- ❑ Introduction (make this brief—one page is ideal)
- ❑ Statement for the need for the study and the problem to be addressed
- ❑ THE PURPOSE OF THE STUDY—Be precise and accurate
- ❑ Questions which guide the study if a qualitative study

- ☐ Use of objectives or hypotheses if your study is quantitative
- ☐ Description of the theory which guides your study
- ☐ Importance of the study
- ☐ Definition of terms if needed
- ☐ Outline of the remainder of the dissertation

CHAPTER TWO: Review of Related Literature
(25–40 pages depending on categories of the review)

- ☐ Organization of the chapter
- ☐ Immediate identification the bodies of literature you are reviewing
- ☐ Acquainting the reader with the state of the art and explaining why you selected this particular set of categories of literature to review
- ☐ Identification of books, monographs, reports, articles which pinpoint exactly what you want to say relative to your purpose statement and the theory which guides your study
- ☐ Serious critique of your literature looking for gaps, contradictions, and criticism of the writing you have selected
- ☐ Relation of your literature directly to your purpose statement and your study emphasizing how this literature led you to the study
- ☐ REMEMBER, A LITERATURE REVIEW IS NOT A SUMMARY OF THE LITERATURE—IT IS A REVIEW.

CHAPTER THREE: Methodology
(20–40 pages depending on methods used)

- ☐ Overview
- ☐ Description of the methodology and the rationale for choosing this method
- ☐ Description of the research design
- ☐ Description of the pilot study
- ☐ Description of how you selected the participants of the study

❏ Exact description of how you plan to collect data, under what conditions, and the length of time involved

❏ Any supplemental charts or tables which help the reader to understand your method

❏ Connection of your method back to your purpose, questions, and literature

❏ Identification of any limitations to your method in this particular study and for your purposes only

❏ Description of how you will analyze your data

❏ Summary

❏ Any appendixes

❏ An About-the-Author paragraph

As you can see, this is a good way to prepare your dissertation proposal. Realize that it may change throughout the process of data collection and analysis and you simply rewrite as needed. Prior to the proposal meeting, all members of your committee should have your proposal for at least 14 days. Your goal at this point is to get your proposal approved after you have a clear idea of what you want to know, what literature relates to your study, and what method is appropriate to your purpose. Never choose a method before you choose a purpose for the study. Once you have this groundwork done, you need only to complete your last two chapters of the dissertation which consists of the following:

CHAPTER FOUR: Presentation of the Data

In this chapter, you present your findings and make sense of them for your reader. Here is your opportunity to analyze and evaluate what you found. This chapter usually is a response to your questions or hypotheses. Be sure to use exact quotations from your participants in the study if doing a qualitative study. These data are from interviews, observations, journals, and written documents, for example.

Be sure to include a RATIONALE for how you present the data, for example, as cases, as one case study, as a narrative, as a dialogue, and so on. Include tables and figures as needed. For direct quotations from interviews, indent and single space substantial quotations.

CHAPTER FIVE: Summary, Conclusions, Recommendations

This chapter ties the dissertation together and defends your thesis about the research. Briefly summarize the chapters and come to your conclusions. Now you may make recommendations of a practical nature for your major audience. In a sense, you are describing how the reader may implement your findings. Be sure to INTERPRET YOUR MAJOR AND MINOR FINDINGS in the study. Be sure to state what you learned as a researcher.

If you do a qualitative study, you must respond to your EXPLORATORY QUESTIONS in this chapter and DEVELOP A MODEL OF WHAT OCCURRED. Your model may be visually represented by diagrams, tables, for example. or verbally. You need to show the reader that your model is GROUNDED IN YOUR DATA.

Note: If you are adding additional chapters in the event you are doing a historical study or any other reason, follow the standards of your given discipline.

APPENDIXES

- ☐ Copy of your consent form
- ☐ Copy of your peer/outside reader form
- ☐ Copies of any letters you sent out to participants
- ☐ Sample of your best section of a transcript
- ☐ Sample of your best example of a field note
- ☐ Sample of your best researcher reflective journal entry
- ☐ Page which lists the costs associated with your dissertation (optional)
- ☐ Any other pertinent information related to the study
- ☐ Copy of your certificate from the IRB indicating you are up to date for research
- ☐ Your own About-the-Author paragraph

Appendix E

Sample Projects From Various Classes

This is a collection of sample topics from qualitative methods classes that students have undertaken.

- Looming Large: Linking Lives and Literacy at the Library
- An Interview Study of Florida's Outstanding Teacher of the Year
- An Interview Study of an Emergency Room Nurse
- Traditional Cuts: Life in a Barber Shop
- Teaching Science: Not for Everyone
- The Ice House Pub: Where People Go to Chill
- Drink: A Study of a Nightclub and Drinking
- Skin Deep: The Waiting Room of a Dermatology Clinic
- Sideline Sidebars on the Soccer Field
- The Life of a Reference Librarian
- An Oral History Study of a Female University Administrator
- An Oral History of a Holocaust Survivor
- A Life History of a Librarian
- Strong Woman: A Study of an Activist Grandmother
- Peace With Bombs: A Study of Military Views on War
- The Road Not Taken: A Doctoral Journey
- Perspectives on the Tampa Bay Writing Project

Appendix F

Examples of Researcher Reflective Journals

EXAMPLE 1: REFLECTIONS ON A QUALITATIVE RESEARCH CLASS (EDITED)   ●

By Ruth Slotnick (2010)

My greatest challenge when doing this project has been my own energy level. Quite frankly, I am exhausted. The writing demands of my dissertation over the past eight months have zapped my ability to fully engage. The next time I do an observation, I need a little recuperative time between projects. This is a valuable lesson learned. I need to rest, relax, read fiction, read qualitative literature, and refuel. As far as meeting my personal goals of systemizing and organization, I feel that I have incrementally improved. Recording entries in a reflective journal, however, still feels like an afterthought. I am not yet regimented and disciplined enough to write immediately upon completing fieldwork. This practice (or laziness) must change or else the process feels half baked.

Sharan Merriam (2009) underscores the painstaking process of honing the researcher's eye and developing a razor-edge focus while systematically recording the descriptive detail required for both participant and nonparticipant observations (p.118). [I feel that my skills to capture complexity have greatly increased over the last week.] The researcher's reflective journal combined with taking copious field notes forms the thick texture and rich dimension that make the researched context come alive. [My field notes and reflective journal have added to these descriptive layers.] Otherwise, Merriam notes, "Data are nothing more than ordinary bits and pieces of information found in the environment" (p. 85). Valerie Janesick (2004) argues that the reflective journal should be used in conjunction with the field notes. The journal becomes an introspective crucible or self-evaluation device that allows the qualitative researcher a place to mix together perceptions, intuitions, and hunches not necessarily explored in descriptive data. Together, these basic skills help the qualitative researcher fine-tune their research skill sets and continuously sharpen the tools of the "descriptive inquirer" (p. 2). In developing these skills, Janesick states that a novice researcher must locate his or her own "personal velocity" and methodology that "resonates" with who he or she is (p. 6). Stated differently, aside from knowing self, the qualitative researcher must find a pattern and a speed that naturally allows him or her to fully observe, efficiently collect, deeply analyze, carefully synthesize, and ultimately construct a compelling account of the study. To accomplish this, one must be "persistent and indomitable" (p. 8) if they are to achieve the painstakingly disciplined and rewarding work of the qualitative researcher. However, Janesick is quick to note that remaining open to the data and arriving to it each time anew with no preconceived notions, no matter how seasoned one is to the process, is paramount (p. 2). Finally, she stresses that the health of the researcher is imperative to successfully accomplish the qualitative quest because the researcher is the collection instrument. Trust me when I say that it is wise to heed her call.

Writing the Dissertation Proposal

October 25, 2008

I'm organizing the literature review. Have a goal to really get better at synthesizing and writing. I think I will always be a slow synthesizer and writer. The goal is to be precise but take it easy on myself as my brain is desperately trying to gnaw on thoughts. I am not a better-than-average writer, which is listed as number 10 on Janesick's (2004) scale of necessary attributes needed to conduct and complete a qualitative dissertation. For the most part, I possess the rest of the attributes, including an intense focus, passion, and authenticity, attributes that top the list. Ambiguity and flexibility are words that I have to have more patience with, but I must admit that, five years ago, I was neither cognitively disciplined enough nor patient enough to pursue a doctorate. Years of feeling a little stupid by a traumatic event that occurred in grade school (I was held back a grade in elementary school after the school year was well underway, which was humiliating in its own right) and a series of academic stumbling blocks, including difficulty with quickly grasping statistical concepts and an inability to fully express myself in writing, led to its own academic paralysis. It haunts me still when I am confronted by these shadowy demons. So, the attempt to organize does help. The papers, the stacks of books from the library, new books with glossy covers—all are just waiting to be read, contemplated, and synthesized. If my head was not such a sieve, I might just remember all the things I underlined and why I thought it linked to something important in my research. Perhaps this journaling process will allow me to have some cognitive dissonance from my dissertation, giving me the freedom to be completely open in the writing process without the fear that it will stand in judgment of my committee. It is my own place to be as stupid and as smart as I feel, a place to record my ideas.

Reflection: On Analysis

May 30, 2009

I am in the process of what Maria Piantanida and Noreen Garman (1999) describe as "living with the study" and "slogging through" as I gather my research "stuff" (p.129). *Stuff* is described as all things pertaining to the study. Stuff is defined as more than the numeric data. It is anything and everything that goes into collection for data analysis. Stuff feels larger and rounder and perhaps less formal or not so cold as the word *data*. Then, they define five distinct phases or facets (their term) of living with the data:

1. Immersing oneself in inquiry

2. Amassing the stuff of the inquiry

3. Slogging through the stuff

4. Coming to the conceptual leap

5. Crafting portrayals

What exactly do they mean by portrayals? Does that mean my interpretation of what was portrayed via the stuff? Does it mean my descriptions or renderings? Or putting together the picture? Is the crafting of portrayals just like doing a textual reading of Shakespeare? As the director or actor, how would I portray the character I am acting? Isn't the reading of a play a hermeneutic journey in itself? Piantanida and Garman continue describing the analysis process, advising the novice researcher that the last step is "generating knowledge through crafting portrayals" (p. 130). The word *crafting* is really important for it implies that the human hand of the researcher interprets and shapes the text. I need to define crafting a bit more. Crafting is defined as a skilled activity. The text becomes the object to be shaped by the hand of the researcher—the researcher's clay. As I craft the portrayal of my study, the integrity and rigor are judged by the depth of analysis that I give to data, the stuff. Even what I am writing here is part of the crafting. I want to write more about my idea of the researcher's clay. The stuff becomes the vessel. Everything goes into stuff. Everything in the studio—lights, electricity, kiln, chemicals, water, clay, potter, and energy—all produce the handcrafted, finished piece.

● EXAMPLE 2: REFLECTION ON BECOMING A RESEARCHER

By Bea Smith (2014)

Reflection

When I was little, I beamed with pride as I announced to every new person I met that I was adopted and proud of it! My mom always made me feel special about that fact and to this day I have never had an inclination to find my birth parents. That is not to say my childhood was perfect but I truly knew both my parents and family members loved me very much. For my parents, it also probably helped that I was an "easy" child to raise; I was the middle child and both my brother, seven years older, and my sister, 20 months younger (she was also adopted) had rebellious periods that challenged my parents while I somehow coasted into early adulthood with few scars (with the exception of the pain over the breakup from my first love at age 15) and I have been described since I was very young as being an "old soul" with a good heart. Even my mom's divorce from my dad when I was in college was more of a relief than a shock (she had vowed to stay with him until my sister graduated from high school despite many unhappy years of marriage).

I started first grade in 1969 in Tampa as a member of the first generation to attend public schools that were desegregated by legal mandate; I never experienced a racial divide and luckily, despite my mom's and grandmother's obvious prejudices (revealed more so when I was older), I was taught to be tolerant, compassionate. I was a teen during the 1970s and literally lived at church during my adolescent years and delayed many experimental activities until I was in college (I'm definitely glad

I waited!) In high school, my AP English teacher instilled in me a love of English, writing, and teaching. I had assumed from age five that I would become an elementary teacher but chose secondary English ed instead and that same teacher who had been my role model hired me as a first-year teacher at my high school at age 20. We are still friends today.

My First Adulthood

For my *First Adulthood* during the 1980s, I followed the *usual path* as described by Gail Sheehy. I got married within a few years of graduating from college. I did prolong my engagement by a year to take my first trip abroad to Europe with three fellow teachers [I was 22; they were in their early 40s; we had a fabulous time and my exposure to life outside the United States with visits to London, Paris, Switzerland and Italy left an invaluable impression as this was the first time I was reminded that here was a world outside of Tampa, Florida.] I then put my teaching career and future aspirations on the back burner and encouraged my husband, who had been adamant when we first met that he would never attend college, to pursue his dream of becoming an Air Force officer and pilot and college grad (he earned both his bachelor's and later his master's with probably a little too much help from me . . .) and I followed him to Alabama, Missouri, and Washington, DC as the dutiful wife and a role model, as the epitome of an "officer's wife" for the next eight years. Per Sheehy, I became the "nurturer who defers achievement." On the positive side, I absolutely embraced the military life and loved the moves, exposure to new places and cultures, and the opportunity to travel.

However, I did begin to get restless in my late 20s and decided virtually overnight to start graduate school and earned my MS in counseling in six semesters and immediately upon graduation was hired as a high school guidance counselor in Knob Noster, Missouri. My husband transferred to the Washington DC area a year later and my career was put on hold once again. I now realize my then husband and I were beginning to go different directions termed by Sheehy as the *Catch-30* syndrome (pp. 40–42) but nothing in my life up to that point prepared me for the excruciating pain I would experience a few years later when he abruptly ended our marriage (we had been together almost 15 years and married nine) over Thanksgiving weekend after having his parents in town; he broke the news to me on the drive back from dropping them off at the airport. I soon discovered (*through my own detective work*) that he had left me for the vice-president of his sports car club. I waited three months for him to admit the affair to me but I was the one to finally confront him with my knowledge. To this day, some of the pain is as raw as it was almost two decades ago and I would never wish the pain of infidelity (being on the receiving end of it anyway) on my worst enemy. It changed my life.

I quickly realized I would not be able to remain in the DC area on my salary so began applying for positions in Florida and ironically, landed back in Tampa much to the delight of my aging parents, and my role as primary caretaker to them officially began in my mid-30s. In hindsight, as I reflect on my *First Adulthood*, I did indeed survive a few significant *marker events* (Sheehy, p. 29), which have served to define me and my future choices and the need for change as I have progressed through midlife. I was only officially single for four months after my divorce was finalized and finally focused on my career and began to advance as a college administrator. A significant event during this time that again changed my life path was experiencing bullying by a veteran colleague who decided I had not paid my dues and was advancing too quickly. I tried as hard as I could to handle the situation but eventually was encouraged by my partner to look for another position as my request for formal mediation to my supervisor and HR office did not improve the climate.

So despite taking a salary cut and lower position when I transferred to a new campus, I quickly made up for lost time both salary- and position-wise. Welcome to my 40s!

I, with the support of my partner, finally decided it was the right time to become a mom. I miscarried and decided that I would try one more time. A little over a year later, I delivered my daughter via C-section at age 41 and also reluctantly married again just prior to her arrival (at 8 ½ months pregnant at the local court house) primarily to give our daughter a "legitimate" last name. I did, however, retain my maiden name this time around and my husband and I just recently surpassed the length of time I had been in my previous relationship. It's more like a partnership this time around, but we both carry scars from past life experiences and relationships and I tend to think that you do things differently in future relationships, some things as the result of learning from past mistakes and maturity as we age and some the result of the reluctance to let down our guards if we've been hurt or betrayed or left behind previously. (I must also admit I suffered from post-partum depression for a couple of months after my daughter's birth [*it's unbelievably humbling to be in total control and then become a late-in-life mom and feel like you have no clue*] and it is indeed a legitimate condition and very scary place to be.

It has become obvious recently that in the world of academia and in my current administrative role that I have reached my career ceiling. I am unable to apply for higher level positions despite having the appropriate experience and background, due to not having a doctorate. At the same time, I have also discovered as a late-in-life mom that I have a drive to provide as well as I can for my family's future, just as my mom had for our family. So with the blessing and amazing support from my husband, who has also been an amazing stay-at-home dad for our daughter since her birth and has taken a back seat to my career progression, **I started my PhD at age 47.** When I announced to my mom, who was beginning to decline over the past few years due to serious health issues, that I was finally going to start my doctorate (*she had encouraged me to do so for many years*), she indicated that she was not sure it was such a good idea with all of my responsibilities including looking out for her; I was taken aback by her response.

I now know that Mom realized that her days were numbered and that she would need to rely on me even more. When it became apparent to us that she would not be able to return to her apartment and that she was dying, we moved her in with us and by then she required around-the-clock care and could no longer walk or do anything without assistance. Ironically, we had just moved my mother-in-law who had lived with us for almost three years to an ALF so literally packed up her stuff and replaced it with my mom's stuff. I still held out hope that we would have her around longer but I knew she did not want to live in the condition she was in. When she passed, a peace came over me as I knew she was no longer suffering. She was 82. I miss her every day. She was my best friend. Life goes on. I turn 50 this fall and then should be sitting for qualifying exams to enter doctoral candidacy next spring. I am looking forward to the prospect of being what Sheehy terms a "late-baby superachiever." As she suggests in the introduction of *Passages*, my Second Adulthood *should* be the most satisfying time of my life both professionally and personally.

Appendix G

Sample Evaluative Rubric for a Qualitative Project

● ASSIGNMENT: INTERVIEW PROJECT

Strengths in Your Work:

_____ Presented data effectively to support themes and model constructed

_____ Work handed in on time

_____ Ideas presented clearly and the title reflects the content

_____ Creativity and imagination evident

_____ Connected texts from the readings in this class in your work (at least five references)

_____ Had appropriate conclusions supported with evidence

_____ Had appropriate summary

_____ Evidence of serious reflection

_____ Integrated technology in the report of findings; visual models, other

_____ Responded to questions listed on syllabus

_____ Use of appropriate research examples as needed

_____ Other—Met page requirement and followed APA 6th edition style

_____ Attached appropriate matter such as field notes, interview transcripts, photographs, and other docs as needed

_____ Responded to questions seriously and practiced self evaluation

Comments:

Areas for Improvement:

_____ Need to show evidence of serious, layered reflection on the topic, conclusions, and/or introductions

_____ Need to develop stronger summary and conclusions

_____ Need to indicate rationale for the selection of site/topic

_____ Need to show evidence that you read the texts

_____ Need to work on punctuation, grammar, and paragraph development

_____ Need to focus on _____

_____ Need to read syllabus and follow critical task requirements

_____ Need to focus on writing and/or narrative writing and APA 6th edition style

Comments:

You have earned the grade of _____ for this assignment.

You have earned the grade of _____ for this course.

Appendix H

Sample Sets of Themes and
Categories From a Completed Study

By Daryl Ward (2014)

● PRELIMINARY THEMES AND SUBTHEMES

The crux of this work has been to explore the research questions at the heart of this research project. By examining Nina's life history and through careful analysis of the co-participant's narratives, I posit that indeed there are generative characteristics found in the teaching behaviors of Nina Brown. Combined with my own reflections, the other educational leaders offered stories that revealed patterns of thoughts and actions in Nina's life. These patterns remained largely unexamined until brought to light through the specific lens of narrative inquiry: What about Nina and the other's stories reveal deeper insights into the phenomenon of generativity? After deep review of the data—living with it, one might say—it became evident that there were four specific generative themes that emerged: flexibility, compassion for all students, passion for teaching/learning, and content knowledge (see Figure H.1). These four areas revealed themselves through stories, poetry, and artifact analysis. The narratives of the co-participants offered examples of how these aspects of Nina's teaching have played out in their own professional lives.

This research project has sought to contribute to the field of educational life history research by creating a teacher's life history from her own recollections, reflections, artwork, and poetry. I used these data-collection methods to draft a narrative that, while it aspires to a high claim of authenticity, is still interpretive in nature; it is *my* version of Nina's story—though many of the stories and thoughts are her own. Thus, in many respects it is a jointly crafted narrative.

Figure H.1   Generative Themes Found Through Data Analysis

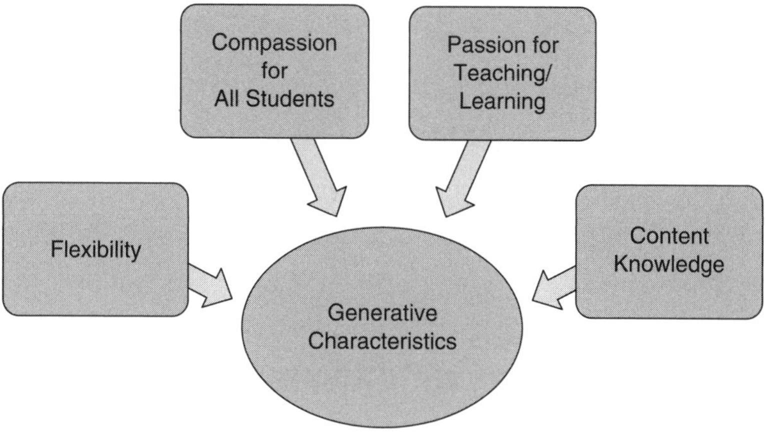

Appendix I

Sample Categories From a Historical Study

on the Portrayal of Native Americans
in High School History Texts

By Gary Padgett (2012)

● THE FIVE GREAT VALUES AUTHENTICITY GUIDELINE

Value 1: Generosity and Sharing

1. Do the Native American people share their possessions?

2. Do they give and share selflessly and humbly?

3. Is the revered bounty of Mother Earth shared?

4. Are they encouraged by family, friends, or tribe to develop and share their talents for the good of all?

5. Are they represented as uniquely separate individuals as well as members of the group?

6. Are children portrayed as "lovingly taken care of" by family, relatives, and nonrelatives?

Value 2: Respect for the Elderly and Women

1. Are male and female elders shown proper respect for their wisdom?

2. Are they portrayed as appropriate role models with whom the young can identify?

3. Are women portrayed as integral, respected, and important, instead of detached and subservient?

4. Are the younger depicted learning from elders, especially through storytelling?

5. Are elders portrayed speaking to the younger without interruption?

Value 3: Getting Along With Nature

1. Are Native Americans depicted as respecting the natural harmony of nature but not as compulsive environmentalists?

2. Are there references to entities possessing a spirit or power to be respected?

3. Is the family unit depicted teaching children love, responsibility, and life?

4. Is the humanness of Native Americans recognized, that is, laughing, playing games, having fun, being with family and friends?

5. Is a language of respect utilized in referring to Native Peoples, that is, avoidance of offensive and stereotypic terminology?

6. Are they portrayed as speaking "broken" English?

7. Is their spirituality and religion respectfully portrayed via ceremony, or is it referred to as superstitious, heathen, meaningless, or trivialized ceremonies, dances, songs, or "war whoops"?

8. Are they depicted with a wide range of physical features, avoiding the "Red Man" stereotype?

9. Are they dressed in culturally authentic garb, or are they all wearing feathers and headdresses regardless of the culture?

10. When depicted in contemporary times, are they dressed in "mainstream" garb depending upon the setting?

11. Do they have stereotyped surnames or authentic translations, including "European" names?

12. Are ceremonial artifacts correctly depicted and explained, such as fetishes, medicine bundles, the wearing of turquoise and silver, the medicine pipe or calumet (not "peace pipe"), and so on?

13. Are they portrayed eating a diverse diet and using utensils or just their hands?

14. Is accurate information provided concerning dwellings (or do they all seemingly live in tipis?), duties of adults and children, ceremonies, and practices?

15. Are they portrayed as contemporary people and not a past people who mysteriously disappeared and no longer exist?

Value 4: Individual Freedom

1. Are the Native American people depicted as accepting responsibility for the consequences of a chosen action or decision?

2. Are they portrayed as not imposing their individual will upon others because of a chosen action?

3. Is the leadership of the tribe properly depicted via multiple chiefs, the role of women in leadership, the Tribal Council, and the leadership operations for the good of the tribe?

Value 5: Courage

1. Is the courage of individuals heroically depicted as an effort to give to or protect one's people, or is it referred to as *fanatic, savage, massacre*, or other terms that give the impression of a totally warlike culture?

2. Are they humble in their exploits and never personally boasting?

3. Are they portrayed as stoics, unable or unwilling to express emotion (unless around strangers)?

4. Do they show proper reverence for the gift of life?

5. Is there a distorted impression that non-Native Americans brought a "superior" civilization to Native Americans such that Native cultures and achievements are demeaned, or are Native civilizations depicted as complex and sophisticated?

Additional Considerations

1. Is the author(s) a true Native American?

2. Is there evidence that the author(s) consulted a Native American?

3. Do the photos or illustrations accurately reflect specific tribal and cultural traditions, symbols, or art forms?

Appendix J

General Rules of Thumb for
Qualitative Researchers

Try to refrain from studying your own group. For many years, researchers have warned against this. In class, students who have studied their own groups have found the difficulties and anguish far greater than any benefits. As a member of a group, you may be too close to that group to be fair and accurate in your reporting. In addition, in hindsight, students who have studied their own schools or their friends' schools have sometimes been turned down for jobs and advancement in their current work situation due to someone's fear of research.

Always have an outside reader or peer reviewer. As you may know, Bronisław Malinowski, Hortense Powdermaker, Margaret Mead, Gregory Bateson, and other classic anthropologists used outside readers of their field notes. Novelists and playwrights also use outside readers to bring a fresh viewpoint and to read for discrepancies and the like. Especially as a researcher in training, it is wise to use an outside reader of your field notes and interview transcripts. Other writers (Lincoln & Guba, 1985) suggest the use of an audit trail from the field of business. This is a fine idea if one has the time and extra money. However, as one who relies on the arts and humanities for my history and being, I prefer the use of the outside reader because it offers a long and dependable history in our field. Lately, students in my doctoral classes have gotten written verification from their outside readers and are calling them *peer reviewers* (see Appendix K). This helps the researcher all the way around. The notion of a peer reviewer is rooted in history and can only add to the final product, the report of the study. This is our history. Can we all agree to honor it?

Design your study to understand. Qualitative work demands that the researcher avoid trying to prove something. Instead, the heart of our work is understanding the social setting and all that it entails. This means that you do not go into the field with the answers. You are always framing questions. It also means that you do not go into the field empty headed either. Before going into any setting, you should already know about yourself as an interviewer, an observer, and a writer, specifically from your pilot study. Often, neophyte researchers appropriate jargon from another paradigm and try to recast qualitative work in another ill-fitting image. Qualitative work just does not work that way. We do not go out to prove something or control something. We go to understand something. The more a prospective researcher can read and practice, the better off he or she will be. Build up your library on method and read and reflect upon these texts. Recently, I asked successful doctoral students—those that finished—what factors contributed to the completion of their projects. Every single person listed the fact that they went out and purchased every text that was of interest to their approach to research, among other factors.

Time in the field equals time in analysis. I have always agreed with those who hold to this guideline. If you spend a year collecting data, expect to spend a year analyzing them. The large amount of text to pore through demands a thorough and just accounting of the data. Many students shortchange their participants by trying to get done with the study as quickly as possible. This is a sad testimonial to our field if this is allowed to prevail. You cannot do justice to your long-term study or your participants if you run in and out to meet arbitrary personal deadlines or some in-house deadline for graduation. Unfortunately, students in education often are so desensitized to their own roles in their organizations that they prefer to let the organizations rule them rather than the other way around. In all my cases of working with doctoral students, I tell them up front that the path is long. They must do equal time in analysis and in the field. Otherwise, we cannot come to agreements. In addition, if a doctoral student wants to rush through and finish quickly for the wrong reasons, it shows. For example, a student recently wanted a particular job, and in her haste to finish, the final chapter looks like a rush job. Do you really want everyone reading Dissertation Abstracts to see a study that is less than complete? The rigor and high standards of qualitative research must be ever present.

Develop a model of what occurred in your study. In qualitative work, theory is grounded from the data: the words of your participants, your field notes, transcripts, reflective journal entries, and other written records. By developing a model of what occurred, the reader of the report is more able to make sense of the data and follow the researcher's argument. This also takes the report to another analytical level. Usually, for the dissertation, this is completed in the final chapter.

Always allow participants access to your data through a member check. As qualitative researchers, we have an obligation to our participants to allow easy access to field notes, journals on the research project, interview transcripts, and initial and final categories of analysis. In fact, this should be built into the informed consent document. In most cases, participants are not very interested in this up to the end of the study. It is always a good idea to give a copy of the completed report or a final copy of the dissertation to one's participants. Some researchers like to show the transcripts to the participants. It is up to you how you do this member checking. Likewise, some doctoral students also give a small gift to participants. For example, one of my former students gave a book from the bestseller list to participants with a thank-you note. I never discourage this because it is obvious that the experience of working on the research project together is totally transformative for both the researcher and participants. In addition, we have currently taken to using written verification from participants regarding access to the data, which avoids misunderstandings later.

Look for points of conflict, tension, and contradiction. Looking for what does not make sense in a study, what does not quite fit, and what exposes points of conflict often yields amazing information and insight. As the researcher goes through mounds of data, points of conflict offer a good grasp of events and are fruitful points of departure for analysis and interpretation. In dance, we call it looking for the asymmetrical. In yoga, we call it looking for the imbalance. Often, new researchers get so caught up in their studies that they forget to look for what is out of the ordinary and what does not fit. Again, having an outside reader and constantly checking your own thoughts through the reflective journal process are most helpful. The rush to finish should not be so strong that you forget to look for the asymmetrical.

Estimate your costs and time and then add some additional costs and time. Inevitably, new qualitative researchers are amazed at the cost of transcriptions, duplication of sections of the report or dissertation, and supplies and equipment. Estimate about $2,500 to $3,000 for completing a long-term qualitative study for the dissertation, excluding tuition.

Currently, transcribers are charging about $100 to $120 for a one-hour recording. One hour of recorded transcript is approximately 21 pages of single-spaced transcription. Some researchers negotiate with a transcriber for the cost of the total package. Voice and video recorders can be purchased used or new at reasonable prices, but for example, a used video recorder is about $200. Likewise, time is your most precious and valuable commodity. Whatever your target date for completion, add another six months to give yourself a reasonable window for reflection and rewriting. Remember that students who do their own transcripts save a great deal of money. Furthermore, copy editors currently charge around $500 for a 300-page dissertation in the Southeast. Prices will vary depending on where you are situated.

Recent estimates from students who completed interview studies show the difference in cost:

a. For a student who did 20 transcriptions personally, the final cost of the dissertation came in at just over $2,000, excluding tuition for dissertation hours.

b. For a student who sent 16 transcripts to a professional transcriber, the final cost of the dissertation came in at around $4,300, excluding tuition for dissertation credit hours.

These guidelines are not meant to be all-inclusive, but they do respond to some of the most often-asked questions about the nuts and bolts of doing qualitative research projects.

Always do pilot interviews and observations. I cannot say enough about the critical nature of conducting pilot interviews and observations and even double-checking one's reflective journal. The idea of pilot studies is as old as the hills. Researchers do pilot studies or at least components of piloting techniques to sharpen their skills at interviewing and observation. From the pilot period, one can learn how to recraft questions in an interview or be reminded of nuts-and-bolts issues.

Write every day. Enough cannot be said about daily writing. Write in your dialogue journal; write in your researcher reflective journal; write narrative descriptions; and practice, practice, practice. Then, go back and rewrite. My own writing schedule is that, no matter what, I write every day for at least two hours. I am a morning person and get more done then so that's when I write. Find your perfect time and write! Then read every day and read in more than your field of study. Then write in your journal every day.

Appendix K

Sample Member Check Form

Dear _____:

Thank you for the insightful and powerful interview(s). Attached please find a draft of the transcripts for your review. Please check for accuracy and that your responses are being reported correctly. Please feel free to contact me at _____ or via e-mail at _____ should you have any questions.

By your act of reading the transcript(s), if I do not hear from you within five working days, I will assume you are in agreement with the transcript(s).

Sincerely,

[Your Name]

Appendix L

Samples of Interview Transcripts (Edited)

By Daryl Ward (2014)

NINA [00:44:12.09]: There's a certain pride when they bring their child into my room to meet me. And they sometimes are embarrassed that they weren't the best for me. And they want me to make their child better than they are. And I look at them and I go, "Why darling, I don't remember any bad thing you did." I, really, sometimes don't. And if they were truly naughty and horrible and miserable—you'll come to this—they become nameless. I forget their names. Because it's not important to keep it. I did what I could. And by this time I think I've taught almost 6,000 people. I remember faces. I remember generalities. [00:44:53.15]. I don't remember specific naughty things. I don't have time for naughty. That's a bad tree . . . don't want to go there.

But I think not feeling welcome there, being on the outs for most of my life, I think that—and I don't . . . I'm having an epiphany . . . I don't engender it or look for it in an egotistical way . . . to be stroked. But I want to feel like my life has meant something. That I'm not weird. I'm not bad. I'm not an outsider, yet I am . . .

DARYL [00:45:33.29]: And that you're making a difference . . .

NINA [00:45:34.14]: I am who I am and if they call it weird, they'll get used to me. I'm old enough now that I'm sure enough that I really don't always fit in well. [00:45:44.12] That's alright. They'll get used to me. I'm a nice person. And they do. And I've made a difference—on that level. I make better students. And yes, their scores come up on the FCAT [said in a derisive, sarcastic tone]. But I think I make them realize something deeper—what does it mean to be human?

DARYL [00:46:06.16]: Good. Next chapter.

NINA [00:46:08.18]: Wow . . . just wanted to think about that and I was also staring at that palm tree [glances to window], it's all green at the top and gnarly at the bottom, but it wouldn't be green at the top without the gnarlies at the bottom. And that made me think about stuff that you'd said and . . .

DARYL [00:46:21.15]: About the tapestry and . . .

NINA [00:46:22.26]: Yes and then I went "Kathy, get back on track" . . . Umm, I want to mention the "Net of Gems." Because if you look at each experience, if we look experientially . . . now I'm going, probably to Victor Frankl, and a little Erik Erikson—is when we step back—to have self-reflection is an important step in becoming a human being. The Net of Gems is very Eastern. If we look at every experience as made of these components [00:46:57.06] [makes hand gestures], they sparkle and then you make another experience and then you realize— and this is where self-reflection comes and why this [points to notes] was interesting—is looking back and seeing the pathway. They don't exist by themselves. They all reflect—it's beautiful—It's the microcosm and the macrocosm. And I look at the stars at night, I realize that the same network is in me, making up my atomic structure . . . in my brain . . . I tell the kids all the time why I'm doing what I'm doing. I want the axon to hook into its little [making hooking gesture with hands] . . . there's like an indentation in the dendrite—I want it hook in there. And then I want to make a pattern to another one and another one and another one. I said, "Look at how many memes you've learned." Every once in a while we sit back and we go. . . . how many single thoughts go with the idea of Zeus?

DARYL [00:47:55.10]: And you create this net . . . this web?

NINA [00:47:58.29]: The neural network. Which is a life network. Which is the cosmos. Which is, "I'm not alone." And that . . . in discovering that moment of humanity . . . I go to a tiny school. Some people would say I have a tiny life. I don't feel that way at all. And maybe that's the beauty of it all. It wouldn't matter where I went, if you stuck me in a room here, I'm going to do . . .

Appendix M

Sample of Dialogic Poetry (Edited)

These poems were created by a participant (Nina) and the researcher (Daryl Ward) during the course of the life history research project.

- ## NINA'S FIRST POEM

On Building Dovetailed Corners With August Wilson

Dovetailed corners
A father's advice on well-built furniture is good to remember—
(Heed)
"It's those little details that only God notices"
hidden misericords on medieval benches
resting perch for tired ecclesiastics . . .
Gargoyles only the dove sees cooing high above the city
one shiny patterned slice of architectural folderol
a buttonhole perfectly stitched with ruby twist
(hidden under the flamboyant Czech bohemian glass button)
Ah, August Wilson knows the perfectly finished dovecote

My grandmother won't let me shortchange the art—
(perhaps that hem that is just uneven turned up material)
Blasphemy
It honors neither the fabric nor the craft

And that is the key—
Pithy intention
He cried that keening moan of knowing
"limitation of the instrument"
It's the dance of creator and creation—
That double loaded brush of Chinese calligraphy
Painted in mind before brush and paper mingle
No excitability here—pause
Square that shoulder
Fret that Sufi song
Hurl hegira and intensity to the four corners
Spin incense and prayer upward on the moon and star of Mary
Arch that Amish framework of plan and commit
Like the keystone in a well-made arch . . .
Connection—
Neatly pinned down with conviction
And all seated in a nice mercy seat
August Wilson's workbench positively hums
Neat chips of wood,

Carefully chosen wood grain
Sanded tidbits gleam
Ebonized wood and inlaid veneer
Oh, this is the fiddly stuff of love
And art like a dovetailed trinity
Resides in hand, head, and heart
Threesome of predilection, patience and patter
And this, I do know, is built on mused ebb and flow
That constant swim and rhythm of pen

No, this is the dovetailed box
Human with that heart beat turning and spinning
Echoed in 10 plays that spoke to me in human

Because

I was born in Gary

Grew up in Pittsburgh and then . . . the South

Strange songs grow in me too

And I felt that keening rhythm in Wilson's jazz,

His front yards and back yards and open and closed fists

● MY RESPONSE

On Cutting (Dovetailed) Corners

They sit there . . . unnoticed,

with matching grain,

sanded and smooth—

tight-fitted joints: the interlocking of

Artistry and Craft.

Folded in on one another as if they are

inseparable hands of prayer.

But the dovetailed corners of teaching—

The bob and the weave;

The zig and the zag;

The warp and the woof

have been cut (we cut corners, you know?)

Replaced by a craft-less metric

That is the new ruler.

And the plumbed depths sound no twain,

Shallow pools reflecting the pedantic apothecary

From whence they've come—

    that prescribes and demarcates.

They are still here . . . interlocked

But looser—with a certain roughness

that comes from dotting I's and crossing T's

not from the zig or the zag

And the twin hands of

Artistry and Craft.

Source: Ward, D. (2014). *Teaching with the end in mind: A Teacher's life history as a legacy of educational leaders* (Unpublished doctoral dissertation). University of South Florida, Tampa

References and Further Reading

Berg, B. L. (2007). *Qualitative research methods for the social sciences* (6th ed.). Boston, MA: Allyn & Bacon.

Best, J. (2004). *More damned lies and statistics: How numbers confuse public issues.* Berkeley: University of California Press.

Burg, C. A. (2010). *Faculty perspectives on doctoral mentoring: The mentor's odyssey* (Unpublished doctoral dissertation). University of South Florida, Tampa. Retrieved from http://scholarcommons.usf.edu/etd/1582/

Chuan, C. T. Y. H. (1963). *The mustard seed garden manual of painting.* Princeton, NJ: Princeton University Press.

Creswell, J. W. (2007). *Qualitative inquiry and research design: Choosing among five approaches* (2nd ed.). Thousand Oaks, CA: Sage.

Csikszentmihalyi, M. (1996). *Creativity: Flow and the psychology of discovery and invention.* New York, NY: HarperCollins.

De Felice, D. (2008). *Living an endangered language: Learning Nahuatl in modern-day Mexico.* Saarbrücken, Germany: Lambert Academic Publishing.

De Felice, D. (2012). *A phenomenological study of teaching endangered languages online: Perspectives from Nahua and Mayan educators* (Doctoral dissertation). Retrieved from http://scholarcommons.usf.edu/etd/4465/

De Felice, D., & Janesick, V. J. (2014). *Understanding the marriage of technology and phenomenological research: From design to analysis* (Unpublished paper under review).

Dewey, J. (1938). *Experience and education.* New York, NY: Collier.

Dewey, J. (1958). *Art as experience.* New York, NY: Capricorn.

Dewey, J. (1967). *The early works.* Carbondale: Southern Illinois University Press.

Edwards, B. (1979). *Drawing on the right side of the brain.* Los Angeles, CA: J. P. Tarcher.

Edwards, B. (1986). *Drawing on the artist within: A guide to innovation, invention, imagination and creativity.* New York, NY: Simon & Schuster.

Edwards, B. (1999). *The new drawing on the right side of the brain.* Los Angeles, CA: J. P. Tarcher.

Einstein, A., & Infeld, L. (1938). *The evolution of physics*. New York, NY: Simon & Schuster.

Eisner, E. W. (1991). *The enlightened eye: qualitative inquiry and the enhancement of educational practice*. New York, NY: Toronto.

Ellis, E. R. (1995). *A diary of the century: Tales from America's greatest diarist*. New York, NY: Kodansha International.

Estes, C. P. (1992/1996). *Women who run with the wolves: Myths and stories of the wild woman archetype*. New York, NY: Ballantine.

Freire, P. (2004). *Pedagogy of indignation*. Boulder, CO: Paradigm.

Goldberg, N. (2005). *Writing down the bones*. Boston, MA: Shambala Press.

Janesick, V. J. (1995). A journal about journal writing as a qualitative research technique: History, issues, and reflections. *Qualitative Inquiry, 5*(4), 505–524.

Janesick, V. J. (1998). The dance of qualitative research design: Metaphor, methodolatry, and meaning. In N. Denzin & Y. Lincoln (Eds.), *Strategies of qualitative inquiry* (pp. 35–55). Thousand Oaks, CA: Sage.

Janesick, V. J. (1999). Using a journal as reflection in action in the classroom. In D. Weil (Ed.), *Perspectives in critical thinking: Theory and practice in education*. New York, NY: Peter Lang.

Janesick, V. J. (2000). The choreography of qualitative research design: Minuets, improvisations, and crystallization. In N. K. Denzin & Y. S. Lincoln (Eds.), *Handbook of qualitative research* (2nd ed., pp. 379–399). Thousand Oaks, CA: Sage.

Janesick, V. J. (2001). Intuition and creativity: A pas de deux for the qualitative researcher. *Qualitative Inquiry, 7*(5), 531–540.

Janesick, V. J. (2004). *"Stretching" exercises for qualitative researchers* (2nd ed.). Thousand Oaks, CA: Sage.

Janesick, V. J. (2007). Oral history as a social justice project: Issues for the qualitative researcher. *The Qualitative Report, 12*(1), 111–121. Retrieved from http://www.nova.edu/ssss/QR/QR12-1/janesick.pdf

Janesick, V. J. (2008). Art and experience: Lessons learned from Dewey and Hawkins. In J. G. Knowles & A. L. Cole (Eds.), *Handbook of arts in qualitative inquiry: Perspectives, methodologies, examples, and issues* (pp. 477–483). Thousand Oaks, CA: Sage.

Janesick, V. J. (2011). *"Stretching" exercises for qualitative researchers* (3rd ed.). Thousand Oaks, CA: Sage.

Janesick, V. J. (2015). *Contemplative qualitative inquiry: Practicing the Zen of research*. Walnut Creek, CA: Left Coast Press.

Jones, S. R., Torres, V., & Arminio, J. (2006). *Negotiating the complexities of qualitative research in higher education: Fundamental elements and issues*. New York, NY: Routledge.

King, S. (2000). *On writing: A memoir of the craft*. New York, NY: Scribner.

Kvale, S. (1996). *Interviews: An introduction to qualitative research interviewing*. Thousand Oaks, CA: Sage.

Kvale, S., & Brinkmann, S. (2009). *Interviews: Learning the craft of qualitative research interviewing* (2nd ed.). Thousand Oaks, CA: Sage.

Lichtman, M. (2011). *Understanding and evaluating qualitative educational research.* Thousand Oaks: Sage.

Lincoln, Y. S., & Guba, E. G. (1985). *Naturalistic inquiry.* Beverly Hills, CA: Sage.

Lortie, D. C. (2002). *Schoolteacher: A sociological study* (2nd ed.). Chicago, IL: University of Chicago Press.

Merriam, S. B. (2001). *Qualitative research and case study applications in education* (Rev. ed.). San Francisco, CA: Jossey-Bass.

Merriam. S. B. (2009). *Qualitative research: A guide to design and implementation* (Rev. ed.). San Francisco, CA: Jossey-Bass.

Meyer, D. Z., & Avery, L. M. (2009). Excel as a qualitative data analysis tool. *Field Methods, 21*(1), 91–112.

Mishler, E. G. (1986). *Research interviewing: Context and narrative.* Cambridge, MA: Harvard University Press.

Mooney, B., & Holt, D. (1996). *The storyteller's guide.* Little Rock, AR: August House.

Morgan, D. (Ed.). (1993). *Successful focus groups.* Newbury Park, CA: Sage

Pascale, C.-M. (2011). *Cartographies of knowledge: Exploring qualitative epistemologies.* Thousand Oaks, CA: Sage.

Perselli, V. (2011) Painting the police station blue: The almost impossible argument for poetry in elite educational research journals. *Power and Education, 3*(1) 64–80.

Piantanida, M., & Garman, N. B. (1999). *The qualitative dissertation: A guide for students and faculty.* Thousand Oaks, CA: Corwin.

Polkinghorne, D. E. (1995). Narrative configuration in qualitative analysis. *International Journal of Qualitative Studies in Education, 8*(1), 5–23.

Progoff, I. (1992). *At a journal workshop: Writing to access the power of the unconscious and evoke creative ability.* New York, NY: J. P. Tarcher.

Rainer, T. (1978). *The new diary.* Los Angeles, CA: J. P. Tarcher.

Roulston, K. (2010). *Reflective interviewing: A guide to theory and practice.* Thousand Oaks, CA: Sage.

Rubin, H. J., & Rubin, I. S. (2005). *Qualitative interviewing: The art of hearing data* (2nd ed.) Thousand Oaks, CA: Sage.

Rubin, H. J., & Rubin, I. S. (2011). *Qualitative interviewing: The art of hearing data* (3rd ed). Thousand Oaks, CA: Sage.

Saldaña, J. (2009). *The coding manual for qualitative researchers.* Thousand Oaks, CA: Sage.

Saturley, M. (2014). *A qualitative look at where I am from* (Unpublished dissertation proposal assignment). University of Southern Florida, Tampa.

Schwandt, T. A. (2001). *Qualitative inquiry: A dictionary of terms* (2nd ed.). Thousand Oaks, CA: Sage.

Slotnick, R. (2010). *University and community college administrators' perspectives of the transfer process for underrepresented students: Analysis of policy and practice* (Unpublished doctoral dissertation). University of South Florida, Tampa. Retrieved from http://scholarcommons.usf.edu/etd/1774/

Spradley, J. P. (1980). *Participant observation*. New York, NY: Holt, Rinehart & Winston.

Stake, R. E.(1995). *The art of the case study research*. Thousand Oaks, CA: Sage.

Stevenson, C. (2002). *A case study on educational leaders' perspectives on technology use in the undergraduate general education curriculum* (Unpublished doctoral dissertation). Roosevelt University, Chicago, IL.

Thornton, D. (2014). *Letter from an antique worth restoring?* (Unpublished class assignment). University of South Florida, Tampa.

Visedo, E. (2013) *From limited-English-proficient to educator: Perspectives on three Spanish-English biliteracy journeys* (Doctoral dissertation). Retrieved from Graduate Theses and Dissertations, http://scholarcommons.usf.edu/etd/4787.

Visedo, E. (2015). *Origin: Identity poetry activity* (Unpublished assignment). University of Southern Florida, Tampa.

Vrobel, O. (2009). *Sample reflection for adding to the reflective journal: Self-evaluation upon observing in a student laboratory for English language learning* (Unpublished class assignment). University of South Florida, Tampa.

Williams-Boyd, P. (2005). *The critical case use of observation of a student: Lessons learned for the professional development of the educator in training* (Unpublished class assignment). Eastern Michigan University, Ypsilanti.

Wolcott, H. F. (1995). *The art of fieldwork*. Walnut Creek, CA: Alta Mira.

Index